International Perspectives on Group Work

The counseling profession in the United States is calling for increased international collaboration, engagement and understanding of the global issues that impact the way in which counselors conduct their professional practice, teaching and research. This book captures the experiences of group workers the world over, inviting them to describe how they facilitate group work to restore wellness, promote healing and create opportunities for reducing isolation and alienation by tapping into the wisdom of multicultural or indigenous practices. The group work profession underscores the importance of training and service delivery that is rooted in humanistic narratives, with a focus on understanding cross-cultural dynamics.

Included in this collection are examples of the rich, creative and diverse world of group work applications, all of which contribute to a greater knowledge, awareness and understanding of many ways in which the power of group membership and leadership can be harnessed for positive change. Group work teachers, practitioners and counselor educators will enjoy learning about these creative and important efforts, and take away ideas to implement in their own group work. This book was originally published as two special issues of *The Journal for Specialists in Group Work.*

Ana Puig is a Scholar and Research Director in the Office of Educational Research at the University of Florida, Gainesville, FL, USA.

Bogusia Skudrzyk is Professor and Director of Counselor Education Program at Palm Beach Atlantic University, Orlando and West Palm Beach Campus, FL, USA.

Julieta Monteiro-Leitner is a Professor in the Department of Educational Leadership and Counseling at Southeast Missouri State University, Cape Girardeau, MO, USA.

A. Michael Hutchins was a licensed professional counselor in private practice in Tucson, AZ, USA.

International Perspectives on Group Work

Leadership, practice, research, and teaching

Edited by
Ana Puig, Bogusia Skudrzyk, Julieta Monteiro-Leitner, and A. Michael Hutchins

Routledge
Taylor & Francis Group
LONDON AND NEW YORK

First published 2016
by Routledge
2 Park Square, Milton Park, Abingdon, Oxon, OX14 4RN, UK

and by Routledge
711 Third Avenue, New York, NY 10017, USA

Routledge is an imprint of the Taylor & Francis Group, an informa business

British Library Cataloguing in Publication Data
A catalogue record for this book is available from the British Library

ISBN 13: 978-1-138-19052-8

Typeset in NewCenturySclbk
by diacriTech, Chennai

Publisher's Note
The publisher accepts responsibility for any inconsistencies that may have arisen during the conversion of this book from journal articles to book chapters, namely the possible inclusion of journal terminology.

Disclaimer
Every effort has been made to contact copyright holders for their permission to reprint material in this book. The publishers would be grateful to hear from any copyright holder who is not here acknowledged and will undertake to rectify any errors or omissions in future editions of this book.

Contents

CONTENTS

Citation Information

The following chapters were originally published in *The Journal for Specialists in Group Work*, volume 40, issue 1 (March 2015). When citing this material, please use the original page numbering for each article, as follows:

Chapter 1
Critical Issues in International Group Counseling
Fred Bemak and Rita Chi-Ying Chung
The Journal for Specialists in Group Work, volume 40, issue 1 (March 2015) pp. 6–21

Chapter 2
Development and Implementation of an International Counseling Outreach Effort in Bhutan: A Group Stage Conceptualization
Lorraine J. Guth, Sonya Lorelle, J. Scott Hinkle, and Theodore P. Remley
The Journal for Specialists in Group Work, volume 40, issue 1 (March 2015) pp. 22–37

Chapter 3
Group Work During International Disaster Outreach Projects: A Model to Advance Cultural Competence
Cirecie West-Olatunji, Rachel Henesy, and Melanie Varney
The Journal for Specialists in Group Work, volume 40, issue 1 (March 2015) pp. 38–54

Chapter 4
International Consultation and Training on Group Work in South Asia
Farah A. Ibrahim
The Journal for Specialists in Group Work, volume 40, issue 1 (March 2015) pp. 55–73

Chapter 5

A Grounded Theory of Western-Trained Asian Group Leaders Leading Groups in Asia
Nattasuda Taephant, Deborah Rubel, and Julia Champe
The Journal for Specialists in Group Work, volume 40, issue 1 (March 2015) pp. 74–101

Chapter 6

Teaching Group Counseling in Botswana: Two U.S.-Trained Counselors Discuss Experiences and Share Cultural Considerations for Practice
Angela D. Coker and Aaron R. Majuta
The Journal for Specialists in Group Work, volume 40, issue 1 (March 2015) pp. 102–116

Chapter 7

International Cultural Immersion: Assessing the Influence of a Group Intervention on Intercultural Sensitivity for Counselor Trainees
Sejal M. Barden, Laura Shannonhouse, and Keith Mobley
The Journal for Specialists in Group Work, volume 40, issue 1 (March 2015) pp. 117–141

The following chapters were originally published in *The Journal for Specialists in Group Work*, volume 40, issue 2 (June 2015). When citing this material, please use the original page numbering for each article, as follows:

Chapter 8

Group Counseling and Satsang*: Learning From Indian Group Practices*
Christopher Rybak, Deepa Sathaye, and Megha Deuskar
The Journal for Specialists in Group Work, volume 40, issue 2 (June 2015) pp. 147–162

Chapter 9

Understanding the Islamic Concept of Usrah *and Its Application to Group Work*
Nabisah Ibrahim, Siti Rozaina Kamsani, and Julia Champe
The Journal for Specialists in Group Work, volume 40, issue 2 (June 2015) pp. 163–186

Chapter 10

Transcending Traditional Group Work: Using the Brazilian Martial Art of Capoeira as a Clinical Therapeutic Group for Culturally Diverse Adolescents
Isaac Burt

The Journal for Specialists in Group Work, volume 40, issue 2 (June 2015) pp. 187–203

Chapter 11

Therapeutic Factors and Members' Perception of Co-Leaders' Attitudes in a Psychoeducational Group for Greek Children With Social Anxiety
Andreas Brouzos, Stephanos P. Vassilopoulos, and Vasiliki C. Baourda
The Journal for Specialists in Group Work, volume 40, issue 2 (June 2015) pp. 204–224

Chapter 12

The Development of Relational Competences in High School Students by Means of Sociometric Methods
Regiane da Silva Macuch and Henrique Malheiro Vaz
The Journal for Specialists in Group Work, volume 40, issue 2 (June 2015) pp. 225–242

Chapter 13

Development and Implementation of a Psychoeducational Group for Ghanaian Adolescents Experiencing Parental Divorce
Anthony K. Nkyi
The Journal for Specialists in Group Work, volume 40, issue 2 (June 2015) pp. 243–264

Notes on Contributors

Vasiliki C. Baourda is a psychologist and Ph.D. candidate in the Department of Primary Education at the University of Ioannina, Greece.

Sejal M. Barden is an Assistant Professor in the Department of Child, Family, and Community Sciences in the College of Education and Human Performance at the University of Central Florida, Orlando, FL, USA.

Fred Bemak is a Professor and Director of the Diversity Research and Action Consortium at George Mason University, Fairfax, VA, USA.

Andreas Brouzos is a Professor in the Department of Primary Education at the University of Ioannina, Greece.

Isaac Burt is Assistant Professor of Counselor Education in the Department of Leadership and Professional Studies at Florida International University, Miami, FL, USA.

Julia Champe is a Contributing Faculty in the School of Counseling – Marriage, Couple & Family Counseling, College of Social & Behavioral Sciences, Walden University, Minneapolis, MN, USA.

Rita Chi-Ying Chung is a Professor in the Counseling and Development Program in the College of Education and Human Development at George Mason University, Fairfax, VA, USA.

Angela D. Coker is an Associate Professor in the Department of Counseling and Family Therapy at the University of Missouri–St. Louis, MO, USA.

Megha Deuskar is an Assistant Professor in the Department of Psychology at Fergusson College in Pune, India.

Lorraine J. Guth is a Professor in the Department of Counseling at Indiana University of Pennsylvania, Indiana, PA, USA.

Rachel Henesy is a doctoral student of Counseling and Counselor Education at the University of Florida, Gainesville, FL, USA.

J. Scott Hinkle is the Director of Professional Development for the National Board for Certified Counselors, USA.

A. Michael Hutchins is a licensed professional counselor in private practice in Tucson, AZ, USA.

Farah A. Ibrahim is Professor of Counseling Psychology and Counseling Education at the University of Colorado, Denver, CO, USA.

Nabisah Ibrahim is Senior Lecturer in the School of Applied Psychology, Social Work & Policy, College of Art & Sciences at University Utara Malaysia, Kedah, Malaysia.

Siti Rozaina Kamsani is Senior Lecturer in the School of Applied Psychology, Social Work & Policy, College of Art and Sciences at University Utara Malaysia, Kedah, Malaysia.

Sonya Lorelle is an Assistant Professor in the Division of Psychology and Counseling at Governor's State University, University Parkway, IL, USA.

Regiane da Silva Macuch is a Professor in the Academic Master's programs of Health Promotion and Knowledge Management in Organizations at Maringá University Center in Maringá, Paraná, Brazil.

Aaron R. Majuta is a Lecturer in the Department of Educational Foundations at the University of Botswana, Gaborone, Botswana.

Keith Mobley is a Clinical Professor in the Department of Counseling and Educational Development at the University of North Carolina at Greensboro, NC, USA.

Julieta Monteiro-Leitner is a Professor in the Department of Educational Leadership and Counseling at Southeast Missouri State University, Cape Girardeau, MO, USA.

Anthony K. Nkyi is a Lecturer, Clinical Psychologist and Counselor in the Counseling Centre, College of Education Studies at the University of Cape Coast, Cape Coast, Ghana.

Ana Puig is a Scholar and Research Director in the Office of Educational Research at the University of Florida, Gainesville, FL, USA.

Theodore P. Remley is Booth-Bricker Endowed Professor at Our Lady of Holy Cross College, New Orleans, LA, USA.

Deborah Rubel is Associate Professor of Counseling in the College of Education at Oregon State University, Corvallis, OR, USA.

Christopher Rybak is a Professor and Chair of the Department of Leadership in Education, Nonprofits & Counseling at Bradley University, Peoria, IL, USA.

Deepa Sathaye is a homeopathic physician and counsellor based in Pune, India.

Laura Shannonhouse is an Assistant Professor at Georgia State University, Atlanta, GA, USA.

Bogusia Skudrzyk is Professor and Director of Counselor Education Program at Palm Beach Atlantic University, Orlando and West Palm Beach Campus, FL, USA.

Nattasuda Taephant is Program Lead and Assistant Professor of Counseling Psychology at Chulalongkorn University, Bangkok, Thailand.

Melanie Varney is a doctoral student in the Counselor Education and Practice at Georgia State University, Atlanta, GA, USA.

Stephanos P. Vassilopoulos is an Assistant Professor in the Department of Primary Education at the University of Patras, Greece.

Henrique Malheiro Vaz is an Assistant Professor in the Faculty of Psychology and Education Sciences at the University of Porto, Portugal.

Cirecie West-Olatunji is Associate Professor of Counseling and Director of the Center for Traumatic Stress Research at the Xavier University, New Orleans, LA, USA.

Introduction

Ana Puig, Bogusia Skudrzyk, Julieta Monteiro-Leitner, and A. Michael Hutchins

This volume on international group work is published at a time when the counseling profession in the United States is calling for increased international collaboration, engagement, and understanding of global issues impacting the way we conduct our professional practice, teaching, and research. Mental health prevention and therapeutic intervention services through group work are increasingly being delivered around the world to address issues from local health crises to parental divorce and psychological trauma. Hohenshil, Amundson, and Niles (2013) recently edited a comprehensive text about counseling around the world that is inclusive of 40 countries and almost every continent. Group work is also featured therein. Theoretical frameworks that inform group work, leadership, practice, research, and teaching must be centered, grounded upon, and informed by local sociocultural, political, and familial practices (Singh, Merchant, Skudrzyk, & Ingene, 2012).

As co-editors of this book, based on a special issue of *The Journal for Specialists in Group Work*, we hoped that group workers around the world would have an opportunity to describe how they strive to facilitate group work which restores wellness, promotes healing, and creates opportunities to reduce isolation and alienation by tapping into the wisdom of multicultural or indigenous practices. The group work profession underscores the importance of training and service delivery that is rooted in humanistic narratives, with a focus on understanding cross-cultural dynamics. The co-editors feel honored by the robust submissions of scholarly work that describe how group leaders integrate group work principles with cultural practices.

Adler (1954) proposed that "the self" is indivisible and purposiveness is central to understanding human behavior. Purposiveness pertains to the extent to which one focuses on major life tasks such as work, friendship, and love, as well as spirituality and self (Mosak, 1989; Myers & Sweeney, 2004). From an Adlerian perspective, in order for individuals to experience wellness in living, major life tasks should be carried out while focusing on relationship building and demonstrating Social Interest (i.e., a sense of mental health) by being "other" oriented and showing concern for others. This concept is not new and has been embedded into a way of being and doing among cultures that represent non-Western perspectives. The co-editors hope that perhaps more than ever, as group workers who strive to eradicate systemic obstacles, we might be able to learn from each other about the wisdom of cultural differences while recognizing the needs of people around the world to be loved, valued, and deemed worthwhile. We hope that this book will indeed illuminate the process of group work that focuses on how we can help individuals feel connected even, or perhaps especially, when life circumstances could tear us apart.

Perhaps more than ever, individuals yearn for connections and belonging; belonging that leads to feeling whole and worthwhile. Cura Personalis—taking care of the Whole Person—is at the heart of Jesuit education and educating others. This focus is not new, yet again; so many cultures have honored the focus on taking care of the whole person, despite the systemic challenges, the unearned privilege, and the oppression that often prevails in everyday lives. These works honor individuals who have made time to create group experiences that indeed could recapitulate primary family dynamics so that we can experience a sense of love, belonging, and feeling worthy. Each culture, community, family, and individual knows what is needed to maintain wellness, to restore healing, and to create connections (Skudrzyk, Brigman, & Rhone, 2003). We need to take and make time to learn with each other and from each other the powerful lessons for living, working, and learning. Dr. Irvin Yalom, Dr. Martin Luther King, Bishop Tutu, and Paolo Freire, among so many others, have illustrated how we can focus on healing and learning how to care for one another.

The co-editors hope that as Gladding (2010) describes in the *Creative Arts in Counseling*, readers will walk away with confirmed perspectives, new perspectives, and clearer ideas that will help them decide how to magnify at times, how to minimize at times, how to substitute, but most of all, focus on how to continue the practice of group work in a way that will bring hope, universality, connections, and courage to discern how things are and how they can be. The belief that collaboration is a shared process of meaning making prevailed in our efforts; the rich and diverse backgrounds of the co-editors has been the lighthouse of the editorial journey in crafting this special issue. Brazilian-American, Polish-American, American, and Puerto Rican mind-spirits came together motivated by a self-assuring confidence that, in honoring the mission of this special issue, these articles would be proof of the reciprocal interaction of the dyad—that the most diverse is still the most universal. We represent a diverse team of group practitioners, teachers, and researchers committed to the understanding and appreciation of multicultural and indigenous practices across the globe. We held extensive discussions about the process of inclusion of the proposed works. In the course of selecting the pieces featured here, we engaged in lively discussions about subjective understandings of society, cultures, family, and self; the mutual construction of meaning and transfer of learning (Orr & Hulse-Killacky, 2006) were central to our efforts. We talked about each one of us representing a different culture and aiming to weave these varied strands into our intentions to give voice to the rich fabric of multicultural practices and approaches, without perpetuating oppression or imposition, without assuming that everything Western does not apply or everything non-Western should be included. We deliberately focused on our value and appreciation of cultural identities and experiences, and creating bridges as global group workers. We wanted to move forward and feature just and caring practices representing our social justice and emancipatory philosophies.

Overview of featured works

The writings that comprise this book represent an overview of international research, outreach efforts, consultation, training, leadership, and teaching practices. Each focuses on culturally informed and competent group work efforts and illuminates aspects of this work across the globe by American and international teachers, scholars, and practitioners. Learning from and with each one of the authors of the submitted pieces and dialoguing with them through our editing inquiries and suggestions, the authors refreshed, charged, and illuminated the very concept of what interpersonal learning really is.

We begin with Bemak and Chung's exploration of critical issues in international group work. They review group work scholarly articles of the past 10 years and underscore the dearth of international group work, even in the face of an increase in globalization and movement of peoples across cultures and countries. They remind us that 75 percent of our world represents collectivistic, group oriented cultures and challenge us to think about the best ways to prepare group practitioners to engage in group work across the globe. Bemak and Chung end by summarizing nine critical areas in need of attention. We hope our readers will take heart and heed their call.

Guth, Lorelle, Hinkle, and Remley highlight the development and implementation of an international counseling outreach program in Bhutan using a group stage conceptualization. They detail the steps taken to engage and include the local expert leaders and practitioners and the visiting group workers and trainers, while attending to, respecting, and integrating indigenous healing practices and cultural norms.

This is followed by West-Olatunji, Henesy, and Varney's description of a disaster outreach training project for counseling students in southern Africa. The authors report results of a study conducted to develop and examine a model to advance cultural competence in beginning students. Group process was employed to enhance students' self-awareness and conceptualization skills and the authors emphasize the importance of integrating these practices during global disaster outreach efforts.

Ibrahim brings us a report of her international consultation and training efforts for faculty and graduate students learning group work in South Asia. She begins with a description of a needs assessment process focused on cultural assumptions and group theory and practice aiming to identify important cultural variables and goals. She highlights the importance of culture- and program-specific approaches to consultation and training and provides concrete tools to help advance these. The role of cultural norms and traditions are also discussed and caveats offered about integrating these into group interventions. Taephant, Rubel, and Champe present results of a grounded theory study of Western-trained Asian group leaders leading groups in Asia. Participants from Japan, Taiwan, and Thailand were interviewed to draw a theory about the process of reconciling Western training with the Asian, international context in which they work. Reflective experimentation was used to integrate personal experiences, Western training, and emic knowledge of cultures in order to develop culturally appropriate group interventions. These works offer us a glimpse into group training, consultation, and practices in the Asia Pacific region.

Teaching practices are also featured here. Coker and Majuta discuss their experiences of teaching group counseling in the African context. Both are U.S.-trained counselors who co-taught counselors-in-training at a university in Botswana. They provide the reader an overview of the country, culture, and issues common to group counseling practitioners and address the challenges and rewards of this work. The authors share cultural considerations for teaching and practice that resulted from this collaboration. Barden reports on a quasi-experimental research study about the impact of a cultural immersion experience on counseling students' cultural sensitivity. The article provides an overview of the Developmental Model of Intercultural Sensitivity and describes the design, analyses, and results of this work. Implications for training and future research are also discussed.

Next we have Rybak, Sathaye, and Deuskar's paper exploring group leadership through the lens of the Indian spiritual practice of Satsang. The authors contend that learning how various cultures approach leadership within small groups can provide insight and perspective into the commonalities and differences of groups. They investigate and inform the reader about the diversity perspective offered through Satsang.

Ibrahim, Kamsani, and Champe's piece sheds light upon the Islamic concept of *Usrah* and illustrate its application to group work with Asian Muslims. They challenge us to learn about the rich cultural and spiritual principles underlying this common practice by Muslims and invite us to consider its adaptation for Asian Muslims living in the West.

Burt presents a creative approach to working with angry and behaviorally challenging youths using principles of the Brazilian martial arts practice of *Capoeira*. He argues that this approach can be a beneficial adjunct to traditional therapy for this population, adding that combining *Capoeira* movements with culturally sensitive principles of traditional therapy practice can help clients from culturally diverse groups. We hope you will find his discussion as compelling as we did.

Vassilopoulos, Brouzos, and Baurda report on a study designed to investigate therapeutic factors and perception of co-leaders' attitudes in elementary school children struggling with social anxiety. They explored how affective, cognitive, and behavioral therapeutic factors changed throughout the stages of group. Changes in the children's perceptions of the group co-leaders were also examined. The study provides implications for group leadership.

Macuch reports results of a three-year study using sociometry as research and intervention tool to explore high school youths' changes in relational skills, perceptions, and communication styles over the course of their high school training. Outcomes support the use of sociometry to assist students in their relationship skills development during this potentially unsettling development stage.

A paper by Nkyi closes our exploration of international group work. He reports his efforts to adapt person-centered and cognitive-behavioral principles and practices to a group of Ghanaian youths whose parents have divorced. Nkyi aims to integrate cultural and spiritual principles into his psychoeducational and therapeutic group sessions. A detailed account of these is provided. He offers us a summary of outcomes and a glimpse into their lives in a rural region of this Sub-Saharan African country.

References

Adler, A. (1954). *Understanding human nature.* New York: Fawcett World Library.

Gladding, S. T. (2011). *The creative arts in counseling (4th ed.).* Alexandria, VA: American Counseling Association.

Hohenshil, T. H., Amundson, N. E., & Niles, S. G. (2013). *Counseling around the world: An international handbook.* Alexandria, VA: American Counseling Association.

Mosak, H. H. (1989). Adlerian psychotherapy. In R. J. Corsini & D. Wedding (Eds.), *Current psychotherapies* (4th ed., pp. 44–94). Itasca, IL: F. E. Peacock.
Orr, J. J., & Hulse-Killacky, D. (2006). Using voice, meaning, mutual construction of knowledge, and transfer of learning to apply an ecological perspective to group work training. *Journal for Specialists in Group Work*, *31*, 3, 189–200, DOI: 10.1080/01933920600777824.
Myers, J. E., & Sweeney, T. J. (2004). The indivisible self: An evidence-based model of wellness. *Journal of Individual Psychology*, *60*, 3, 234–245.
Skudrzyk, B., Brigman, G., & Rhone, A. (2003). Fostering success through group work with children who celebrate diversity. *Journal for the Specialists in Group Work*, *28*, 166–184.
Singh, A., Merchant, N., Skudrzyk, B., & Ingene, D. (2012). Multicultural and social competence principles for group workers. *Journal for Specialists in Group Work*, *37*, 4, 312–325.

Critical Issues in International Group Counseling

Fred Bemak
Rita Chi-Ying Chung
George Mason University

Three-quarters of the world come from collectivistic group-oriented cultures. As the world becomes more globalized it is inevitable that group counseling will be a major choice of healing and psychological intervention internationally. However, a review of scholarly articles from The Journal for Specialists in Group Work *and* Group Dynamics *during the past 10 years reveals that there are few articles that address international group work. To better prepare group counselors to do group counseling across international boundaries this article discusses 9 critical cross-cultural themes in international group work and the importance of having an international group counseling training curriculum.*

As globalization creates a world that is more closely connected it is inevitable that group counseling becomes more prominent as a mental health intervention that bridges international, national, and regional boundaries and cultures. This is particularly relevant given that 70% of the world's population originates from collectivistic group-oriented cultures (Chung & Bemak, 2012) where societal values are based on interconnectedness and cooperation. The emphasis on social connectedness in the majority of the worlds' societies would make group counseling a natural choice as a means of healing and psychological intervention (Bemak & Chung, 2004; Conyne & Bemak, 2004).

Although group counseling would be a culturally responsive intervention in collectivistic cultures, there is very little that has been published on this topic in Western-based English language journals.

We suspect that most of the group counseling work that is done internationally is either not published in Western English language academic journals or published in journals that are in languages other than English. Regardless, a wealth of information on international group work is not shared globally. Pedersen (2003) stated that "American psychology is in danger of being left behind," because "U.S. psychologists know far less about psychology in other cultures than international psychologists know about us" (p. 400). We believe this can be generalized to group counseling in Western countries.

The purpose of this article is to review issues relevant to global group counseling and provide recommendations about how group counselors can be better prepared and culturally responsive when conducting group counseling in international settings. The article will examine nine critical cross-cultural themes that are essential for effective transnational group counseling, and will provide recommendations for modifications in international group counseling practice. The article will also discuss the importance of addressing international issues in group counseling training that will provide a basis for global group counseling cultural competence. We will begin with content analyses of international group work articles in *The Journal for Specialists in Group Work* (*JSGW*) and *Group Dynamics: Theory, Research, and Practice* which will lay the foundation for discussing the importance of global group counseling, followed by a discussion of the nine international cross-cultural group counseling critical issues and themes.

CONTENT ANALYSES OF GROUP COUNSELING ARTICLES

The results of a content analyses of international group work articles for the past 10 years (2003 to 2013) published in *JSGW* and *Group Dynamics* found that for *JSGW*, out of 248 published articles, only 10 (4%) were about international group counseling/psychotherapy. Within that time period *JSGW* published seven special issues, none of which were specifically focused on international group counseling. For *Group Dynamics,* out of 245 articles, there were 93 (37.9%) international group counseling articles and out of 93 only 21 (22.6%), or 8.6%, were about actual group counseling and group psychotherapy. The remaining 72 articles focused on a variety of group work topics that ranged from group dynamics (i.e., group identification, ambivalence, bias, cohesion, climate, trust, prejudice, intergroup relations, and group leader-member relationship; e.g., Hornsey, Olsen, Barlow, & Oei, 2012; Stathi, Crisp, & Hogg, 2011); group functionality (i.e., group team building, task, decision making, and information exchange; e.g., Kooij-de Bode, van Knippenberg, & van Ginkel, 2008; Marques-Quintero, Curral, Passos, & Lewis, 2013); group leadership (i.e., group leader behavior and traits; e.g., Leicht, Crisp, & Randsley de Moura, 2013; Seppälä, Lipponen, & Pirttilä-Backman, 2012; Tjosvold, Coleman, & Sun, 2003); and types of groups (i.e., short-term, homogenous vs. heterogeneous, and virtual groups; e.g., Kösters, Burlingame, Nachtigall, & Strauss, 2006; Martinez-Moreno, Zornoza, González-Navarro, & Thompson, 2012; Piper, Ogrodniczuk, Joyce, & Weideman, 2009).Within the 10-year period *Group Dynamics* had published three special issues, again none were specifically about international group work.

For both journals only a small percent of articles were on actual international group counseling and psychotherapy (e.g., Harel, Zipora, & Cutrona, 2011; Maxwell et al., 2012; Shechtman, Goldberg, & Cariani, 2008; Shechtman & Halevi, 2006). For *JSGW* less than 5% of articles focused on international group counseling and group psychotherapy. Sixty percent ($N = 6$) of the international articles were from Asia, and the others were from Botswana ($N = 1$), Canada ($N = 1$), Greece ($N = 1$) and Israel ($N = 1$). For *Group Dynamics* just over a third of the articles focused on different aspects of international group work, but only 8.6% focused on group counseling and psychotherapy. Interestingly, 22.6% ($N = 21$) of the international articles were from Canada, 16.1% ($N = 15$) from the United Kingdom, 15.1% ($N = 14$) from Israel and The Netherlands respectively, 20.4% ($N = 19$) from other European countries, 8.6% ($N = 8$) from Australia and New Zealand, 1.07% ($N = 1$) from Lebanon and China respectively. Noteworthy is the fact that approximately 90% of international articles in *Group Dynamics* were from the global north, none of the international articles in *Group Dynamics* were from the continent of Africa, Central or South America, the Caribbean, and only one article was from Asia. Although a majority of *JSGW* international group counseling articles were from Asia, they only accounted for 6 (2.4%) articles out of a total of 248 within a 10-year period. *JSGW* also had only one article (.4%) from Africa within the 10-year period. Given these findings it is clear that group counselors in the United States are missing out on the rich information that could be gained from knowing about international group work from other regions in the world.

The content analyses strongly suggests there needs to be a greater focus on international group work, especially group counseling and group psychotherapy, particularly from the global south regions. As globalization fosters greater contact and knowledge across cultures, and challenges the development and growth of the mental health field (Casas, Park, & Cho, 2010; Marsella, 2007) it is essential that group counselors know how to do group counseling and group psychotherapy across international borders and learn from group counseling practices that are occurring in other parts of the world. The next section will discuss nine themes that address critical issues in doing international group counseling.

CRITICAL INTERNATIONAL GROUP COUNSELING THEMES

To conduct effective culturally sensitive global group counseling requires additional competencies that are specific to international settings. The Association for Specialists in Group Work Multicultural and Social Justice Competencies (ASGW Multicultural and Social Justice Competence Principles for Group Workers, 2012) provides a good starting foundation for doing effective group work internationally. These competencies incorporate the ASGW Best Practice Guidelines (Thomas & Pender, 2008) and offer a set of guidelines on how to work effectively with different cultural groups. The competencies address the areas of: Awareness of Self and Group Members, Strategies and Skills, Group Workers Performance and Processing, and Social Justice Advocacy. The ASGW Multicultural and Social Justice Competencies equip group workers to be culturally responsive and social justice minded in working with diverse populations in the United States. However, we believe that an additional set of competencies building on the ASGW Multicultural and Social Justice Competencies is required to do group work internationally.

It is important to note that the ASGW competencies must be successfully acquired as a foundation to attaining the skills and abilities to do international group counseling. Although the ASGW Multicultural and Social Justice Competencies flag the importance of understanding cultural, historical, and sociopolitical backgrounds and experiences of group members, there are added dimensions working in international settings. Working internationally, group counselors must also be mindful of their home country's mainstream dominant cultural, social, and political viewpoints about that culture and country that influence personal attitudes, beliefs, and values towards group members. Below is a discussion of nine international themes and critical issues that builds on the ASGW Multicultural and Social Justice Competencies that we would suggest are necessary to acquire competency to do effective international group counseling.

Theme 1: Understanding the Context of Collectivistic Cultures and Group Work

The fields of psychology and counseling in the United States have been criticized as being deeply rooted in the cultural values, worldviews, and behaviors based on Western Euro-Anglo principles of individuality, abstract ideals, and rationalism (Chung, 2005; Leong & Ponterotto, 2003). With most of the world's population being from collectivistic cultures effective group work in these settings may be in sharp contrast to Western individualistic cultural worldviews and group practice. Group counseling, regardless of the context, aims for group members to work cooperatively and assist each other in addressing group and personal issues. Group counseling is rooted with similar values as collectivistic cultures and therefore is an ideal intervention in those cultures within the international arena. Ironically, even though there is an emphasis on social relationships in collectivistic cultures and group counseling, traditional group counseling training and practice founded on principles of Western individualistic concepts may be contradictory to group counseling internationally. Subsequently it is essential that international group counselors have a clear understanding of the fundamental values inherent in collectivistic societies and facilitate groups accordingly.

Theme 2: Awareness of Political Countertransference

Providing counseling in an international setting poses new challenges that are related to issues of countertransference. In doing group work internationally group counselors frequently encounter new dimensions in their countertransference that incorporate political, historical, and social issues that we call political countertransference (Bemak & Chung, in press; Chung, 2005, Chung & Bemak, 2012). Political countertransference encompasses those issues that are heavily influenced by historical oppression and the contemporary sociopolitical climate that impact the counselor or psychotherapist. Political countertransference is promoted by mass media and politics regarding certain countries, cultures, religions, and political issues related to members of specific cultural groups. Regardless of how aware we are about our biases, prejudices, and privilege we still are influenced directly and indirectly, overtly and covertly, and subliminally by public media coverage about certain groups of people. For example, after 9/11 the United States experienced numerous terrorist alerts. The outcome of each alert reinforced the culture of fear (Bemak & Chung, in press; Chung & Bemak, 2012), that specifically targeted Arabs, Muslims, and Middle Eastern people and resulted in hate crimes which escalated 1600% from 2000 to 2001 (Chung, Bemak, Ortiz, & Sandoval-Perez, 2008). Although group counselors were aware of stereotypes and the danger of stereotyping every Middle Eastern person as being a terrorist, they were bombarded with public media information that resulted in promoting a culture of fear and created the danger of experiencing political countertransference. Working internationally it is essential that group counselors are aware, acknowledge, examine, and understand the origins of their own political countertransference and how it may interfere with effective and successful international group counseling. Being exposed to different media outlets rather than relying solely on one media source or their home country's interpretation of the international events can assist group counselors in gaining a more comprehensive perspective of political issues.

Theme 3: Mental Health Colonialism and Imperialism

As stated in the ASGW Multicultural and Social Justice Competencies, group workers must be mindful of their personal worldviews, beliefs, attitudes, values, stereotypes, biases, and privileges. All these variables can create deep and strong reactions and feelings by group counselors that have the potential to interfere with effective group counseling on a global level. Furthermore, counselors from Western countries are often trained in Euro-American individualistic methods of group work, which is sometimes erroneously interpreted by Western group workers as the "best" or "only" way to do group counseling. We cannot make the assumption that U.S. or Western theories, models, interventions, and strategies, are universal unless they have demonstrated extensive cross-cultural validity and applicability (Chung, 2005; Leong & Ponterotto, 2003). Underscoring group counseling theory and practice are psychological and counseling concepts which are also viewed from a Western perspective that are based on Western ideas, theories, and notions and have the potential to hinder effective international group counseling work.

For example, the term "diversity" or "diverse groups" as it relates to race and the ethnicity is often used in the global north to refer to groups that are dissimilar to the Anglo European-American cultural background. Therefore the term "diversity" or "diverse groups" is a Eurocentric and ethnocentric term using the Western Anglo European-American group as a baseline to view, judge, assess, interpret, evaluate, and perceive non-Western groups. This type of Western colonial and imperialist thinking can be problematic working internationally because group workers may have the mindset that they the "experts," "superior," they know what is best, or have a higher status of skills compared to non-Western cultures. In fact, using the term "American" by U.S. citizens is an ethnocentric term that excludes the rest of the Americas, and can create cross-cultural tension for U.S. group workers working in other parts of the Americas (i.e., Central and South America). Furthermore, Western public media may also reinforce this Eurocentric ethnocentric worldview that promotes Western superiority. In Australia, for example, many of the indigenous population, the Aboriginals, do not identify themselves under the diversity umbrella that has been established, called *Culturally and Linguistically Diverse* (CALD). CALD is a term that was created by White Australians and designates everyone else but them as diverse (Bemak, 2013). If one was to reverse the baseline for the CALD designation from the vantage point of Aboriginals, then White Australians would be categorized under the CALD label. This type of structure and definition that is done in Western countries is rooted in colonialism and perpetuates imperialism since it ignores not only the indigenous populations but also other ethnic and racial groups, and has the potential to incorporate these dynamics within the framework of international group counseling.

It is therefore important that group workers in international settings do not carry the colonial imperialist mentality that they are the "expert"; they know the best way to conduct group counseling with the "we" showing "you" how it is done mentality (Chung, 2005). This type of oppressive attitude only creates further challenges in doing international group work and sets up a power dynamic where the group counselor may be viewed, consciously or unconsciously, as the oppressor rather than the guest. This construct relates to Freire's (1972) banking concept of characterizing non-Western cultures as empty vessels, ignorant, and passive recipients who eagerly and willingly accept the information, in this case from the Western "expert" group worker. By forcing Western knowledge without the consideration of cultural, historical and sociopolitical background of the country we are working in promotes disempowerment rather than authentic empowerment since this attitude fosters a reliance on the Western group worker as the sole expert (Chung, 2005; Chung & Bemak, 2012; Freire, 1972).

Theme 4: International Group Work Voyeurism

Many international group counselors have the intention of conducting culturally responsive group work as a result of believing they have a genuine understanding, acceptance, and appreciation of cultural differences, combined with self-awareness of their own prejudices, biases, and privileges. Even so, we have often witnessed group workers who hold strongly felt ethnocentric and Eurocentric viewpoints, who are motivated to do international group work, and yet are unaware of their ethnocentric and Eurocentric biases that can potentially cause them to be ineffective in conducting group counseling across international boundaries. We have labelled this type of international group counseling as *international voyeurism*. International voyeurism may result in false idealizations of international cultural competence, accompanied by the denial about the lack of cultural awareness and responsiveness, and more insidiously the arrogant assumption that spending minimal time in a country results in them becoming "experts" of that culture. Traveling to other countries for conferences or workshops for short periods of time provides a very limited cultural exposure and a cursory cultural immersion, but does not make group counselors experts about that culture. We have encountered group counselors who excitedly talk about their adventures at a conference in a particular country and speak as if they are experts both about the country and about doing group counseling in that particular culture/country. This type of attitude and worldview unintentionally reinforces and perpetuates an international voyeuristic curiosity of those from Western countries, especially towards those in the global south and other developing countries. This voyeuristic curiosity enhances and reinforces the exoticism of being in a different culture/country and more insidiously reinforces and perpetuates the colonial imperialistic perspective of superiority as stated in Theme three. Kleinman and Kleinman (1977) addressed this idea stating, ". . . voyeurism is another outcome of construing suffering at a safe distance, without the social responsibility of real engagement" (pp. xviii). By keeping a safe distance group workers are avoiding, evading, excluding, denying, and escaping from the realities of their clientele which in some cases may be a painful reality of living in constant and pervasive poverty, violence, oppression, discrimination, injustice, and human rights violations. To deal with these painful realities from a safe distance promotes international voyeurism that results in "let me save you" mentality as stated in Theme three. Subsequently, being an international voyeur inhibits genuine dialogue and authentic group counseling and promotes superficial outcomes. To begin to truly understand the culture in which they are working group counselors must spend adequate time and dedication to doing cross-cultural group counseling, rather than a whimsical "one-off" trip or one-time conference or workshop and belief that they have become the "expert." The voyeuristic mindset therefore creates more harm than good.

Theme 5: Redefining Ethics and Boundaries for International Group Counseling

Working internationally will require adaptation, modification, alterations, and changes to Western traditional group counseling practices. International environments do not have the same narrowly defined legalistic practices as the United States and some other Western countries, which require different responses that are consistent with the national and cultural context in other countries. Barnett, Lazarus, Vasquez, Moorehead-Slaughter, and Johnson (2007) pointed out how codes of ethics in the major U.S. professional national associations were based on Western European-American cultural values and may not have applicability across cultures. Certain national and cultural practices must be embedded into international counseling such as giving and receiving gifts or socializing with clients (Bemak & Chung, 2015). For example it is considered good etiquette and manners to give and receive gifts on auspicious holidays or at special celebrations in many societies. For a group counselor to reject thoughtful personal gifts for a New Year's celebration would be considered rude and disrespectful. Similarly, to attend a client's wedding or join for festivities for a birthday party in many cultures would be expected and normative, rather than a violation of ethical boundaries.

Another concept that impacts boundaries when working internationally is how one defines and approaches time. In less time conscious cultures group counseling sessions may be far more flexible and fluid so that being late for a group counseling session would not be perceived as resistance and defensiveness that may require therapeutic interpretation and attention. Similarly, confidentiality is viewed very differently in collectivistic cultures and relates to boundary issues. Given that social connectedness is a dominant value in collectivistic cultures compared to individualistic cultures, in these cultures it is acceptable to speak more freely with others about one's group experience and group members (Bemak & Chung, 2011). We have facilitated numerous group counseling sessions in other countries where the boundaries related to privacy are very different, so that when a group member is having difficulty other group members may feel that this problem is a larger community problem, and believe sharing information outside the group is helpful rather than a violation of confidentiality (Bemak & Chung, 2011; Bemak & Chung, 2014). Given the different perspective about confidentiality and personal boundaries has bearing on where groups meet in international settings. In our experience private physical locations for international group counseling sessions may not be available or may not be very private, related to both a lack of space and less overall concern about privacy. We have held group counseling sessions in open outdoor physical spaces in schools and outside office buildings, in gymnasiums, in open spaces in churches and other religious institutions, etc. (Bemak & Chung, 2011; Bemak & Chung, 2014). Therefore group counselors working in international settings must exercise flexibility and creativity on where and how group counseling takes place.

Theme 6: Three Major Globalization Issues Impacting Mental Health and Group Counseling

There are three major global issues that we believe have significant impact on mental health and group counseling. The first issue is migration, which is a growing issue in the world today. Approximately 3.1% of the world's population, or 1 of every 33 people, is a migrant, with a 10-year increase in international migrants from 150 million to 214 million people (United Nations Department of Economic and Social Affairs, 2008). Major global trends such as migration should be kept in mind when considering future needs for mental health work and group counseling. Given that global migrants come from collectivistic societies group counseling would be an appropriate means to provide the clinical interventions that this population so desperately needs (Bemak & Chung, in press).

The second global issue that impacts mental health and group counseling is bicultural identity. Many individuals are struggling with bicultural identities as they attempt to retain the values and behaviors of their home culture with the increasing access and awareness of global culture. Globalization is influencing local cultures throughout the world with regards to technological access and information, education, food, media, governance, traditional beliefs, and practices, etc. The result of the confluence of local and global cultures is confusion about oneself and one's identity. Berry (1998) identified the conflict between a new culture and one's culture of origin as "acculturative stress." Group counseling is an excellent means of intervention to assist in sorting through the stress associated with identity confusion based on conflicting cultural values.

The third major issue is global environmental change. The impact of the environment that includes global warming and environmental racism has created a significant increase in environmental refugee migration (Chung, Bemak, & Kudo Grabosky, 2011) with estimates of 25 million environmental migrants or refugees (United Nations Environment Programme [UNEP], 2010). Studies have found increased risks for high levels of distress, depression, and anxiety and poorer mental health outcomes after exposure to repeated trauma (Kolassa et al., 2010), such as in the aftermath of environmental disasters. It is projected that with environmental degradation such as global warming, the rapid melting of ice, rising sea levels, and deforestation that 200 million people will become environmental refugees by 2050 (UNEP, 2010). Group counseling and therapy may be helpful in addressing these global environmental changes (Bemak & Chung, 2013; Pandya, 2011).

Theme 7: Partnership With Traditional Healers

The World Health Organization (WHO) defines traditional healing as health practices, approaches, and beliefs incorporating spiritual therapies, manual techniques, and plant, animal, and mineral-based medicines used singularly or in combination to maintain well-being and to treat, diagnose, and prevent illnesses (WHO, 2008). International group counselors will be working in societies where there are longstanding traditional healing practices. Many of the practices have centuries of recognition with healers such as *Sangomas* (in Southern Africa), the *Curanderos* (in Latin America), *Shamans* (in Asia), *Witch Doctors* (in Africa), *Medicine Men* (in First Nation cultures), *Inyangas,* or *Santeros/as* (in Southern Africa) who provide healing in different parts of the world. Given the longstanding history and recognition of various alternative and complementary healing practices, it is essential that group counselors are aware of and appreciate the work of healers and are able to facilitate collaboration when helpful for clients (Bemak & Chung, in press; Chung & Bemak, 2012). Forming an alliance with an authentic traditional healer who is from the same culture as the group members establishes not only credibility of the group counselor, but also an invaluable partnership that combines traditional healing with culturally responsive group counseling.

Theme 8: International Group Workers as Learners

For group counselors to be culturally and social-justice competent in the global arena requires a paradigm shift from traditional group counseling methodologies (Chung & Bemak, 2012). Since group counselors working in an international setting are only guests of that culture, the experts about ecological and systemic issues encountered by group members are the group members themselves. Group counselors may have acquired knowledge about the culture and the historical and sociopolitical context of the country in which they are working, and may be updated about current sociopolitical issues, however, they are only guests in that culture and not environmental experts. In an international setting for group counselors to truly understand group members' cultural, historical, sociopolitical, and ecological experiences they may at times need to be "learners" rather than the "teachers" (Bemak, 1996). To prevent an unequal balance of power where the group counselor holds all the authority and in a sense domination over group members the relationship between group counselor and group members must cultivate a two-way communication where at times the group worker is the "learner" and the group members are the "teachers" (Bemak, 1996; Freire, 1972). When the first author conducted a group with street children in Brazil it was a "give and take" and sharing power that allowed the children to teach the author about the ways of the street which established trust and credibility, and the children's acceptance of the author to facilitate groups conducive to healing and growth (Bemak, 1996).

Theme 9: International Group Work Training

As stated in the beginning of the article, globalization has enabled the world to be more connected and provided an easier access to cultures and countries that in even the past 10 years seemed unreachable. With dramatic increases in global migration, natural disasters, and mobility, group counseling has the potential to be a viable choice of healing worldwide, since three-quarters of the world's cultures are collectivistic in nature and group oriented. However, to be internationally competent requires additional skills and awareness as stated in the aforementioned critical international group counseling themes. We have met many motivated group workers who are eager to do international group work, but do not have the training about how to conduct international group counseling. It is our belief that this training is essential in our rapidly changing world.

The literature points towards the need for mental health to achieve a clear understanding of the impact of globalization on training (Ægisdóttir & Gerstein, 2010; Chung & Bemak, 2012; Marsella, 2007; Marsella & Pedersen, 2004; Ng & Noonan, 2012). Extending the need more specifically to group counseling training is imperative given that the global majority of the world's population lives in collectivistic societies. Important recommendations have been made to internationalize mental health training curriculums which would also be applicable to group counseling training, such as increasing the awareness of social, political, historical, and cultural factors; teach about the interrelationship of economics, politics and environment and psychology; integrate culture into theory and human development; enhance transnational research; providing internships in international settings, embed social justice and human rights; infuse training applications to vulnerable populations, e.g., the impoverished, refugees, street children, and survivors of post-disasters and survivors of human trafficking; learn about different cultures; and insert global problems as an aspect of training curriculums (Chung & Bemak, 2012; Heppner, Leong, & Gerstein, 2008; Marsella & Pedersen, 2004). Training group counselors to work within an international context is essential for our future as a profession.

CONCLUSION

Transnational group counseling work has been largely ignored in the field. The studies demonstrate the lack of scholarship and research in this area, leaving many group counselors to carry Western constructs into their work internationally. Effectively providing group counseling across international borders must include internationalized group counselor training. The ASGW Multicultural and Social Justice Competencies must be expanded and further developed to include international competencies. Additionally, a deep appreciation and awareness of the critical international group counseling themes discussed in this article must be cultivated to closely examine how Western practices can fit within the context of other countries and cultures. It is essential that group counselors continue to update themselves with new information by reading and accessing current scholarly and public media articles that go beyond work that is focused on their home country alone, and maintain a broad view of social, political, economic, and historical factors that comprise the countries where they are or will be working. Furthermore, we strongly believe that for group counseling to be viewed globally as a culturally viable means of healing and intervention then future group counselors must be globally connected, globally aware and trained from an international perspective.

REFERENCES

Ægisdóttir, S., & Gerstein, L. (2010). International counseling competencies. In J. G. Ponterotto, J. M. Casas, L. A. Suzuki, & C. M. Alexander (Eds.), *Handbook of multicultural counseling* (3rd ed., pp. 175–188). Thousand Oaks, CA: Sage.

Association for Specialists in Group Work. (2012). *Multicultural and social justice competence Principles for group workers*. Retrieved from http://www.asgw.org/pdf/ASGW_MC_SJ_Priniciples_Final_ASGW.pdf

Barnett, J. E., Lazarus, A. A., Vasquez, M. J. T., Moorehead-Slaughter, O., & Johnson, W. B. (2007). Boundary issues and multiple relationships: Fantasy and Reality. *Professional Psychology: Research and Practice, 38*, 401–410.

Bemak, F. (1996). Street researchers: A new paradigm redefining future research with street children. *Childhood, 3*, 147–156.

Bemak, F. (2013, October). *Critical dimensions in transforming and responsive transcultural mental health*. Keynote speaker at 4th Transcultural Mental Health and 2nd Refugee Health Conference, Perth, Australia.

Bemak, F., & Chung, R. C-Y. (2004). Teaching multicultural group counseling: Perspectives for a new era. *The Journal for Specialists in Group Work, 29*, 31–41.

Bemak, F., & Chung, R. C-Y. (2011). Post-disaster social justice group work and group supervision. *The Journal for Specialists in Group Work, 36*, 3–21.

Bemak, F., & Chung, R. C-Y. (2013). Post-disaster group counseling: A multicultural perspective. In Delucia-Waack, J. L., Gerrity, D. A., Kalodner, C. R., & Riva, M. *The handbook of group counseling and psychotherapy* (2nd ed., pp. 571–584). Thousand Oaks, CA: Sage.

Bemak, F., & Chung, R. C-Y. (2014). Post-disaster group counseling: A multicultural perspective. In J. L. DeLucia-Waack, D. Gerrity, C. Kalodner, & M. Riva (Eds.), *Handbook for group counseling and psychotherapy* (2nd ed., pp. 571–584). Thousand Oaks, CA: Sage.

Bemak, F., & Chung, R. C-Y. (2015). Cultural boundaries, cultural norms: Multicultural and social justice perspectives. In B. Herlihy & G. Corey (Eds.), *Boundary issues in counseling: Multiple roles and responsibilities* (3rd ed., pp. 84–91). Alexandria: VA: American Counseling Association.

Bemak, F., & Chung, R. C-Y. (in press). Counseling immigrants and refugees. In P. B. Pedersen, J. Draguns, W., Lonner, & J. Trimble, Scharron del Rio, M. (Eds.), *Counseling across cultures* (7th ed.). Thousand Oaks, CA: Sage.

Berry, J. W. (1998). Acculturative stress. In P. B. Organista, K. M. Chun, & G. Martin (Eds.), *Readings in ethnic psychology* (pp. 117–122). New York, NY: Routledge.

Casas, J. M., Park, Y. S., & Cho, B. (2010). The multicultural and internationalization counseling psychology movement: When all is said and done it's all multicultural, isn't it? In J. G. Ponterotto, J. M. Casas, L. A. Suzuki, & C. M. Alexander (Eds.), *Handbook of multicultural counseling* (3rd ed., pp. 189–200). Thousand Oaks, CA: Sage.

Chung, R. C-Y. (2005). Women, human rights and counseling: Crossing international boundaries. *Journal of Counseling and Development, 83*, 262–268.

Chung, R. C-Y., & Bemak, F. (2012). *Social justice counseling: The next steps beyond multiculturalism*. Thousand Oaks, CA: Sage.

Chung, R. C-Y., Bemak, F., & Kudo Grabosky, T. (2011). Multicultural-social justice leadership strategies: Counseling and advocacy with immigrants. *Journal of Social Action in Psychology and Counseling, 3*, 86–102.

Chung, R. C-Y., Bemak, F., Ortiz, D. P., & Sandoval-Perez, P. A. (2008). Promoting the mental health of migrants: A multicultural-social justice perspective. *Journal of Counseling and Development, Multicultural and Diversity Issues in Counseling, 38*, 310–317.

Conyne, R., & Bemak, F. (2004). Teaching group work from an ecological perspective. *The Journal for Specialists in Group Work, 29*, 7–18.

Freire P. (1972). *Pedagogy of the oppressed*. London, England: Penguin Books.

Harel, Y., Shechtman, Z., & Cutrona, C. (2011) Individual and group process variables that affect social support in counseling groups. *Group Dynamics: Theory, Research & Practice, 15*, 297–310

Heppner, P. P., Leong, F. T. L., & Gerstein, L. H. (2008). Counseling within a changing world: Meeting the psychological needs of societies and the world. In W. B. Walsh (Ed.), *Biennial review of counseling psychology* (pp. 231–258). New York, NY: Taylor & Francis.

Hornsey, M., Olsen, S., Barlow, F., & Oei, T. (2012) Testing a single-item visual analogue scale as a proxy for cohesiveness in group psychotherapy. *Group Dynamics: Theory, Research & Practice, 16*, 80–90.

Kleinman, A., & Kleinman, J. (1977).The appeal of experience; the dismay of images: cultural appropriations of suffering in our times. In A. Kleinman, V. Das, & M. M. Lock (Eds.), *Social suffering* (pp. 1–23). Berkeley: University of California Press.

Kolassa, I.-T., Ertl, V., Eckart, C., Kolassa, S., Onyut, L. P., Elbert, T. (2010). Spontaneous remission from PTSD depends on the number of traumatic event types experienced. *Psychological Trauma: Theory, Research, Practice, and Policy, 2*, 169–174.

Kooij-de Bode, H., van Knippenberg, D., & van Ginkel, W. (2008). Ethnic diversity and distributed information in group decision making: the importance of information elaboration. *Group Dynamics: Theory, Research & Practice, 12*, 307–320.

Kösters, M., Burlingame, G., Nachtigall, C., & Strauss, B. (2006). A meta-analytic review of the effectiveness of inpatient group psychotherapy. *Group Dynamics: Theory, Research & Practice, 10*, 146–163.

Leicht, C., Crisp, R., & Randsley de Moura, G. (2013). Need for structure predicts leadership experience. *Group Dynamics: Theory, Research & Practice, 17*, 53–66

Leong, F. T. L., & Ponterotto, J. G. (2003). A proposal for internationalizing counseling psychology in the United States: Rationale, recommendations and challenges. *The Counseling Psychologist, 31*, 381–395.

Marques-Quintero, P., Curral, L., Passos, A., & Lewis, K. (2013). And now what do we do? The role of transactive memory systems and task coordination in action teams. *Group Dynamics: Theory, Research & Practice, 17*, 194–206.

Marsella, A. J. (2007). Education and training for a global psychology: Foundations, issues and actions. In M. J. Stevens & U. P. Gielen (Eds.), *Toward a global psychology: Theory, research, intervention, and pedagogy* (pp. 333–361). Mahwah, NJ: Lawrence Erlbaum.

Marsella, A. J., & Pedersen, P. (2004). Internationalizing the counseling psychology curriculum: toward new values, competencies, and directions. *Counselling Psychology Quarterly, 17*, 413–423.

Martinez-Moreno, E., Zornoza, A., González-Navarro, P., & Thompson, L. (2012) Investigating face-to-face and virtual teamwork over time: when does early task conflict trigger relationship conflict? *Group Dynamics: Theory, Research & Practice, 16*, 159–171.

Maxwell, H., Tasca, G., Gick, M., Ritchie, K., Balfour, L., & Bissada, H. (2012) The impact of attachment anxiety on interpersonal complementarity in early group therapy interactions among women with binge eating disorder. *Group Dynamics: Theory, Research & Practice, 16* 255–271.

Ng, K., & Noonan, B. M. (2012). Internationalization of the counseling profession: Meaning, scope and concerns. *International Journal for the Advancement of Counselling, 34*, 5–18. doi:10.1007/s10447-011-9144-2

Pandya, A. (2011). Group and Family Interventions. In F. J. Stoddard Jr., A. Pandya, & C. Katz, (Eds.), *Disaster psychiatry: Readiness, evaluation, and treatment* (pp. 213–226). Arlington, VA: American Psychiatric Publishing, Inc., Committee on Disasters and Terrorism Disaster Psychiatry Outreach.

Pedersen, P. D. (2003). Culturally biased assumptions in counseling psychology. *The Counseling Psychologist, 31*, 396–403. doi:10.1177/0011000003031004002

Piper, W., Ogrodniczuk, J., Joyce, A., & Weideman, R. (2009). Follow-up outcome in short-term group therapy for complicated grief. *Group Dynamics: Theory, Research & Practice, 13*, 46–58.

Seppälä, T., Lipponen, J., & Pirttilä-Backman, A. (2012) Leader fairness and employees' trust in coworkers: the moderating role of leader group prototypicality. *Group Dynamics: Theory, Research & Practice, 16*, 35–49.

Shechtman, Z., Goldberg, A., & Cariani, R. (2008). Arab and Israeli counseling trainees: a comparison of ethnically homogenous and heterogeneous groups. *Group Dynamics: Theory, Research & Practice, 12*, 85–95.

Shechtman, Z., & Halevi, H. (2006). Does ethnicity explain functioning in group counseling? The case of Arab and Jewish counseling trainees in Israel. *Group Dynamics: Theory, Research & Practice, 10*, 181–193.

Stathi, S., Crisp, R., & Hogg, M. (2011). Imagining intergroup contact enables member-to-group generalization. *Group Dynamics: Theory, Research & Practice, 15*, 275–184.

Thomas, R. V., & Pender, D. A. (2008). Association for Specialists in Group Work: Best Practice Guidelines 2007 revisions. *The Journal for Specialists in Group Work, 33*, 111–117. doi:10.1080/01933920801971184

Tjosvold, D., Coleman, P., & Sun, H. (2003). Effects of organizational values on leaders' use of informational power to affect performance in China. *Group Dynamics: Theory, Research & Practice, 7*, 152–167.

United Nations Department of Economic and Social Affairs. (2008). *Trends in international migrant stock: The 2008 revision*. Retrieved from http://esa.un.org/migration/index.asp?panel=1

United Nations Environment Programme (UNEP). (2010). *Climate change and environmentally induced migration*. New York, NY: United Nations Environment Programme. Retrieved from http://www.unep.org/conflictsanddisasters/Policy/DisasterRiskReduction/ClimateChangeAndMigration/tabid/282/Default.Aspx

World Health Organization. (2008). *Fact sheet no. 134: Traditional medicine*. Retrieved from http://www.who.int/inf-fs/en/fact134.html

Development and Implementation of an International Counseling Outreach Effort in Bhutan: A Group Stage Conceptualization

Lorraine J. Guth
Indiana University of Pennsylvania

Sonya Lorelle
Governor's State University

J. Scott Hinkle
National Board for Certified Counselors

Theodore P. Remley
Old Dominion University

This article highlights the development and implementation of an international counseling outreach program in Bhutan using a group stage conceptualization that includes the initial, transition, working, and final stages. The initial stage included a counseling initiative started by one of the queens as well as meetings with key leaders from the National Board for Certified Counselors International and Bhutan. The transition stage involved developing plans for an international counseling outreach effort in Bhutan that involved formal collaborations between the two countries. The working stage included selecting counselors/educators from the United States who provided counseling/training in Bhutan. Future work is discussed, and also implications for the counseling profession.

The development and implementation of international counseling outreach programs around the world is increasing. Leaders of many nations recognize that "professional counseling is one of the tools that can help advance the mental health of their people. . . . Although the profession is at varying developmental stages in different countries, significant advancements in counseling are progressing with increasing momentum" (Hohenshil, Amundson, & Niles, 2013, p. 3). The need for effective counseling by mental health professionals goes beyond borders and continents and is truly needed in every culture. As people become increasingly connected across the globe, counselors must learn "how to work across, through, and beyond cultural and continental differences" (Hohenshil et al., 2013, p. 9).

Since the counseling profession is growing globally, counselors need to be prepared to tailor theories, techniques, and programs to other cultures and countries (Hohenshil, 2010). "The concerns experienced by people around the globe speaks concerns experienced by people around the globe speak to the importance of a highly effective profession that can function appropriately and successfully across borders and between cultures" (Gerstein, Heppner, Stockton, Leong, & Ægisdóttir, 2012, p. 97). It is important to note that the concepts of wellness and healing have existed globally with some practices being in existence for thousands of years (Barnett & Shale, 2012; Witmer, 2013). As counseling practices expand in other countries, it is imperative to understand the indigenous healing practices that are part of the particular culture. For example, the National Board for Certified Counselors International (NBCC-I) only operates in countries when invited and develops comprehensive plans from mutual perspectives using local experts.

This internationalization of the counseling movement underscores that growth of counseling around the world is a significant and exciting trend in the counseling profession (Hohenshil, 2010). In fact, in 2010 there was a special issue of the *Journal of Counseling & Development* devoted to counseling efforts that are emerging in several countries. The development of counseling in countries such as China (Lim, Lim, Cai, & Schock, 2010), Botswana (Stockton, Nitza, & Bhusumane, 2010), Malaysia (See & Ng, 2010), Romania (Szilagti & Paredes, 2010), Italy (Remley, Bacchini, & Krieg, 2010), and Mexico (Portal, Suck, & Hinkle, 2010) show how these countries have responded to current trends and needs in this rapidly changing world. The most recent publication of the book *Counseling Around the World: An International Handbook* (Hohenshil et al., 2013), speaks to the importance of counseling efforts taking place in over 100 countries around the globe, including Bhutan.

Bhutan, a small country of 683,407 people, is nestled between India and the Himalayan border of Tibet, and is referred to as the *Last Shangri-La* because of its leaders' efforts to preserve their unique cultural traditions and beautiful natural environment (Wangchhuk, 2010). The influence of religion is visible in everyday life (e.g., temples, prayer flags, prayer wheels) with about three fourths of the population practicing Buddhism (Walcott, 2011). Bhutanese law requires all citizens to wear traditional national dress in public areas that consists of a knee-length robe (*gho*) tied at the waist for men and an ankle length skirt (*kira*) tied at the waist, long-sleeved blouse (*wonju*), and jacket (*tego*) for women (Wangchhuk, 2010). People of Bhutan are generally divided into three ethnic groups based on location in the country. People who live in the East are referred to as the *Sharchops*, people in the West are called the *Ngalops*, and people from the South part of the country are known as the *Lhotshampas* (Wangchhuk, 2010).

Considered one of the least developed countries in the 1960s with no infrastructure such as roads or communications systems, modern development of the country did not begin until the early 1970s. In the last 15 years the country has rapidly developed including the introduction of television and Internet service to the once secluded population (Wangchhuk, 2010), as well as the introduction of school and mental health counseling. Bhutan has recently increased efforts to more formally establish the counseling profession in the country. Since 1996, a handful of Bhutanese counselors have been trained in Western countries and Australia due to there being no formal university counselor education program in Bhutan.

Rapid growth has had significant effects on the population of Bhutan including the rise of urban migration, divorce rates, and substance abuse (Walcott, 2011; Wangchhuk, 2010). While there are not reliable statistics on mental health issues in the country, the only national hospital reported 2,846 patients were treated for mental health problems in 2008. Depression, anxiety, alcohol abuse, and substance abuse were prominent diagnoses. Stigma surrounding mental illnesses is influenced by traditional beliefs which explain mental illness to be a result of evil spirits, witchcraft, or karma (Pelzang, 2012). It is thought that 99% of the people in Bhutan seek religious help when someone is physically or mentally ill. Therefore, as mental health service delivery in the country is further developed, a holistic approach is needed that integrates this religious dimension and traditional beliefs into counseling practice (Pelzang, 2012).

At the beginning of the 21st century, a monarchy was established in Bhutan. Bhutan's fourth king developed the term *Gross National Happiness* (GNH) which captured the government's guiding philosophy for promoting the wellbeing of the people and the growth in this country. The concept of GNH provides a vision for environmental and cultural preservation, psychological wellbeing, and health for the country and its citizens (Dakpa, Rabten, Rai, & Garung, 2011). The GNH is measured by a multidimensional index and provides data to policy makers and the government on how to "increase the percentage of people who are happy or decrease the insufficient conditions of people who are no-yet-happy" (Ura, Alkire, Zangmo, & Wangdi, 2012, p.1).

Buddhism remains central to the cultural and spiritual part of the country's heritage (Walcott, 2011). In the book, *Educating for GNH: A Guide to Advancing Gross National Happiness,* Dakpa et al. (2011) provide an overview of the psychological wellbeing domain that contains the variables of emotional balance, mental health, spirituality, and quality of life. Practices such as meditation and prayer as well as values such as compassion and empathy are congruent with the concept of counseling.

The purpose of this article is to highlight the development and implementation of an international counseling outreach program in Bhutan using a group stage conceptualization. Although there are different models that demonstrate how groups develop over time (Brabender, 2010), this article will use the initial, transition, working, and final stages conceptualization (Corey, Corey, & Corey, 2014). This stage conceptualization helps to provide a framework for understanding how the counseling profession evolved in Bhutan in collaboration with professionals from the United States.

INITIAL STAGE: DEVELOPING THE COUNSELING PROFESSION IN BHUTAN

The initial stage of a group is often characterized by orientation, search for meaning, and exploration (Yalom, 2005). This is a time when rapport is being built among members, expectations are discussed, norms are developed that guide how the group functions, fears and hopes are explored, trust is being established, and goals are often formed (Corey et al., 2014). These characteristics were present as key Bhutanese leaders worked to spark the development of the counseling profession in Bhutan. During this phase of development, goals were mutually established for the movement and rapport was built among key leaders from Bhutan and the United States. Trust, norms (spoken and unspoken), and expectations were developed as the ground work was laid.

Several historical events led to the initiative to establish the counseling profession in Bhutan. First, the development of counseling in Bhutan began with Queen Ashi Sangay Choden Wangchhuk who founded RENEW (Respect, Educate, Nurture, and Empower Women) in 2004, which is an organization to provide support and empowerment to women and girls, in particular around the issue of domestic violence. Additionally, a counselor from Bhutan contacted the National Board for Certified Counselors (NBCC) to become a National Certified Counselor (NCC). NBCC evaluated additional education that the counselor needed for certification and helped her obtain the required training. Subsequently, leaders from NBCC went to Bhutan in 2008 to present the first NCC certificate to this Bhutanese counselor. This person went on to become a driving force for counseling in her country. In 2008, NBCC leaders also met with the Queen to discuss collaboration with NBCC-I.

NBCC-I has a mission of strengthening the counseling profession globally and has worked with international organizations and leaders of several countries in order to support the development of community projects, counseling services, and mental health support where needed. In these projects, counselors and counselor educators from the United States often travel to international sites to offer consultation, collaboration, training, and counseling services. NBCC-I projects are developed only in situations in which counselors in another country request assistance in helping the profession of counseling develop in that country. NBCC-I and the counselors who participate in international projects are cautious to ensure that values or cultural norms found in the United States are not imposed on the counseling profession that is developing in another country. However, often counselors and leaders in other countries are interested in learning more about the model of counseling in the United States so that they can determine how that model might be adopted in their own culture. Project participants from the United States often explain how counseling, supervision, group work, etc. are applied in the United States, while being aware that cultural differences always exist in another country. Project participants learn about the culture and values of people within the other country as they prepare for the project and during the time they are visiting the country.

TRANSITION STAGE: DEVELOPING INTERNATIONAL COUNSELING OUTREACH EFFORT IN BHUTAN

The transition stage of a group is sometimes characterized by fear, anxiety, reluctance, challenges to the leader(s), and control issues (Corey et al., 2014; Yalom, 2005). The transitional phase can be a time of uncertainty as trust continues to be built and members work though the hesitancy that emerges. In establishing the counseling profession in Bhutan, the transition stage was marked by establishing agreements and creating plans for collaboration. As these interactions took place there were some issues that needed to be addressed such as who would be in control of the various programs and plans that were being developed. At times, fears and reluctance were observed in planning meetings. There also was observed a sense of hopefulness and anticipation at the end of this stage.

Group work within political and governmental organizations involves negotiating existing relationships that are well-established and complex. An additional challenge for the project in Bhutan included counselors from the United States interacting with numerous professionals in a vastly different culture (Chandratilake, McAleer, & Gibson, 2012). Fear, anxiety, reluctance, challenges to the leader(s), and control issues (identified by Corey et al., 2014; Yalom, 2005) were all evident during this transition stage up to the working stage of the relationship that later emerged (addressed in further detail in the working stage discussion). It is important to note that the professionals from the United States worked to ensure that the needs and goals for this initiative were generated by the Bhutanese professionals and the training/work that occurred was culturally responsive.

There were several events that led to a more formal collaboration between NBCC-I and leaders in Bhutan to further develop counseling in the country. For example, two formal memorandums of understanding between NBCC-I and RENEW have been signed that outline collaborations in the effort to develop the counseling profession in Bhutan. NBCC-I also signed a similar agreement with the Ministry of Health that places a professional counselor from the United States in the psychiatric unit at the national hospital on a continual basis. The role of the counselors who are placed in Bhutan for three month periods is to assist the only two psychiatrists in Bhutan with inpatient care and staff training. In addition, the *Thunder Dragon Counseling Institute* was formed by NBCC-I and Old Dominion University. This institute was designed to send counseling professionals from the United States to Bhutan to help with counseling initiatives. A primary component of the institute was to give counseling professionals from the United States a multi-week experience in Bhutan as counseling service providers so that they might consider returning to the country for long-term volunteer counseling experiences. The participants of this institute also provided training and services in a variety of settings based on the established needs expressed by the leaders in Bhutan.

WORKING STAGE: PROVIDING COUNSELING AND TRAINING IN BHUTAN

The working stage is the "core of the group process" (Jacobs, Masson, Harvill, & Schimmel, 2012, p. 37). This stage of a group is marked by a deeper level of exploration where significant work takes place, learning occurs, cohesion increases, and progress on goals is made (Fall, McMahon, & Hays, 2011). As the counseling profession grew in Bhutan, this stage occurred when the initiatives that were planned in the transition stage were implemented. Counselors from the United States provided service and training to Bhutanese residents and professionals. This collaboration was essential in sparking the working stage where counselors from Bhutan learned more in-depth counseling skills. The participants from both countries involved themselves in the learning process, interacted with one another, and engaged in culturally responsive counseling services with clients and students.

During this stage, work took place in Bhutan to further establish the counseling profession. Two *Thunder Dragon Counseling Institutes* were held in 2011 and 2012 with over 20 counseling professionals from the United States participating in this international counseling outreach effort designed to further establish the counseling profession in Bhutan. The counseling professionals from the United States were masters or doctoral level professionals who were counselor educators, school counselors, and clinical mental health counselors holding a broad range of specialties.

The delegations from the United States spent 2 weeks providing direct counseling services to Bhutanese residents in schools, an inpatient psychiatric unit, university counseling centers, and a women's center. The scope of the counseling work varied depending on the expressed needs at each site. Generally, the counseling services were provided daily to clients or students who presented with counseling issues. A counselor from the United States and a helping professional from Bhutan (e.g., teacher/counselor, psychiatrist, and counselor) were sometimes both present during the counseling sessions. The sessions were typically held in English since this language is widely spoken in the main towns and is the mode of instruction in the schools. On occasion, translation was needed (from native Dzongkha language to English or vice versa) and provided by a Bhutanese helping professional. The delegation also met with counseling leaders in Bhutan to understand the current state of counseling in the country and the related cultural considerations. Training and recommendations for the future practice of counseling in the country also were provided. In order to highlight the efforts in the working stage, several examples of the counseling initiatives that have taken place in Bhutan are described.

Counseling in the Schools

In the 1960s, modern education in Bhutan was expanded to form an organized school system with free and universal education. Wangchhuk (2010) explains the educational structure in Bhutan includes 7 years of Primary Education (including Pre-Primary) and 6 years of Secondary Education (including 2 years each at the lower, middle, and higher secondary levels). The educational system today includes "1,651 schools and institutes with 197,832 students/learners and 8,418 teachers. . . . The literacy rate is 59.5 percent" (Wangchhuk, 2010, p. 264).

The schools are one of the primary settings where counseling is being developed in Bhutan and collaboration with counselors from the United States has taken place. During the initial *Thunder Dragon Counseling Institute* in 2011, there were no official positions for school counselors. A representative from the Ministry of Education informed the institute participants that governmental job descriptions of school counselors had been approved (S. Pelden, personal communication, October 2011); however, the majority of schools did not have a full-time school counselor. Instead schools had teacher/counselors who were teachers interested in counseling and had some training in counseling. The teacher/counselors offered services and support to students during their limited free time. During the institute, professionals from the United States provided additional training to the teacher/counselors on individual/group counseling.

During the institutes, there were six professionals from the United States who volunteered in the schools to enhance the counseling services. Collaboration was emphasized in the process to ensure cultural norms were addressed. The counselors from the United States explored their primary concerns and encouraged principals, teachers, and teacher/counselors to generate the goals they wanted for their counseling program and what difference in the children and classrooms they hoped to see as a result. When consulting with the school stakeholders, the concerns and goals varied depending on the age level of students. High school personnel were concerned with substance abuse, truancy, and the stress of family problems of the students. At the pre-primary and primary grade levels, personnel were primarily concerned with student misbehavior, hyperactivity, attention span, parental divorce adjustment, and classroom management.

The professionals from the United States began the collaboration by asking the stakeholders what they hoped to gain by the participant's visit. School personnel specifically asked for teacher training on positive student-teacher relationships, basic listening, and classroom management. This training was conducted in a large group setting and began with discussion questions to try to engage participants. After providing information on specific skills as well as modeling the skills, groups were asked to practice in pairs. Teachers were initially reluctant to answer discussion questions or participate in the practice in the beginning of the session. The principals took on a leadership role in the group and encouraged everyone to share. By the end of the training, participants shared stories about their experiences with students as well as asked questions. They discussed how they could see these skills being useful in their setting. After the training, participants continued to talk among themselves about what they learned and ideas they wanted to incorporate with students.

Group work also was utilized in classrooms within the schools. Since counseling is a newer concept in Bhutan, stakeholders asked the institute's counseling professionals who were providing services and training to talk with students about what counseling is and how it can be helpful. This information was provided in individual classrooms in a large group format. Stakeholders were asked about what their ideas about counseling were. This question helped to illuminate stigmas and misconceptions. Information was provided to help counteract stigmas, such as seeking counseling help doesn't mean someone is "crazy." The reactions from the groups varied from quiet and polite listening to a more energetic curiosity. Several students asked questions at the end of the discussion about how to solve their specific problems such as, "How do you stop drinking alcohol?" Others requested to see counselors individually to ask their questions such as: "How can I get my parents back together?" These questions seemed to show that students were eager to receive help, but were unsure how to obtain help to bring about the changes they wanted in their lives. Individual counseling sessions were provided to students and growth was noted as they processed their issues.

The concept of group counseling was introduced in one of the schools. Lorelle and Guth (2013) reported how the teacher/counselors were provided with information and training on group counseling in Bhutan. One of the institute participants worked with the teacher/counselors to co-facilitate counseling groups on divorce, anger, and hyperactivity which were topics requested by the principal based on student needs. The students responded positively during the group experience and the teacher/counselors reported they would like to continue to learn more about group work and utilize groups in the future.

Other work was done on a more individual basis and included providing collaborative consultation to individual teachers and parents regarding specific students. Several schools had a vision for a comprehensive school counseling program that would provide consistent support for struggling students and instill core values of their culture which included problem solving and mindful decision-making skills. Ways to implement interventions or programs to help them achieve their goal of having comprehensive counseling programs were discussed with the principals and teacher/counselors. The school personnel asked about the models of school counseling in the United States. Information about the American School Counselor Association (ASCA) National Model (2012) and International Model of School Counseling Programs (Fezler & Brown, 2011) was shared, and the school personnel decided what components fit the direction they wanted for their school counseling programs within their culture. The International Model was designed to be culturally sensitive with language considerations, content that reflects the unique environment of a country, and cross-cultural perspectives (Fezler & Brown, 2011). The principal and the teacher/counselors in one of the pre-primary/primary schools decided that they wanted to focus on character building in their students and thought the curriculum lessons could be a piece of the model incorporated into their school. Strengths of the school and current effective practices were identified in order to build on positive aspects of the schools. For example, one school had club times established for the students which could be an ideal forum for classroom lessons or where a peer helper club could be initiated.

The main barrier each of the schools had regarding implementing these ideas for counseling was a limited amount of time available to the teacher/counselors, given that there was not a full-time counselor to continue with the school's interest in implementing a comprehensive school counseling program that they desired. Another barrier that the school personnel expressed included a lack of resources; one high school described not having access to counseling books/resources and had limited space to provide individual or group counseling to students. Because of this lack of time in the role of counselor for the teacher/counselors and resources, school officials hoped for continued collaboration in the future where counselors from the United States could return for longer periods of time to provide counseling services and consultation so that they could develop a counseling program that is congruent with the Bhutanese culture.

Counseling Services at the Royal University of Bhutan

During the 2011 institute, two volunteer participants of *The Thunder Dragon Institute* provided direct counseling services to students and consultation on the development of university counseling centers on two campuses of the Royal University of Bhutan. These counselors from the United States spent a week at the campus in Paro which is located about an hour from the capital city of Thimphu and a week in Samtse, a campus located south of Thimphu near India.

Each campus had a full-time counselor who had earned a master's degree in counseling. One had studied in Australia and the other in India; both counselors received their training prior to NBCC-I's involvement. Although these individuals had the title of counselor, they actually functioned as full-time faculty members teaching several academic courses each semester; one served as chair of his academic department. The time allotted to these professionals to provide counseling services to students was limited to only a few hours each week. The campus in Samtse had an active college peer counseling program in which upper class students were trained to talk with other students about academic, personal, and social concerns.

In order to gain an understanding of the students and their needs, the institute counselors met in individual counseling sessions with about 10 students from each campus and interacted with groups of students. In Bhutan, students apply to the Royal University of Bhutan and are then assigned to a university campus based on their preferred major. There are 10 campuses of the university and the campuses are located throughout the country (http://www.rub.edu.bt). Most students live in small villages in Bhutan and travel to and from their assigned university campus can include more than a day of travel by bus or car followed by up to 12 hr of walking from a main road to a student's village. Before departing for the university, many students have not left their home village for significant periods of time. Student concerns expressed to the counselors from the United States included adjustment to living in residence halls with other students, loneliness, distress about being separated from their family members, anxiety about their job placements after graduation, failure to meet academic standards, alcohol abuse, and thoughts of suicide. As with many countries, alcohol abuse and suicide are significant problems in the universities in Bhutan ("Rising Substance Abuse," 2014).

Counseling Services in the Psychiatric Unit of the National Hospital

During the institutes, six participants were assigned to the inpatient ward of the Department of Psychiatry, Jigme Dorji Wangchuck National Referral Hospital (JDWNRH) in Thimphu, the capital city of Bhutan. The counselors from the United States provided inpatient and outpatient counseling services to patients as well as supervision, consultation, and training to the staff of the psychiatric unit. They participated in three-times-weekly multidisciplinary team rounds that included diagnosis, treatment, and social support. Problems addressed were primarily as depression, anxiety, and substance abuse. These services led to the Ministry of Health encouraging the aforementioned MOU for direct inpatient services, training, and supervision.

Trainings and Workshops

Numerous trainings and workshops were provided during this collaboration. The first national counseling conference was held in February, 2011 in Thimphu. During the first *Thunder Dragon Counseling Institute*, 10 volunteer participants from the United States provided training to 75 Bhutanese helping professionals. Presentation topics included the roles of school counselors, values clarification, grief and loss counseling, avoiding burnout, family counseling and assessment, substance abuse counseling, cultural awareness, child development, adventure based counseling, and an overview of group counseling skills. The concept of group work was new to many of the conference attendees. At the beginning of the group work presentation, selected participants were invited to participate in the "Ball in Play" activity (Halbur, 2002) that was a culturally appropriate method to illustrate group stages. The participants were instructed to take a ball that was provided and play a game for 10 min. At first the participants were unsure what to do. However, as the time progressed they engaged in a traditional Bhutanese dance where they moved in a circle using the ball as a prop. It was beautiful to witness the members move into a working stage during the dance. This activity is a metaphor for the stages of group development. After the activity was over, the audience was able to identify the initial, transition, working, and ending stages of the group. The participants were also interested in learning more about group counseling and how they could use the skills at their respective school or agency.

NBCC-I has developed a mental health curriculum in collaboration with the World Health organization in order to attempt to bridge the gap of unmet mental health needs in international communities. The *Mental Health Facilitator (MHF)* program provides training on basic helping skills and how to recognize mental health issues. The examples used in the curriculum were customized to the Bhutanese culture. There have been five 30-hr training sessions offered in Bhutan, some by institute participants. The training is designed to be given in a large group format. After providing information to the large group, participants were divided into small groups to practice skills they were learning and discuss how they envision applying these skills in their culture and community. By the end of the week, the group had many ideas on how to use their new knowledge.

Further Developments Resulting From the Counseling Institutes

After the institutes, there have been continued collaborations. The two *Thunder Dragon Counseling Institutes* held in 2011 and 2012 brought a total of 20 volunteer counselors from the United States to Bhutan for approximately 3 weeks to introduce them to the country and set the stage for counselors to return as volunteers for longer periods of time. The short-term institutes served their purpose and long-term volunteer counselors from the United States have been serving in Bhutan. To date, five counselors have returned to Bhutan and spent a minimum of 3 months each assisting the country's only two psychiatrists with inpatient care and staff training. These follow-up initiatives providing more in depth clinical mental health services such as assessments and evaluation, behavioral diagnosis, treatment planning, and inpatient mental health counseling. Professional development training and consultation also was offered. Counselors at the hospital worked as clinical staff members providing clinical intakes, assessments and evaluations, differential clinical diagnosis, treatment planning, and on-going treatment of both inpatient and outpatient mental health and addictions patients. They averaged counseling 3–4 patients each morning in addition to participating in three clinical staffings weekly, and co-leading specialized group counseling sessions (e.g., anxiety group counseling).

The counselors also worked with the Ministry of Health's National Mental Health Program to provide professional development training for Bhutan's new cohort of physicians from across Bhutan. Twenty-two physicians and seven nurses and other allied health workers from Bhutan's Basic Health Units and Regional Hospitals were trained in mental health assessment and evaluation, diagnosis, treatment, and mental health counseling; alcohol and other drug clinical assessment and treatment; and needs assessment and organizational planning for the nation's drug and mental health services. Specialized training also was provided for the Tarayana Foundation, training an all-Bhutan cohort of child care workers in child development, mental health and addictions assessment, counseling theory, and planning mental health and early education related services for the first national cohort of trained child care workers. The Tarayana Foundation is a non-profit organization that has the mission to enhance the lives of vulnerable communities in rural Bhutan (Tarayana Foundation, 2014). Additionally, two counselors also returned to Bhutan and provided more extensive services working with the Ministry of Education in the schools.

An outgrowth of the collaboration also includes two individuals from Bhutan being educated as counselors in the United States. One Bhutanese counselor recently received her master's degree in counseling from Eastern Michigan University and a second Bhutanese student has completed her first year of doctoral study at Old Dominion University.

FINAL STAGE: FUTURE WORK IN BHUTAN

The final stage of group is characterized by having members consolidate learning, express the meaning of the group experience, and see how the new behaviors and skills can be used in everyday life (Corey et al., 2014). As some of the working stage initiatives ended such as the *Thunder Dragon Counseling Institute* which was discontinued after 2 successful years, participants from Bhutan and the United States reflected on the meaning of the experience on multiple levels. For example, Bhutanese professionals took their new learning and applied it in their continued counseling work with students and clients. The professionals from the United States also were deeply impacted as a result of their service-learning experience. The connections that were made across cultures have remained for many who were involved in this initiative.

Consultation also has taken place on the development of a Bhutan counseling organization to represent the interests of professional mental health services, their professional staff, and the people they serve. On August 9, 2013, a memorandum of understanding was signed to establish the Bhutan Board for Certified Counselors which will help to professionalize counseling in the country (http://www.bbs.bt/news/?p=30271). Although this milestone is significant, it also demonstrates that more work is needed to establish the national organization and counselor certification.

Although Bhutan is still in the working stage with several initiatives, implications for counseling include:

1. *Remember the Power of Group Work*. His majesty Jigme Singye Wangchuck stated "Gross National Happiness is far more important that Gross Domestic Product" (Wangchhuk, 2010, p. 185). This shared vision and guiding philosophy of the country emphasizes collective happiness for the people. It is evident from this initiative in Bhutan that group work can be impactful on many levels in helping to promote this GNH philosophy. The Institute for Intercultural Studies provides the following Margaret Mead quote: "Never doubt that a small group of committed citizens can change the world." (http://www.interculturalstudies.org/faq.html#quote). During the *Thunder Dragon Counseling Institutes* and the other NBCC-I projects, several small groups of people from the United States collaborated with small groups of people in Bhutan to further the development of counseling in Bhutan. These efforts will hopefully continue to positively impact the citizens of Bhutan who will benefit from the new counseling initiatives taking place.
2. *Start Small When Making Changes*. Rather than trying to build a comprehensive counseling program all at once, it could be helpful to pick one goal or one program at a school or agency that is realistic. For example, one of school's officials stated it was not feasible to hire a full time counselor at the moment. Since these stakeholders in the school were interested in seeing students coming to class prepared to learn, the teacher/counselor can make a small step by collaborating with the teachers on implementing a few interventions at a school wide level to address this issue. They can assess the impact of these interventions and make needed changes that are informed by data.

3. *Take Advantage of Technology*. With technological advances including virtual meetings, ongoing collaboration from afar is now possible. Weekly or monthly supervision or consultation could be done online to assist in facilitating the development of counseling in Bhutan. Webinars on specific topics could also be offered.

In conclusion, this article highlights how the stages of group development apply to an international initiative to establish the profession of counseling in Bhutan. This meaningful initiative demonstrated that positive change can occur when there is collaboration, advocacy, training, consultation, and commitment. The dynamic interactions during this process helped to promote interpersonal learning (Yalom, 2005) and growth for all involved. It is unknown what the future holds, but with the power of the group process, anything is possible.

ACKNOWLEDGMENTS

The authors would like to thank all who were involved in this initiative including counselors/educators/leaders from Bhutan and the United States.

REFERENCES

American School Counselor Association (2012). *The ASCA national model: A framework for school counseling programs* (3rd ed.). Alexandria, VA: Author.

Barnett, J. E., & Shale, A. J. (2012). The integration of complementary and alternative medicine (CAM) into the practice of psychology: A vision for the future. *Professional Psychology: Research and Practice*, *43*, 576–585.

Brabender, V. (2010). Group development. In R. Conyne (Ed.), *The Oxford handbook of group counseling* (pp. 182–204). New York, NY: Oxford.

Chandratilake, M., McAleer, S, & Gibson, J. (2012). Cultural similarities and differences in medical professionalism: A multi-region study. *Medical Education*, *46*, 257–266.

Corey, M., Corey, G., & Corey, C. (2014). *Groups: Process and practice* (9th ed.). Pacific Grove, CA: Brooks/Cole.

Dakpa, K., Rabten, W., Rai, A., & Gurung, N. (2011). *Educating for GNH: A guide to advancing gross national happiness*. Paro, Bhutan: Department of Curriculum, Research, and Development.

Fall, K. A., McMahon, H. G., & Hays, D. G. (2011). The working stage. In B. Erford (Ed.), *Group work: Process and applications* (pp. 121–145). Upper Saddle River, NJ: Pearson.

Fezler, B., & Brown, C. (2011). *The international model for school counseling programs*. Retrieved from http://www.aassa.com/uploaded/Educational_Research/US_Department_of_State/Counseling_Standards/International_Counseling_Model_Handbook.pdf

Gerstein, L. H., Heppner, P. P., Stockton, R., Leong, F. T. L., & Ægisdóttir, S. (2012). The counseling profession in- and outside the United States. In L. H. Gerstein, P.

P. Heppner, S. Ægisdóttir, S. M. A. Leung, & K. A. Norsworthy (Eds.), *Essentials of cross-cultural counseling* (pp. 79–102). Los Angeles, CA: Sage.
Halbur, D. (2002). Ball in play. In J. L. DeLucia-Waack, K. H. Bridbord, & Kleiner, J. S. (Eds.), Group *work experts share their favorite activities: A guide to choosing, planning, conducting, and processing* (pp. 45–46). Alexandria, VA: Association for Specialists in Group Work.
Hohenshil, T. H. (2010). International counseling introduction. *Journal of Counseling & Development, 88*, 3.
Hohenshil, T. H., Amundson, N. E., & Niles, S. G. (2013). *Counseling around the world: An international handbook*. Alexandria, VA: American Counseling Association.
Jacobs, E. E., Masson, R. L., Harvill, R. L., & Schimmel, C. J. (2012). *Group counseling: Strategies and skills* (7th ed.). Pacific Grove, CA: Brooks/Cole.
Lim, S. L., Lim, B. K. H., Cai, R. M. R., & Schock, C. K. (2010). The trajectory of counseling in China: Past, present, and future trends. *Journal of Counseling & Development, 88*, 4–8.
Lorelle, S., & Guth, L. J. (2013). Establishing the school counseling profession in Bhutan: Reflections from the field. *Journal for International Counselor Education, 5*, 1–13. Retrieved from http://digitalscholarship.unlv.edu/jice/
Pelzang, R. (2012). Mental health care in Bhutan: Policy and issues. *WHO South-East Asia Journal of Public Health, 1*, 339–346.
Portal, E. L., Suck, A. T., & Hinkle, J. S. (2010). Counseling in Mexico: History, current identity, and future trends. *Journal of Counseling and Development, 88*, 33–37.
Remley, T. P., Jr., Bacchini, E., & Krieg, P. (2010). Counseling in Italy. *Journal of Counseling & Development, 88*, 28–32.
Rising substance abuse challenges Bhutan's reputation as the world's happiest country. (2014). Retrieved from http://enews.buddhistdoor.com/en/news/d/46501
See, C. M., & Ng, K. M. (2010). Counseling in Malaysia: History, current status, and future trends. *Journal of Counseling & Development, 88*, 18–22.
Stockton, R., Nitza, A., & Bhusumane, D. B. (2010). The development of professional counseling in Botswana. *Journal of Counseling & Development, 88*, 9–12.
Szilagti, A., & Paredes, D. M. (2010). Professional counseling in Romania: An introduction. *Journal of Counseling & Development, 88*, 23–27.
Tarayana Foundation. (2014). *Bhutan Foundation*. Retrieved from http://www.bhutanfound.org/tarayana
Ura, K., Alkire, S., Zangmo, T., & Wangdi, K. (2012). *A short guide to gross national happiness index*. Retrieved from http://www.grossnationalhappiness.com/wp-content/uploads/2012/04/Short-GNH-Index-edited.pdf
Walcott, S. M. (2011). One of a kind: Bhutan and the modernity challenge. *National Identities 13*, 253–266.
Wangchhuck, L. (2010). *Facts about Bhutan: The land of the Thunder Dragon*. Thimphu, Bhutan: Absolute Bhutan.
Witmer, J. M. (2013). Evolution of wellness. In Paul F. Granello (Ed.) *Wellness counseling* (pp. 11–28). Upper Saddle River, NJ: Pearson.
Yalom, I. D. (2005). *The theory and practice of group psychotherapy* (5th ed). New York, NY: Basic Books.

Group Work During International Disaster Outreach Projects: A Model to Advance Cultural Competence

Cirecie West-Olatunji
University of Cincinnati

Rachel Henesy
Melanie Varney
University of Florida

Given the rise in disasters worldwide, counselors will increasingly be called upon to respond. Current accreditation standards require that programs train students to become skillful in disaster/crisis interventions. Group processing to enhance self-awareness and improve conceptualization skills is an essential element of such training. This article disseminates information from a case study analysis on the experiences of 7 counselor-trainees during a 28-day international outreach trip to southern Africa, which involved daily group processing. The authors identified 2 major themes: (a) Struggle and Discomfort and (b) Growth. Working through struggle/discomfort strengthened group cohesion and facilitated the participants' growth. Significant findings for group workers who engage in international outreach, implications for counselor development, and recommendations for future research are discussed.

Professional counselors and other mental health professionals have an obligation to respond to mass disasters and should offer services that are both multicultural and social justice oriented (Substance Abuse Mental Health Services Administration [SAMHSA], 2003; U.S. Department of Health and Human Services, 2003; West-Olatunji, 2010). While scholars in the area of group work have called for an increase in multicultural and social justice competence (Singh, Merchant, Skudrzyk, & Ingene, 2012; Smith & Shin, 2008;

West-Olatunji, Templeton, Goodman, & Mehta, 2011), few researchers have focused on group work and international disaster outreach. This case study analysis explored how participants in a 28-day international outreach trip to southern Africa developed characteristics vital to multicultural and social justice competence through daily group processing.

BACKGROUND

According to the American Red Cross (American Red Cross, 2013), a mass disaster can be described as a catastrophic event that is unexpected and causes a serious disruption in the functioning of a community or society. Natural disasters are caused by a natural physical phenomenon and can be geophysical, hydrological, climatological, meteorological, or biological. Human-made disasters are often by accident or neglect, such as industrial accidents, or intentional, such as in acts of terrorism. The 2009 Council for Accreditation of Counseling and Related Educational Programs (CACREP) standards (2009) called on counselors to be prepared to respond to events that can lead to trauma, such as disasters and other crises, both nationally and internationally. Counselor training is available through the American Red Cross and through counselor training certificate programs that integrate service learning and outreach (Goodman & West-Olatunji, 2009).

Effective models of group work for international disaster outreach should be based on best practices for group counseling and should be aligned with multicultural, social justice, and advocacy competencies as outlined by the Association for Specialists in Group Work (ASGW) Best Practice Guidelines (Thomas & Pender, 2007). Counselors who engage in group interventions should practice in accordance with the American Counseling Association (ACA) Code of Ethics, as well as the ASGW guidelines, the multicultural competencies, and best practices set forth by the Association for Multicultural Counseling and Development, national, state, and local laws, and cultural customs in all stages of group facilitation: (a) planning, (b) performance, and (c) processing. This includes: (a) appropriate training, (b) knowledge, skills, and awareness, (c) ongoing evaluation of self and of group, and (d) an ecological evaluation of community needs, available resources, and organizational standards. Competent group counselors have gained personal awareness and continue to seek professional supervision and consultation to deal with personal conflicts that arise throughout the course of their careers.

In addition to the Best Practice Guidelines for group work, ASGW outlined the Multicultural and Social Justice Competence Principles for Group Workers based on current literature in the areas of group work, diversity, multiculturalism, social justice, and advocacy in counseling (Singh et al., 2012). The Competence Principles consist of three domains encompassing awareness, skills, and advocacy. In addition to the necessary knowledge and skills, group facilitators need an awareness of their own worldviews and how these views interact with diverse client worldviews. Counselors have a responsibility to be aware of their values, beliefs, and biases, as well as how those values, beliefs, and biases impact clients and group dynamics. Additionally, the Competence Principles call for counselors to address cultural conflicts within the group and to not avoid such discussions due to fear or discomfort.

Moreover, the ACA Advocacy Competencies highlight the integral nature of social justice and advocacy for professional counselors, while emphasizing the importance of client empowerment and community collaboration. Counselors engaging in international and/or outreach counseling should take these issues into strong consideration when considering the sustainability of their efforts and the impact on client and community empowerment (Lewis, Arnold, House, & Toporek, 2002).

Social justice in group work involves both reflection and action. Awareness includes being aware of not only overt oppression and discrimination, but also of covert oppression and historical contexts. Counselor resistance to both multicultural and social justice paradigms can be a result of (a) denial of one's own social privilege, (b) guilt or confusion, (c) a lack of awareness, and/or (d) a lack of emphasis on multicultural and social justice issues in counselor preparation programs (Smith & Shin, 2008; West-Olatunji, Shure, & Goodman, 2011). According to Smith and Shin, it is vital that group counselors develop self-awareness and ethnic self-knowledge in order to be culturally competent and social justice-oriented. They state that this awareness is a precursor to group facilitation that highlights the need for such awareness to be discovered by counselors-in-training. Smith and Shin (2008) emphasized the importance of counselors' understanding of social privilege, both in their clients and in themselves.

Multiculturalism is an integral part of the group process. Culturally competent group interventions can be applied through culturally responsive techniques with specific homogeneous groups, or through the synthesis of indigenous and mainstream models with diverse-member groups (Torres-Rivera, Phan, Garrett, Wilbur, & Schwartz, 2007).

International cultural immersion can be an opportunity for counselors and counselors-in-training to learn new perspectives while increasing cultural competence and developing critical consciousness

(McDowell, Goessling, & Melendez, 2012; West-Olatunji & Goodman, 2011). West-Olatunji and Goodman found that group connection helped to promote growth and critical consciousness among members of an outreach group, whereas resistance and unawareness hindered their growth. McDowell et al. (2012) also studied the impact of group processing during an outreach experience on the development of cultural competence and critical consciousness in counseling students. Participants in their study experienced a range of emotions that included excitement and discomfort during their experience. Participants also reported that they struggled with the amount of time spent with the group, and they felt frustrated by group conflicts. Additionally, participants reported guilt and discomfort associated with gaining self-awareness of their own privilege.

Although there are several models for disaster counseling, such as the use of psychological first aid and psychosocial interventions, the focus of this paper is on the Culture-Centered Disaster Mental Health Counseling (CDMHC) model. Developed by Goodman and West-Olatunji (2009), this approach is built upon critical consciousness theory (Freire, 1970). The authors asserted that CDMHC has three major objectives. First, it facilitates counselors' efforts to reach out to culturally diverse individuals and communities. Second, use of this model enables counselors to better conceptualize and intervene with culturally diverse clients. Finally, CDMHC promotes awareness, knowledge, and skills in order to prevent counselors' cultural encapsulation.

The authors stated that working in partnership with community members fosters mutuality, inclusion, and collaboration. Thus, counselors can cultivate self-awareness, peer learning, exposure to differing realities, and community-centered perspectives. Key aspects of this approach include the use of journaling to portray increased awareness of environmental influences on individuals' responses to disasters. Additionally, proponents of this approach see dialogue as a core element of culture-centered disaster counseling. Trainers mandate group process, peer supervision, and live supervision as key elements of critically conscious disaster response. Finally, advocates of culture-centered disaster counseling seek to facilitate community action and emphasize community empowerment. Outcomes for participants of culture-centered disaster counseling deployments have included increased cultural awareness, self-knowledge, psychological healing, sense of social justice, group cohesion, and an emphasis on self-care (West-Olatunji & Shannonhouse, 2013; West-Olatunji et al., 2011). This study asked the question, "How do participants of an international outreach experience articulate their multicultural and social justice competence following intensive daily group process over a 28-day period?"

METHODS

The researchers utilized an instrumental case study method in order to provide insight regarding how daily group processing affected counselor development and development of cultural competence. The researchers employed a grounded theory approach to identify and conceptualize latent themes within the dataset and the relationships among those themes (Creswell, 2008). The facilitator/principal investigator and the process observer were both African American females. Two female graduate counseling students, one European American and one Eurasian American, assisted with data analysis.

Subjectivity Statement

My identity and lived experiences as a seasoned African American female counselor educator with extensive clinical training and experience informed my conceptualization of the study as well as interpretation of the data collected. In addition to my role as principal investigator, I also served as the co-facilitator of the process groups and clinical director of the outreach project. It is to be noted that many of the participants had previously interacted with me in my role as adviser, instructor, supervisor, and research mentor. These identities allowed me to act as insider witness (Tillman, 2002) to the participants' experiences during the outreach experience.

Participants

There were six participants in the sample, all of whom attended a counselor education program in a large university in the southeastern United States. Five of the participants were female and one was male. The participants were between the ages of 24 and 31 (mean age of 26.5). Four of the participants were doctoral level students and two were at the master's level. The cultural background of the participants consisted of one Asian American and five European American students. Participants had varying levels of exposure to cultural communities but none reported experience with either disaster training or clinical outreach. None of the participants had significant work experience as a professional counselor.

Protocols

The purpose of the outreach endeavor was to provide disaster counseling services to HIV/AIDS infected and affected individuals in South Africa and Botswana. This trip was a replication outreach project of a previous trip to post-Katrina New Orleans that was directed by the same leader (Goodman & West-Olatunji, 2009). In developing a model for culture-centered disaster counseling, the researcher sought to engage participants in outreach activities involving the development of interventions situated in clients' historical, social, and cultural realities. While much of the literature on disaster counseling focuses on natural disasters, other forms of human-made disasters can be as catastrophic, including terrorist acts, health epidemics (e.g., HIV/AIDS and various flu strains), and industrial accidents (West-Olatunji & Goodman, 2011).

The principal investigator solicited applications to participate in the outreach experience through various electronic communication channels, such as counseling listservs and emails to counseling program chairs. Applicants were asked to provide information on their clinical experience, coursework, and prior outreach trips. Additionally, applicants were asked to submit an essay articulating their multicultural and social justice perspectives and provide two letters of recommendation from counseling professionals. An independent review panel conducted a blind review of the applications using a scoring rubric. Applicants with the highest scores were invited to participate in the outreach experience. Those who agreed to participate were given IRB-approved documents for review and signature, including demographic and IRB participant consent forms.

Two months prior to the outreach trip, participants were required to attend weekly 1-hr informational workshops over a 6-week period on various topics, such as historical background, sociopolitical context, counseling issues, compassion fatigue, and a brief language course. Workshop presenters were professionals with expertise in the specific topics of concern. These sessions were designed to prepare participants for immersion into the southern African cultures they would encounter. During the outreach experience, the group leader held 2-hr group processing sessions each evening in their hotel. Participants were instructed to maintain a daily journal over the course of the trip to reflect on their outreach experiences and group processing experiences. Approximately 3 weeks following the conclusion of the trip, participants were asked to submit electronic versions of their completed journals to the principal investigator. Two follow-up debriefing sessions were held at the host university at the 2-week and 4-week points. Both sessions, 2 hr in duration, were facilitated by the principal investigator.

Prior to the departure date, the leader conducted a needs assessment to learn what services the stakeholders articulated as needed. This information provided the framework for program development and participant assignments. Over the 28-day period, the participants: (a) provided professional development trainings, (b) shadowed professional counselors and community outreach workers during their normal routines in community agencies, schools, and neighborhoods, and (c) offered consultation on difficult clinical cases. Other activities included visiting university campuses to exchange ideas with counseling faculty and students and participating in cultural tours to become more familiar with the socio-political context of their disaster outreach activities. During the day-to-day shadowing, participants engaged in crisis counseling in individual, group, family modalities, psychoeducational workshops, and whole classroom guidance in the schools. Participants were encouraged to employ culturally relevant theories, such as NTU Therapy (Wynn & West-Olatunji, 2009), Multicultural Counseling Therapy (MCT; Sue, Ivey, & Pedersen, 1996), and Relational-Cultural Therapy (RCT; Comstock et al., 2008), when working with clients. Some of the placements included a women's shelter, two middle schools, and a non-governmental agency specializing in HIV/AIDS interventions. All of the settings offered opportunities for culture-centered disaster counseling as HIV/AIDS was a major theme at all of the sites.

One of the core assumptions of the culture-centered disaster counseling model used for this project is sustainability. Reflecting on the basic tenets of counseling, culture-centered disaster counseling relies upon client voice and empowerment, respect for clients' lived experiences and strengths, and a belief in clients' ability to self-actualize (West-Olatunji, 2012). Thus, participants were encouraged to build on the communities' existing resources (both human and material) to facilitate an expeditious recovery. Therefore, this model counters the "rescue" focus of many well intentioned clinicians who provide "drive by" disaster assistance without thought to sustainability (West-Olatunji, 2010, 2012; West-Olatunji et al., 2011). Using a culture-centered disaster counseling model, the team offered training, consultation, ongoing resources and clinical support, as well as referral to other organizations. During the needs assessment phase, prior to the onset of the trip, the outreach leader also identified what material resources are needed. Whenever possible, these resources are brought to the desired communities. During the particular trip, the host university identified counseling textbooks as needed. The outreach team was able to bring over $7,000 worth of new textbooks to be added to the university library's holdings. Following the trip, there were debriefings with the stakeholders. These discussions led to a follow up trip 2 years later to visit the same institutions.

Data Analysis

First, researchers independently read through the complete data set to get an overall idea of common themes. Researchers then independently coded the data set and subsequently compared themes

Table 1 Themes and Subthemes Taxonomy

Struggle and Discomfort (i.e., feelings of guilt, incompetence, self-doubt, and confusion) *Conflict and Tension* (i.e., confrontation, racial dynamics, anger) *Disconnection* (i.e., group role confusion, isolation, dissociation, exhaustion)	*Growth* (i.e., change in the individual and how they view the world) *Group Cohesion* (i.e., feelings of safety and support from the group) *Self-Awareness* (i.e., acknowledgement that that one's personal reality is subjective in nature and not a universal reality) *Excitement* (i.e., expression of curiosity and energy)

through a process of consensus building. Themes found independently by at least two out of three researchers were written on index cards. The researchers categorized and organized the labeled index cards according to main themes and sub-themes that were later presented to an external research team via email communication. The external research team was comprised of mixed-level graduate counseling students who provided feedback on the themes, offered implications, and suggested recommendations based on the findings.

FINDINGS

Two main themes that emerged from the data were: (a) Struggle and Discomfort and (b) Growth (see Table 1). The first main theme of Struggle and Discomfort was apparent through group members' feelings of guilt, incompetence, self-doubt, and confusion. The second main theme, Growth, was related to evident change in the individual and how they view the world, as well as increased self-awareness which could potentially lead to improved clinical practice.

Struggle and Discomfort

Group members expressed struggle and discomfort with both the immersion experience and group processing. This struggle and discomfort appears to be related to feelings of guilt, perceived incompetence, self-doubt, and role confusion among group members. Group members expressed guilt about the historical context for the issues presented by the community members. For example, one participant stated, "My overall feeling was guilt; guilty at my own selfishness about how I was feeling in light of what we had seen that day and all that people had gone through as a result." For some, this guilt was related to gaining an awareness of both their own privilege and cultural encapsulation.

In this process of struggle, some group members attempted to focus on other group members rather than themselves. For example, one participant stated, “As I shared this with the group during group process I began to cry. It was difficult for me but soon I became even more uncomfortable as the focus remained on me and what I needed.” Further, some group members attempted to gain approval from the group facilitator, perhaps in an attempt to avoid exploring their self-doubt by gaining the group leader’s approval rather than their own.

> Dr. Reed [pseudonym] shared her reaction to my comment the night before and said how badly she was hurt and felt disrespected by my comment . . . I cannot express the devastation I felt to hear that she felt that way as a result of me . . . I tried to explain . . . that it was out of my deep respect for her and desire to want to be near her and learn from her.

Struggle and Discomfort could, however, lead to self-exploration and self-disclosure, which appeared to enhance awareness and strengthen group cohesion for some participants: “I know I rush people. I know I am impatient and knowing that now maybe I can work on being more flexible.” “I shared first because I have been aware of the fact that I have not been truly connecting with my experiences emotionally but instead have been looking at them from a distance.” “Even as I am writing I can feel my resistance as I let my mind wander to other random things. . . . Avoiding has always been my method.”

Two sub themes emerged from the main theme of Struggle and Discomfort: (a) Conflict and Tension and (b) Disconnection. Conflict and Tension (i.e., confrontation, racial dynamics, anger) was defined as cultural and interpersonal differences with other group members and facilitators. This conflict and tension appeared to drain energy from the individuals; however, for some participants it raised issues of privilege and racial dynamics that could lead to greater awareness and growth if worked through. There appeared to be an inner dialogue related to inner tension and self-doubt, yet the focus was externalized (e.g., blame was placed on other people’s behaviors or views, people felt excluded by others rather than by their choice to remain silent about issues); this again may have served as a temporary distraction from self-exploration. The following quotes were selected to demonstrate this subcategory: “Tolerance of other members is at a low. . . . I don’t know how I will get by the next two weeks.” “I am disappointed . . . [with] some of the other professionals and their behavior around the group and disrespect for students. . . . I miss every[one] from home. . . . this will be a trial of my patience and emotions.”

> Last night in processing it was said that since many of us may never be back, we have to get what we want and need to make this experience

> worthwhile. If this was the way the group really felt I would not be forced into activities because of the desires of other group members to include that as part of their experience. I am looking forward to possibly never seeing some of these people ever again.
>
> Process group was also really emotional tonight. It seemed like there was more separation based on race than before in the group. I felt tension between members and was not sure what to do about it. Situations like today make me realize all over again how things can be offensive and sensitive to different racial groups in very different ways.
>
> Unfortunately, this conversation carried on for too long and no real resolution came about. That is extremely sad because again it was simply a difference in perception and communication . . . I was even approached following the meeting and asked if I thought race was playing a role in the situation. Sadly, I had to admit yes and my heart sank.

The sub-theme of Disconnection was best evidenced by participants' disengagement from the group, either physically (exhaustion and escapism) or emotionally (feeling alone and isolated.) The researchers theorized that the internal disconnection may have been experienced in the body, as evidenced by statements from participants such as, "To be honest, I was not as attentive as usual because I was so tired" and "We had group process that night but to be honest I can't remember much about it right now." As such, they may have experienced their inner struggles as exhaustion, which may have served as a distraction. The researchers also hypothesized that the participants experienced group role confusion as a result of the disconnection. For example, one participant stated,

> I started crying and disclosed that I was incredibly uncomfortable, it was a pretty deep cry and I addressed Paula's comment. Felt like I couldn't go up to the front [because] I might disrupt that fun. I felt like I couldn't understand, I wasn't on the inside, and I wouldn't "get it."

Hence, they may have hid themselves for fear of being uncovered (i.e., feeling like a fraud). Such behavior is representative of classic training-group dynamics, suggesting that group work during international outreach may be a multilayered group experience.

Struggle and Discomfort, and the sub-themes of conflict, tension, and disconnection, contributed to group cohesion as participants learned more about themselves and each other, and took the time to question their worldviews in context of their past and what they had learned during the outreach experience and from other group members. One participant stated, "I think it just highlights how impervious White people are to the lives of African Americans and what they deal with on a daily basis."

Dr. Reed [pseudonym] disclosed feeling "unsafe" because of all the talk and energy given to individualistic needs:

> I know I come from not only a place of privilege, but I'm an only child so I feel like my needs have more than been met over the years. . . . Seems like just about every practitioner was a minority and the majority of students were white Eurocentric. I wonder if this plays a role in the perception of neediness.

Growth

Participants demonstrated increased intuitive knowledge related to enhanced counseling competence, particularly in cross-cultural counseling, as a result of both the immersion experience and the daily group processing. "I think it was a great experience for all of us, each learning from the other. I personally had a boost in confidence in my own abilities as a counselor as I realized that I know a little more than I thought as I shared ideas and conceptualizations."

The theme Growth was also related to how participants' new knowledge and experiences impacted their pre-existing worldviews. Two participants shared their shift from a more Western, individualistic worldview to one that is more connected and communal: The first participant stated, "this group of healers from SA [South Africa] and helpers from the U.S. coming together is something much bigger, greater, beautiful, and healing. . . . I am deeply touched by this even now as I reflect and write." Another participant wrote, "some of the powerful words include: *witness, more love and healing for us and them*, and this is not a job or a career but *their life*. The dedication of these workers is indescribable." The experience not only changed the way in which participants viewed the world, but also increased their awareness of how they interact within groups and systems, as expressed by one female participant: "Perhaps, the groups I've been a part of the past 2 days have been a part of my healing process, too. I wonder how I will bring them and this experience back home with me."

Additionally, three sub-themes were found under the main theme of Growth: Group Cohesion, Self-Awareness, and Excitement. Group Cohesion was found to be a sense of feeling supported by the group and empowered by the connection and experiences within the group. It helped participants to feel safe and supported which, in turn, facilitated growth. Additionally, the participants felt more confident in their sense of belonging within the group and the profession as a whole. Growth and Group Cohesion were dynamically interactive. "It was clear that bonds were established and the group was unified. [. . .] It was very reciprocal." "We stood with hands joined and appreciated one another's presence and the energy of our group. It was warm, strong, and solid. We sang and prayed. We hugged and embraced . . . and then went to lunch." "I felt happy and connected. I felt as if the collectiveness of our team and their team was something bigger and greater than myself. In my spirituality, this is what 'God' is and why I feel the most connected and spiritual in nature and in my close relationships with people."

Self-Awareness was illustrated by understanding that one's personal reality is subjective in nature and not a universal reality. It was the ability to know what one knows, what one doesn't know, and the difference between the two. It was portrayed through group members' demonstration of being more open to the realities of others, as well as through openness to feedback. One participant recorded the following passage:

> Perhaps I am frustrated about how I have been able to disconnect from what I am seeing and experiencing and keeping it at such a cognitive level. . . . I am wondering if this is a defense mechanism, but I am not sure. I want to go deeper at times . . . but instead stay on the surface or more superficial, easy going level. I am wondering how this impacts my relationships with clients as a counselor. . . . What am I scared of with going deeper?
>
> There was a lot that went on in process, but this was the moment that stood out for me. I learned I couldn't make as many hypothesis [sic] as I would have liked to and I certainly understood the importance of context and seeing from another's perspective. It is so important to have that ability in doing this work.
>
> It's interesting to feel it on a personal level and then try and look at it from a larger perspective in a totally different context. I'm certainly feeling things, but am confused. I think that is because I don't understand the context here as much as I would like.

Self-Awareness was also related to Growth as it contributed to a cycle of teaching, learning, and reflection which led to authenticity and action. Two participants' accounts of this are as follows: "I shared first because I have been aware [. . .] of the fact that I have not been truly connecting with my experiences emotionally but instead have been looking at them from a distance." "I realize that though my feelings of invisibility were what was on top, I could have approached it differently by making personal efforts with the professors." In relation to discomfort, one student stated "I acknowledge that much of what I was undergoing was to my own issues of worth and that I needed to step out and make contact as well." In response to concerns shared by a Black group member, one White student gained Self-Awareness in regards to how her life experiences had shaped her empathy up to this point: " I just had no idea that it was that big of a deal and that is just a result of living in my White bubble."

The sub-theme Excitement emerged and is evident in the curiosity that participants articulated in relation to learning something new about the world and about themselves. This curiosity seemed to serve as a source of energy that was present during their outreach activities. "I felt so inspired by the day, I was extremely anxious to open up about my recent feelings. It was great to let it out and hear the support from the group. I was also proud to hear Sara divulge some information as well. She and I had spent a great deal of time together preparing for this journey and I was honored that we opened up at the same time." The participants also noted a gratitude toward their group facilitator that was particularly energizing, thus demonstrating the catalytic validity of the outreach experience overall.

DISCUSSION

The findings from this study highlight the dynamics that can take place during group processing when responding to international disasters, especially when working with counselors-in-training, and how the combination of an immersion experience and daily group processing can contribute to the development of multicultural and social justice competencies. Standards for group work within an international context may involve more specialized group counseling, training, and multicultural competence than previously considered (Singh et al., 2012). Additionally, the findings from this study show an increased need for group cohesion and self-care when responding to international disasters, as these may help counselors push through the struggle and discomfort in order to achieve growth. Furthermore, best practices for internationally conducted group work may need to involve more emphasis on self-care as counselors work through struggle and discomfort to achieve growth and transformation (West-Olatunji et al., 2011).

In line with the CDMHC model (Goodman & West-Olatunji, 2009), participants growth, particularly in the areas of multicultural and social justice competence, was facilitated by tenets of critical consciousness theory (Freire, 1970); specifically, through the process of dialogue in daily group processing. The struggle and discomfort experienced by the participants appears to be related to the resistance often faced by counselor-trainees of the dominant culture when presented with multicultural and social justice paradigms (Smith & Shin, 2008; West-Olatunji et al., 2011). Working through this struggle and discomfort to explore its origins may have helped participants to gain new awareness of their own worldviews and biases, develop stronger connections to others in the group, and to break free from their previous cultural encapsulation (Goodman & West-Olatunji, 2009; Torres-Rivera et al., 2007). For some, this growth led to a new excitement related to their own abilities and their roles as counselors.

As counselor education programs consider how to infuse disaster counseling training in their programs in response to the 2009 CACREP standards, it may be important to explore how disaster training is related to each of the core content areas, as well as the ACA Advocacy Competencies and the ASGW Multicultural and Social Justice Competence Principles for Group Workers. In particular, pedagogical concepts within group work and disaster counseling need to be revisited for integration of concepts.

Recommendations for Practice and Policy

The researchers offer several recommendations based on the findings of this study. First, participants in international outreach should be required to engage in process groups prior to disaster outreach trips in order to identify areas of struggle and discomfort that may impede their work with clients in disaster-affected areas. Second, we recommended that disaster outreach competencies are established that heavily rely upon group counseling skills. Third, due to the developmental aspect of working with counselors-in-training, there is a need for more preparation prior to deployment.

In anticipation of the struggles and discomfort that may be intrinsic to international outreach work, additional group-related trainings are suggested. Specifically, pre-deployment process groups would be beneficial. This would allow participants the opportunity to become familiar with the facilitator's group counseling approach and style. This would also afford the group facilitator the opportunity to become familiar with each of the participants and their individual group counseling skill sets. Hence, we recommend that group leaders incorporate process groups as standard pre-, during, and post-outreach components.

Further, given the relatively new development of international outreach research, scholars have yet to establish disaster outreach competencies. Competencies in this area would necessitate advanced group, multicultural, and advocacy counseling skills. Particularly within international contexts, expertise in group work would be a requirement for participants and facilitators alike. It is recommended that ASGW develop disaster outreach competencies that have a heavy focus on group work skills.

Finally, due to the range of developmental levels evidenced by the counselor trainees in this study, it may be necessary to intensify applicant screenings to consider participants with more advanced group work training. The introductory group counseling course that counseling students take may not be sufficient training for the complex demands during an international outreach trip. Thus, in some way, participants on international outreach trips are ensured to have sufficient preparation to engage in group process and have the intended outcomes of increased clinical competence.

It should also be noted that one of the recommendations for future research was later adopted by one of the participants. This participant investigated the long-term outcomes of international outreach on student participants and found that such training opportunities increased cultural competence overall (Barden & Cashwell, 2014).

Limitations and Future Research

One limitation of this study is that the responses were from a limited number of seven participants at one specific geographic location that may not be generalizable to other international outreach groups. An additional limitation is related to the demographic nature of the participants, as well as the mixed training levels of the participants. Finally, there is no measure of a baseline for the participants prior to the outreach experience.

Given the findings from this study, a follow up investigation with a more heterogeneous group is warranted. The resistance and struggles articulated by the participants suggest that mainstream students from European American, middle-class backgrounds experience substantial angst in moving outside of their own worldviews to appreciate the realities of dissimilar and diverse clients, peers, and facilitators. Yet, very little is known about how culturally diverse counseling students would respond to an international outreach experience under the supervision of a group facilitator. It would be of interest to learn how the peer-to-peer interactions would differ with a critical mass of diverse students among the participants. Further, an outreach team consisting of only culturally diverse counseling students may yield outcomes of interest for faculty teaching at historically Black colleges (HBCU's), Hispanic-serving institutions (HSIs), and tribal colleges. A replication study is therefore warranted.

In sum, the researchers sought to explore how an intensive group work experience within an international context enhanced the cultural and social justice competence of seven counselor trainees. The findings suggest that trainees would benefit from additional group counseling training prior to deployment. Facilitators of international outreach groups may wish to include more stringent application criteria for selection of participants, such as an advanced group counseling course and/or require that selected participants engage in intensive group process as pre-deployment activity. Recommendations for future research include a replication study that involves a more diverse group of participants.

REFERENCES

American Red Cross. (2013). *Disaster relief*. Retrieved from http://www.redcross.org/what-we-do/disaster-relief

Barden, S. M., & Cashwell, C. (2014). International immersion: An exploratory study of critical factors and counselor development. *Journal of Multicultural Counseling and Development, 42*, 42–60.

Comstock, D. L., Hammer, T. R., Strentzsch, J., Cannon, K., Parsons, J., & Salazar II, G. S. (2008). Relational-cultural theory: A framework for bridging relational, multicultural, and social justice competencies. *Journal of Counseling & Development, 86*, 279–287.

Council for Accreditation of Counseling and Related Educational Programs. (2009). *2009 CACREP Standards*. Retrieved from http://www.cacrep.org/wp-content/uploads/2013/12/2009-Standards.pdf

Creswell, J. W. (2008). *Educational research: Planning, conducting, and evaluating quantitative and qualitative research* (3rd ed.). Upper Saddle River, NJ: Pearson Education.

Freire, Paulo. (1970) *Pedagogy of the oppressed*. New York, NY: Herder and Herder.

Goodman, R. D., & West-Olatunji, C. A. (2009). Engaging students in outreach as an extension of advocacy to achieve praxis. *Journal for Civic Commitment, 12*. Retrieved from http://www.mc.maricopa.edu/other/engagement/Journal/Issue12/Goodman.shtml

Lewis, J. A., Arnold, M. S., House, R., & Toporek, R. L. (2002). *ACA advocacy competencies*. Retrieved from http://www.counseling.org/resources/competencies/advocacy_competencies.pdf

McDowell, T., Goessling, K., & Melendez, T. (2012). Transformative learning through international immersion: Building multicultural competence in family therapy and counseling. *Journal of Marital & Family Therapy, 38*, 365–379.

Singh, A. A., Merchant, N., Skudrzyk, B., Ingene, D., Hutchins, A., & Rubel, D. (2012). Association for specialists in group work: Multicultural and social justice competence principles for group workers. *The Journal for Specialists in Group Work, 37*, 312–325. doi:10.1080/01933922.2012.721482

Smith, L. C., & Shin, R. Q. (2008). Social privilege, social justice, and group counseling: An inquiry. *The Journal for Specialists in Group Work, 33*, 351–366. doi:10.1080/01933920802424415

Substance Abuse Mental Health Services Administration. (2003). *Developing cultural competence in disaster mental health programs: Guiding principles and recommendations* (Pub. No. SMA 3828). Rockville, MH: Author.

Sue, D. W., Ivey, A. E., & Pedersen, P. B. (1996). *A theory of multicultural counseling and therapy*. Pacific Grove, CA: Brooks/Cole.

Thomas, R., & Pender, D. A. (2008). Association for Specialists in Group Work: Best practice guidelines 2007 revisions. *The Journal for Specialists in Group Work, 33*, 111–117. doi:10.1080/01933920801971184

Tillman, L. C. (2002). Culturally sensitive research approaches: An African-American perspective. *Educational Researcher, 31*(9), 3–12.

Torres Rivera, E., Phan, L. T., Garrett, M. T., Wilbur, J., & Schwartz, E. (2007). Comparing the color of fear and evolution of a group: A pilot study. *Revista Interamericana De Psicología, 41*, 323–328.

U.S. Department of Health and Human Services. (2003). *Developing cultural competence in disaster mental health programs: Guiding principles and recommendations* (DHHS Pub. No. SMA 3828). Rockville, MD: Center for Mental Health Services, Substance Abuse and Mental Health Services Administration.

West-Olatunji, C. (2010). If not now, when? Social justice, advocacy, and counselor education. *Professional Issues in Counseling, 42*, 1–11.

West-Olatunji, C. (2012). The engaged practitioner: Reaching out to marginalized communities. In J. Carlson, & J. Kottler (Eds.), *Helping beyond the 50 minute hour: Therapists involved in REAL social action* (pp. 245–256). New York, NY: Routledge.

West-Olatunji, C., & Goodman, R. (2011). Entering communities: Social justice oriented disaster response counseling. *Journal of Humanistic Counseling Education and Development, 50*, 172–182.

West-Olatunj, C., & Shannonhuse, L. (2013). One counselor-trainee's journey toward multicultural counseling competence: The role of mentoring in executing intentional cultural immersion. *Professional Issues in Counseling* (Winter). Retrieved from http://www.shsu.edu/~piic/documents/OneCounselorTrainee'sJourneyToward MulticulturalCounselingCompetence.pdf

West-Olatunji, C., Shure, L., & Goodman, R. D. (2011). Use of multicultural supervision with school counselors to enhance cultural competence. *Journal of School Counseling, 9*. Retrieved from http://www.jsc.montana.edu/articles/v9n16.pdf

West-Olatunji, C., Templeton, L., Goodman, R., & Mehta, S. (2011). Creating cultural awareness: An outreach immersion experience in southern Africa. *International Journal for the Advancement of Counselling, 33*, 335–346.

Wynn, R., & West-Olatunji, C. (2009). Culture centered case conceptualization using NTU psychotherapy with an African American male gay client. *The Journal of LGBT Issues in Counseling, 2*, 308–325.

International Consultation and Training on Group Work in South Asia

Farah A. Ibrahim
University of Colorado Denver

This article presents a consultation and training for faculty and graduate students in South Asia under the auspices of the United Nations' Transfer of Knowledge Through Expatriate Nationals (TOKTEN) Program. It describes the development of a consultation relationship and training on group work. Needs assessments focusing on both cultural assumptions, and group theory and practice were conducted to identify cultural variables, and goals for the group work training. An outline of the process used and outcomes are presented.

This article presents a consultation experience and the development of a training program on group counseling for the Institute of Applied Psychology for its training program in counseling and psychotherapy in South Asia. The Institute is at a major university in a large urban city in South Asia. The author, a South Asian woman, was brought in as a consultant. However she was not familiar with the local culture and needed to understand the local cultural context. In addition, she had been away from her culture of origin for over 30 years. The United Nation's Transfer of Knowledge Through Expatriate Knowledge (TOKTEN, 2008) program invites expatriates to share their knowledge and skills, especially in third world nations. There is no salary, however, airfare and a modest *per diem* allowance are provided. It is a voluntary service to country of origin. Countries participating in the program request assistance in educational and/or technical domains on their identified needs. A challenge in international consultation is to understand the local cultural context, and to develop a training program consistent with cultural assumptions of the constituents, and enhancing participants' learning about group process and practice (Higginbotham & Marsella, 1988; Ibrahim, Ohnishi, & Sandhu, 1997; Squarcini, 2011).

South Asia, and specifically, the Indian subcontinent with its deep historical and cultural roots, and civilizations dating back to 5000–7000 years B.C., can be difficult to interpret (Squarcini, 2011; United Nations Economic and Social Commission for Asia and the Pacific, n.d.). South Asian culture is collectivistic; although colonialization, advances in technology, and the current global economy have mediated the cultural context. Implementation of Western perspectives in counseling and group work is difficult in the South Asian context due to the complexities of the culture. The primary conflict is between South Asian collectivism and the rugged individualistic roots of counseling theory, which are grounded in the belief in individualism that allows individuals to set the course of their lives (Kleinman, Eisenberg, & Good, 1978; Sue & Zane, 1987; Westermeyer, 1985).

Several concepts in Western training models (e.g., setting boundaries; advocating and taking action for personal development; and taking charge of one's own destiny without consideration of the family, its values, and the culture or society) are difficult to apply within a collectivistic system (Higginbotham & Marsella, 1988). Consequently, before developing the training program the consultant assessed faculty and students' cultural values and needs as well as their educational needs to prepare them to facilitate groups.

CULTURAL AND LEARNING NEEDS ASSESSMENTS

The consultation with faculty and development of the training in group work necessitated two separate needs assessments to understand the cultural and learning needs of the constituents: (a) cultural assessments to make the training consistent with the culture of the participants and the context, and (b) identification of learning needs to establish goals for the training. Cultural assessments were conducted to clarify the underlying beliefs, values, and assumptions and to understand the cultural identities of all participants. Knowledge gained would help the consultant develop positive working relationships with the faculty and students (Ibrahim, 2007a).

The cultural assessments included worldview (beliefs, values, and assumptions) and cultural identity assessments, using the Scale to Assess World View© (SAWV; Ibrahim & Kahn, 1984, 1987) and the Cultural Identity Check List–Revised© (Ibrahim, 2007a, 2009). To facilitate the relationship building process, using data gathered from the two assessments the consultant collaborated with faculty and students to create a sociometric map using the cultural information provided by all involved (Treadwell, Kumar, Stein, & Prosnick, 1998). Sociometry helps in categorizing similarities or differences, or connections and social distance among group members (Treadwell, Stein, & Leach, 1985). The information gained seemed to help in developing trust as individuals learned about each other's cultural values and identities. After the experience of sharing information about worldview and cultural identity, one participant noted, "I did not realize we had so many similarities." Another participant stated "we have been together in the program for two years, and I now feel that I hardly knew anyone." Creating a shared worldview among the participants seemed to enhance relationships in the group and increase members' comfort with each other, paving the way for mutually supportive interactions (Ibrahim, 1999).

The South Asian context requires establishing a personal relationship to successfully gather information on learning needs. The consultant conducted focus groups to assess learning goals, with separate focus groups for faculty and students to identify the challenges in translating group theory to practice (Das & Ibrahim, 1990). The questions and concepts explored were: (a) what aspects of group work are difficult to implement in the local context? (b) What issues do you want to explore during the training to conduct effective group counseling? (c) What aspects of group training should be reviewed again in this training? And (d) are there any individual concerns that were not addressed by the previous questions?

OUTCOME OF NEEDS ASSESSMENT: TRAINING GOALS

The needs assessment was conducted using focus groups and taking notes during the sessions. The notes were summarized and shared with participants to establish accuracy. This process was repeated twice, and each time the results were summarized and shared with the group, and after minor edits, the faculty and student participants accepted the identified learning goals. The main issues identified from the focus groups were (a) the difficulty in translating theory and practice of group work for clients in the local context; and (b) inability to translate skills identified in group textbooks to local culture. The assumptions and constraints of collectivism characteristic of South Asian cultures made it difficult to implement Western concepts when dealing with clients and their families in areas such as primacy of the individual versus the family, boundary issues, and free will (McCarthy & Hart, 2011; Pistole, Kinyon, & Keith, 2008). The faculty and the students had training and education on group work and had been exposed to Western educators and consultants on group counseling. However, as noted by several scholars, individualistic assumptions cannot be easily applied in collectivistic settings (Barlow, 2004; Burlingame et al., 2007; Markus

& King, 2003). The faculty and students reported that all the training they had received was content-focused on group theory and practice issues with no experiential component. For example, they lacked training and practice using structured group exercises to understand group concepts, processing the outcomes of structured exercises, and essential group leadership skills (Corey, Corey, & Corey, 2014; Ivey, Pedersen, & Ivey, 2008; Pistole et al., 2008). The training program developed during this consultation focused on translating theory to practice using experiential exercises. The faculty endorsed the approach and believed that it would be a useful aspect of group leadership training, recognizing that the process would help trainee group leaders in addressing cultural issues specific to South Asia to help clients and their families. The faculty was invited to be a part of the training and they agreed to assist with the training process by facilitating discussions, especially related to the local culture and treatment modalities.

Training Outline and Process

A 3-week training program was developed for experiential group training to help translate group theory to practice effectively in South Asia. Training was conducted from 9:00 a.m. to 5:00 p.m., recommended as an effective schedule for professional training (DeViva, 2006); with 1 hr open for lunch and one 10-min break, in the morning and afternoon sessions each. The program was conducted for 6 days each week. An outline of the 3-week training program appears in Appendix A. Below, highlights of the group process are discussed.

Each 3-hr component (morning and afternoon sessions), began with a mini-lecture on the assigned readings, from both Corey et al. (2014) and Ivey, Ivey, and Zalaquett (2009) texts. A structured group exercise was conducted based on the assigned readings, followed by processing the exercise to identify concepts from group theory (e.g., phase of group development, climate, goal development, and setting norms, along with skills of group communication). The consultant developed a *Process Observation Form for Diverse Settings* (Ibrahim, 2008; Appendix B) to help participants in understanding the process dimension along with the skills using a culture-centered perspective, by focusing on cultural intentionality and empathy (Ibrahim, 2008; Ivey et al., 2008). For example, in the initial session, the focus was on developing group goals, to make the goals participant-specific and to gain commitment from the group members on the training goals. To accomplish this, in the initial session the group was divided in two, and they alternately shared in a fishbowl format what they wanted to learn. Using Fishbowl in training for group work helps build community by providing a model for direct group interaction and focuses the group to work more productively (Case, 1995; McClosky, 2013). The final phase of the exercise was conducted in the large group, finding common ground among the goals articulated and getting group consensus on the goals. After the exercise was completed, the facilitator/consultant modeled processing the exercise, and seeking input from members on their observations using the *Process Observation Form for Diverse Settings*. The final step was to summarize the observations, linking the information from the processing session to group theory and practice. Initially, the facilitator conducted the processing of exercises and linking theory to practice. Eventually, the faculty and students took over this aspect as the group moved into the working stage (Corey et al., 2014).

During the training, faculty and students were encouraged to bring up issues and concerns that they anticipated they would be dealing with, and learning how to bridge the cultural gaps in theory and practice of group work for the South Asian context. Several issues were addressed, ranging from problems of living (transitions and changes), to anxiety, depression, and severe mental illness. Allowing time to confront specific cultural differences, and address the needs of the community seemed to help in integrating the information to the constituents' cultural context (Barlow, 2004; Burlingame et al., 2007; Corey et al., 2014; Markus & King, 2003; McCarthy & Hart, 2011; Romano, & Sullivan, 2000; Schumaker, Ortiz, & Brenninkmeyer, 2011).

The training group members articulated additional goals for group work from the ongoing formative evaluations using the *Group Counseling Training: Session Feedback Form* (Ibrahim, 2007b; Appendix C). These goals included learning about the ethics of group work (confidentiality, involuntary membership, and discomfort with sharing family issues), boundary issues, diversity competencies, and addressing social justice and advocacy (Association for Specialists in Group Work [ASGW], 2012; Ibrahim, 2010). Members were assured that they were not required to participate in any group exercise that could make them uncomfortable and to share only information, thoughts, and feelings they were comfortable in sharing. The training focus was emphasized; throughout the sessions members were encouraged to share only information that pertained to the learning goals and to stay in the here-and-now. It took a while for the anxiety level to go down; however it appeared that group members eventually became comfortable, and the learning that took place was meaningful, as noted in the session feedback forms by the participants. Some of the comments shared were: "I was nervous about discussing parent-child conflict issues today and I'm glad I brought it up, the discussion was useful it helped me to learn to pose it as a query, rather than a judgment;" "It took courage to address the issue of having faculty in the group session, and I am glad we were able to resolve it, because I do not want to be rude or impolite;" and "Thank you for helping me understand that this is not a therapy group for us, and we do not have to talk about our personal issues."

In the initial phase the trust-building issues the group addressed were focused on hierarchy within the group because authority figures (faculty) were functioning as participants in the training; this made it difficult for the student participants to voice their concerns, especially when they did not agree with a faculty member's perspective. The resolution was to have everyone share their anxieties and concerns, with no judgment or evaluation by the group members. If members continued to experience discomfort and were hesitant to speak up they were encouraged to share their concerns with the facilitator either by using the anonymous daily session feedback form or by speaking to the facilitator individually. The students did use the anonymous feedback form to share their concerns. The facilitator summarized the feedback information and shared a summary of the feedback at the beginning of the next session. Based on the feedback, new learning goals as well as issues and concerns, were addressed in the next session. This process seemed to allay anxiety and was useful in addressing ongoing concerns in the group.

The group made a commitment to focus on understanding the experiential process, along with setting boundaries, and learning about appropriate self-disclosure in a training group. Further, group members made a commitment to support each other and to provide feedback in a positive manner by first addressing the strengths and assets of members, instead of evaluating, judging, or criticizing other members. Rules for feedback were provided, and the participants were supported throughout the training process as they practiced the new skills. The combination of learning about group communication skills, and group theory and practice, both in week one and two of the training, seemed to help in creating a positive, learning climate (Corey et al., 2014; Harel, Schectman, & Cutrona, 2012; Ivey et al., 2008). Group exercises appeared to facilitate the development of trust among the participants, and also helped with focusing on the specific goals. For example, learning about the phases of group development and processing the experience in each session (Corey et al., 2014; Ivey et al., 2008). During the transition phase, a dilemma arose regarding the use of first names, an unacceptable practice in a hierarchical culture (Ibrahim & Ingram, 2007). The group achieved a compromise to address faculty by title (Dr. or Professor) and first name and to address students as Mr., Ms., or Mrs., with first names only, as the local custom required. At the conclusion of the training, a summative evaluation was conducted to assess learning and to develop future learning goals for the participants. This was part of the termination exercise, in which group members identified their specific learning goals, and what they had accomplished in the 3-week intensive training.

Outcomes

Based on group members' comments on the daily *session feedback form* and the final assessment of learning goals during the termination exercise, it appeared that the 3-week training was helpful in demystifying the process of applying group theory to practice. The training helped in delineating for the members the principles of experiential learning, group process, and practice. In addition it helped in clarifying how cultural assumptions can be incorporated into group work. Training outcomes included: (a) learning the skills of group communication; (b) understanding the process of developing group goals and norms; (c) using structured exercises to understand the process and phases of group development; and (d) evaluating a group experience for knowledge and skills, as well as personal growth in the group context.

The feedback on the daily *session evaluation forms* indicated that participants found it helpful to learn through personal experience about addressing anxieties, and concerns, and developing mutually acceptable goals for group work, a finding consistent with group work literature (e.g., Barlow, 2004; Burlingame et al., 2007; Corey et al., 2014; Fuhriman & Burlingame, 2001; Ivey et al., 2008). The group seemed to move through the phases of group development comfortably, and issues were resolved as they emerged. Member feedback indicated it was especially helpful for the group to share cultural concerns and issues in the sessions, and during processing. Overall, the daily feedback was very helpful in making the training successful. The feedback provided input for the facilitator, and gave her an opportunity to make changes and accommodations for the next day, to meet the needs of the group.

Using Western assumptions in a collectivistic setting can be problematic; an example is the issue of direct communication, which is implicit in Western culture. The communication process is indirect in South Asia and it is difficult for people to be direct in their communication, especially when they have a divergent perspective or are addressing an emotionally difficult issue, or when communicating with people in authority (Ibrahim et al., 1997; Kleinman et al., 1978; Squarcini, 2011). The facilitator encouraged members to use "I" statements, and own one's feelings and discomforts without blaming anyone. She also emphasized that therapeutic work requires courage to address sensitive issues. She helped participants recognize how leader and group members work together to establish a supportive therapeutic relationship, based on knowing the strengths and the challenges each person faces and using empathy and support to facilitate the counseling process (Corey et al., 2014; Ivey et al., 2008). Several additional cultural issues were addressed, such as setting boundaries in a collectivistic hierarchical setting, and understanding the basic human rights of individuals within a cultural system using the United Nations Universal Declaration of Human Rights (Das & Ibrahim, 1990; Ibrahim et al., 1997; United Nations, 1948). Addressing these issues helped in clarifying the priority of individual human rights, and the strategies needed to negotiate the social and familial systems. Further, the training addressed effective and ineffective methods and strategies in dealing with familial and cultural constraints, along with hidden agendas and their effect on the therapeutic process, e.g., spousal abuse, rights of women in a marriage, or a woman's right to refuse an arranged marriage (Aziz, 2011b; Higginbotham & Marsella, 1988; Ibrahim, 2010; Ibrahim et al., 1997; UN Economic and Social Commission for Asia and the Pacific, n.d.).

The issue of boundaries was critical to address in the training group, given that South Asian culture is very stoic, hardworking, and private (Das & Ibrahim, 1990; Farver, Narang, & Badha, 2002; Ibrahim et al., 1997; Squarcini, 2011). Participant feedback indicated that learning to share personal information in a non-familial setting was useful for the group members. The training emphasized developing trust, and establishing guidelines for confidentiality and professional ethics, to ensure that if personal information were shared it would be held in confidence. The need to establish these conditions was critical, given the cultural norms and to prevent psychological harm. The facilitator and the Institute faculty modeled maintaining confidentiality in the experiential group training, by only discussing group training concerns during group meetings when all the members were present. The facilitator explained that discussing group concerns outside of the training group takes away the energy needed to address the concerns in the setting where they should be resolved. If such concerns are not addressed among group members during group meetings the issues may go underground, and become a hidden agenda (Corey et al., 2014; Ivey et al., 2008). The courage it took for group members to be honest and in the moment was admirable, and it seemed to help them in relating to the experience of their future clients. The facilitator offered support to group members and encouraged them to trust the group process. By reinforcing the importance of confidentiality throughout the training (i.e., anything discussed in the group sessions was confidential), and reminding the group about professional ethics regarding confidentiality, it helped to create an environment where group members were able to take risks.

Another cultural issue that was important for the participants pertained to individual rights in a collectivistic setting. This was a difficult issue as societal rules in South Asian cultures emphasize the wellbeing of the family as more important than the individual's needs or goals (Farver et al., 2002; Ibrahim et al., 1997; Squarcini, 2011). To clarify this concern, it was important to explore with the group ways to strike a balance between individual needs and family needs and recognize that when individual wellbeing is overlooked, eventually, the family or group suffers. This discussion provided an opportunity to focus on a social justice issue of importance in South Asia: basic human rights must be honored, specifically in situations involving abuse, violence, or lack of affection (Aziz, 2011a, 2011b; Ibrahim, 1994; United Nations (UN) Economic and Social Commission for Asia and the Pacific, n.d.). Solutions were offered, such as engaging supportive family members to assist clients by using intermediaries to advocate for them (Farver et al., 2002; Ibrahim, Dinsmore, Estrada, & D'Andrea, 2011; Sue & Zane, 1987).

The group addressed another significant cultural issue, the role of "victim." In South Asian settings this role is celebrated and recognized as "patience," and is considered a virtue (Ibrahim, 1994; Srivastava, 2012). There are several populations vulnerable to oppression in South Asia, especially women, children, sexual and religious minorities, and people with limited resources. Although culturally "victims" of oppression are considered virtuous if they display patience and forbearance, the victim role takes a toll on individuals and families. The training emphasized that it is imperative to help clients recognize they have human rights, especially where safety is concerned. It is critical to help clients negotiate a path to personal rights and safety, carefully and judiciously. The facilitator emphasized that the final decision on the actions the client is willing to take must rest with the client. The client must make the decision to move toward empowerment before change can take place (Aziz, 2011a, 2011b; Farver et al., 2002; Gerhart, 2012; Ibrahim, 1994). In addition, the facilitator helped increase group members' awareness of the importance of helping clients develop familial and social networks to enhance empowerment, and work toward developing community action groups to advocate for basic human rights to reduce societal oppressions (Aziz, 2011a; Ibrahim et al., 1997; Ibrahim et al., 2011; UN Economic and Social Commission for Asia and the Pacific, n.d.).

Implications for International Group Counseling Training and Recommendations

Providing international consultation on group work requires ethical professionals to address (a) understanding of the culture, the context and its parameters, and social justice concerns; and (b) modifying group process and practice, knowledge, and skills to match the cultural and social context (Das & Ibrahim, 1990; Higginbotham & Marsella, 1988; Kleinman et al., 1978). The discussion below expands on some of the issues addressed in this international consultation.

The Cultural Context

South Asia is a collectivistic culture, with a patriarchal system. There is extreme poverty although there are also some very rich people; wealth is unequally distributed. Most South Asian countries do not have a social welfare system (e.g., Social Security, Medicare, or unemployment benefits). In a collectivistic system, it is assumed that group work would be a natural mode to resolve conflicts and dilemmas that arise in everyday life. However, given the culture of South Asia, which emphasizes patriarchy, hierarchy, traditional culture, along with stoicism, a high need for privacy, and concerns about "losing face," it can be very challenging to conduct counseling and therapy in general, and especially difficult to do group work (Farver et al, 2002; Ibrahim, 1994; Ibrahim et al., 1997; Ibrahim & Ingram, 2007; Squarcini, 2011; Srivastava, 2012).

An example of hierarchy and the limitations this imposes on communication with authority figures came up during the training. During week one, after 2 days of training, using the daily anonymous feedback forms, the group members shared discomfort about being in a group with their faculty. Challenging faculty is not acceptable in the culture, and students did not want to clarify some of the statements made by faculty; depending on the individual's personality, clarifying and exploring an issue can also be considered a challenge (Ibrahim & Ingram, 2007). Using counseling theories and skills from Western cultures needs to be handled carefully by keeping the cultural assumptions of the setting at the forefront (Das & Ibrahim, 1990; Higginbotham & Marsella, 1988; Kleinman et al., 1978). This situation was handled by reviewing all the skills and their definitions and having members discuss what would work in their setting. The facilitator modeled the technique of clarifying using the microskills of *feedback* with cognitive and affective *empathy* and *eliciting meaning* (Ivey et al., 2009). Group members discussed using the skills in the training group, and reached an agreement that if used in the manner modeled the skills would not be considered a challenge to authority figures. The issue of challenging authority was not brought up again in the feedback forms. The group climate became warmer as people relaxed and interacted using the skills of feedback, empathy, and eliciting meaning when clarifying, as the facilitator had modeled.

It is important to recognize principles of social justice and basic human rights when handling the complexities of collectivism (Ibrahim, 2010; Ibrahim et al., 2011). To do so involves encouraging people to take back their power, and to move toward a meaningful life without losing acceptance of their primary familial, and cultural group. The process of negotiating change needs to be mediated within the cultural and familial context.

Modifying Group Process and Practice

In this consultation it was important to conduct the needs assessment on cultural values to understand the local context. Although most Asian cultures appear similar to outsiders there is considerable variability, with several regional cultural differences within South Asian cultures (Ibrahim et al., 1997; Ibrahim & Ingram, 2007). Knowledge of the cultural context in which the training took place, allowed the consultant to provide culturally responsive and effective consultation and training. She was able to provide training with respect according to local customs, and honor the culture of the constituents to avoid cultural malpractice (Das & Ibrahim, 1990; Dana, 1998). In South Asia, hierarchical relationships and positional authority are honored (Ibrahim et al., 1997). As an outsider, the consultant had to gain respect and trust of individuals in positions of authority before any work could take place (Das & Ibrahim, 1990; Higginbotham & Marsella, 1988).

The process employed for conducting cultural assessments, and collaboratively developing a sociometric map helped participants connect with each other and the consultant, and helped facilitate a positive working relationship. The cultural assessments provided information that was useful in designing the training program by matching the cultural assumptions and expectations of the region. The changes included: (a) modifying the egalitarian focus in group work to recognize the social positions of the members, exemplified by not using first names unless there was a respectful prefix or suffix; and (b) modifying the rules for communication from direct communication to the accepted cultural mode of indirect communication style (Ibrahim et al., 1997; Ibrahim & Ingram, 2007). An unexpected outcome of conducting the cultural assessments and sharing about beliefs, values, ancestry, and other aspects of culture was that the director of the Institute realized the consultant was the niece of her best friend in college, and both the director and the consultant had Kashmiri ancestry. This connection enhanced the consulting and relationship-building process, with faculty and students because of perceived similarity contributing to source credibility (Hogg & Hardie, 1991; Klohnen & Luo, 2003).

CONCLUSION

Conducting an international consultation, and training on group work can be facilitated using cultural and learning needs assessments tools. This process can help make the information and skills provided in training, both culture- and program-specific. The daily assessments of goals achieved, learning accomplished on both knowledge and skill levels, and feelings experienced during the training were helpful in keeping the facilitator on track. Keeping the group members' needs and goals in the forefront, along with adapting strategies to make them meaningful for the South Asian context contributed to the success of this consultation. The daily use of the *Process Observation Form for Diverse Settings* was also useful in making abstract concepts from the textbook real for the participants and seemed to enhance their ability to process group work. The training process was enhanced through use of the cultural assessments. As group members learned about each other-their cultural assumptions, the struggles they had encountered and overcome, and their goals in life—the group process became warm and supportive. The assessments conducted by the author and the climate created in the training group also made it easier to bring up several cultural issues that were taboo, such as incest, abuse, violence, and mental illness, and how counselors can negotiate these issues with clients and their families.

It is recommended that in international consultations it would be helpful to identify both cultural issues and learning goals, and to conduct formative (daily process observations, and feedback on learning goals to the consultant) and summative evaluations (a final assessment on learning goals) to seek input from the constituents. In this consultation, cultural issues regarding empowering clients and focusing on basic human rights was not as successful as it might have been in a different cultural context, primarily because the participants shared their culturally- based discomfort with placing the needs of a person above the family. Although, in principle they agreed with the UN Declaration of Human Rights (1948), the group members believed that mediating with the family and helping them compromise would be the best option. However, in situations involving violence, it could have dire consequences for victims, and the group members acknowledged this and discussed the need for social, and political action to support vulnerable populations, with legal mandates, and shelters (Aziz, 2011a, 2011b; Ibrahim, 1994; Olson, Viola, Fromm-Reed, 2011; UN Economic and Social Commission for Asia and the Pacific, n.d.; Westermeyer, 1985).

ACKNOWLEDGMENTS

The author wishes to express sincere appreciation to Dr. Carmen Salazar for review and support of this manuscript.

FUNDING

The development of this article was supported by the United Nations Transfer of Knowledge Through Expatriate Nationals (TOKTEN) Program.

REFERENCES

Association for Specialists in Group Work. (2012). *Multicultural and social justice competence principles for group work*. Retrieved from http://www.asgw.org/pdf/asgw_mc_sj_priniciples_final_asgw.pdf

Aziz, N. (2011a). The psychological and human rights condition of Afghan women. In J. Heath & A. Zahedi (Eds.), *Land of the unconquerable: The lives of contemporary Afghan Women* (pp. 244–290). Berkeley: University of California Press.

Aziz, N. (2011b). What self-immolation means to Afghan women. *Peace Review: Journal of Social Justice, 23*, 45–51.

Barlow, S. (2004). A strategic three-year plan to teach beginning, intermediate, and advanced group skills. *The Journal for Specialists in Group Work 29*, 113–126.

Burlingame, D. E., Earnshaw, D., Ridge, N. W., Matsumo, J., Bulkley, C., Lee, J., & Huang, A. D. (2007). Educational group treatment for the severely and persistently mentally ill: How much leader training is necessary? *International Journal of Group Psychotherapy 57*, 187–218

Case, C. M. (1995). Fishbowl training in group process. *The Journal for Specialists in Group work, 20*, 183–188.

Corey, M., & Corey, G., & Corey, C. (2014). *Group process and practice* (9th ed.). Belmont, CA: Wadsworth/Cengage.

Dana, R. H. (1998). *Understanding cultural identity in intervention and assessment.* Thousand Oaks, CA: Sage.

Das, A., & Ibrahim, F. A (1990). International consultation: Case study. In B. Herlihy & L. Golden (Eds.), *American Association for Counseling and Development ethics handbook* (4th ed., pp. 91–100). Alexandria, VA: American Association for Counseling and Development.

DeViva, J. C. (2006). The effects of full-day and half-day workshops for health care providers in techniques for increasing resistant clients' motivation. *Professional Psychology: Research and Practice, 37*, 83–90.

Farver, J. A., Narang, S. K., & Bhadha, B. R. (2002). East meets west: Ethnic identity, acculturation, and conflict in Asian Indian families. *Journal of Family Psychology 16*, 338–50.

Fuhriman, A., & Burlingame, G. M. (2001). Group psychotherapy training and effectiveness. *International Journal of Group Psychotherapy: 51*, 399–416. doi:10.1521/ijgp.51.3.399.49889.

Gerhart, D. (2012). *Theory and treatment planning in counseling and psychotherapy*. Belmont, CA: Cengage Learning.

Harel, Y., Shechtman, Z., & Cutrona. C. (2012). Exploration of support behavior in counseling groups with counseling trainees. *The Journal for Specialists in Group Work 37*, 202–217.

Higginbotham, N., & Marsella, A. J. (1988). International consultation and the homogenization of psychiatry in Southeast Asia. *Social Science Medicine, 27*, 553–561.

Hogg, H. G., & Hardie, E. A. (1991). Social attraction, personal attraction, and self-categorization-a field study. *Personality and Social Psychology Bulletin, 17*, 175–180. doi:10.1177/0146167291017002O9

Ibrahim, F. A. (1994). Suicidal behavior in Asian-American women. In S. S. Canetto & D. Lester (Eds.), *Women and suicide* (pp. 144–156). New York, NY: Springer/Verlag.

Ibrahim, F. A. (1999). Transcultural counseling: Existential world view theory and cultural identity: Transcultural applications. In J. McFadden (Ed.), *Transcultural counseling* (2nd ed., pp. 23–57). Alexandria, VA: ACA Press.

Ibrahim, F. A. (2007a). *Cultural Identity Check-List–Revised*. Denver, CO: Author.

Ibrahim, F. A. (2007b). *Group counseling training: Session feedback form*. Denver, CO: Author.

Ibrahim, F. A. (2008). *Process observation form for diverse settings*. Denver, CO: Author.

Ibrahim, F. A. (2009). Cultural identity exploration. In C. F. Salazar (Ed.), *Group work experts share their favorite multicultural activities: A guide to diversity-competent choosing, planning, conducting, and processing* (pp. 153–158). Alexandria, VA: Association for Specialists in Group Work.

Ibrahim, F. A. (2010). Innovative teaching strategies for group work: Addressing cultural responsiveness and social justice. *The Journal for Specialists in Group Work, 35*, 271–280.

Ibrahim, F. A., Dinsmore, J., Estrada, D., & D'Andrea, M. (2011). Counselors for Social Justice (CSJ): Ethical standards. *Journal for Social Action in Counseling and Psychology, 3*. Retrieved from http://jsacp.tumblr.com

Ibrahim, F. A., & Ingram, M. A. (2007). Counseling South Asian international students. In R. Singaravelu, & M. Pope (Ed.), *Counseling international students* (pp. 195–211). Alexandria, VA: ACA Press.

Ibrahim, F. A., & Kahn, H. (1984). *Scale to Assess World View*. Storrs, CT: Author.

Ibrahim, F. A., & Kahn, H. (1987). Assessment of worldviews. *Psychological Reports, 60*, 163–176.

Ibrahim, F. A., Ohnishi, H., & Sandhu D. (1997). Asian-American identity development: South Asian Americans. *Journal of Multicultural Counseling and Development, 25*, 34–50.

Ivey, A. E., Ivey, M. B., & Zalaquett, C. (2009). *Intentional interviewing and counseling*. Belmont, CA: Wadsworth/Cengage.

Ivey, A. E., Pedersen, P. B., & Ivey, M. B. (2008). *Group microskills: Culture-centered group processes & strategies*. Alexandria, VA: ACA Press.

Kleinman, A. K., Eisenberg, L., & Good, B. (1978). Culture, illness and care: Clinical lessons from anthropologic and cross-cultural research. *Annals of Internal Medicine, 88*, 251–258.

Klohnen, E. C., & Luo, S. (2003). Interpersonal attraction and personality: What is attractive-self similarity, ideal similarity, complementarity, or attachment security?

Journal of Personality and Social Psychology, 85, 709–722. doi:10.1037/0022-3514.85.4.709.

Markus, H. E., & King, D. A. (2003). A survey of group psychotherapy training during predoctoral psychology internship. *Professional Psychology: Research and Practice 34*, 203–209.

McCarthy, C. J., & Hart, S. (2011) Designing groups to meet evolving challenges in health care settings. *The Journal for Specialists in Group Work, 36*, 352–367.

McClosky, A. (2013). *Using Fishbowl discussion to encourage post-formal thinking*. Psychology Teacher Network. Retrieved from http://www.apa.org/ed/precollege/ptn/2013/02/fishbowl-discussions.aspx

Olson, B., Viola, J., & Fromm-Reid, S. (2011). A temporal model of community organizing and direct action. *Peace Review: A journal of Social Justice, 23*, 52–60. http://dx.doi.org/10.1080/10402659.2011.548253.

Pistole, M. C., Kinyon, J., & Keith, C. D. (2008). Group experiential learning with undergraduate nursing students: An interdisciplinary approach. *The Journal for Specialists in Group Work 33*, 161–178.

Romano, J. L., & Sullivan, B. A. (2000). Simulated group counseling for group work training: A four-year research study of group development. *Journal for Specialists in Group Work, 25*, 366–375.

Schumaker, D, Ortiz, C., & Brenninkmeyer, L. (2011). Revisiting experiential group training in counselor education: A survey of Master's-level programs. *The Journal for Specialists in Group Work 36*, 111–128.

Squarcini, F. (Ed.), (2011). *Boundaries, dynamics and construction of traditions in South Asia*. New York, NY: Anthem.

Srivastava, D. (2012). *The effect of ethnic identity, family conflict, and acculturation on racial discrimination and mental distress of second generation Asian Americans* (Doctoral dissertation). Proquest Dissertations and Theses database. (UMI No. 1039156975)

Sue, S., & Zane, N. (1987). The role of culture and cultural techniques in psychotherapy: A critique and reformulation. *American Psychologist, 42*, 37–45.

Treadwell, T. W., Kumar, V. K., Stein, S. A., & Prosnick, K. (1998). Sociometry: Tools for research and practice. *International Journal of Action Methods, 51*, 10967–10980.

Treadwell, T. W., Stein, S., & Leach, E. (1989). The social atom-revised. *International Journal of Small Group Research, 5*, 65–68.

United Nations. (1948). *The universal declaration of human rights*. Retrieved from: http://www.un.org/en/documents/udhr/

United Nations Economic and Social Commission for Asia and the Pacific. (n.d.) *Harmful traditional practices in three countries of South Asia: Culture, human rights and violence against women*. Bangkok, Thailand: Author.

Westermeyer, J. (1985). Psychiatric diagnosis across cultural boundaries. *American Journal of Psychiatry, 142*, 798–805.

APPENDIX A
CONSULTATION AND TRAINING PROCESS

Preparation for Consultation and Training	Cultural Assessments: (a) Worldview (beliefs, values, and assumptions on five core value areas: human nature, nature, social relationships, time, and activity). (b) Cultural identity exploration. (c) Learning needs assessment, separate focus groups with faculty and students with five to eight members, lasting one and 1 half hr.
Initial Phase: Week I	(a) Ethics of group work, required competencies, cultural dimensions of the training theory and the cultural context in South Asia. (b) Developing a group climate as a learning community. The focus was on building trust and learning about confidentiality and understanding local cultural norms and mores. (c) The skills of group work were introduced, starting with the basic listening sequence, responding with empathy, intentionality, cultural intentionality, paraphrasing, and summarizing.
Working Phase: Week II	(a) Group development process, initial, transition, working, and termination stages. (b) Working through the stages using experiential exercises to develop trust, goals, norms, and learning about processing the group experience (Appendix B: Group Experience Processing Form).
Final Phase: Week III	(a) Practice issues, adaptation of Western theories and practice to local context and making group theory and practice culturally relevant. (b) Focusing on specific issues that emerged in the training regarding boundaries, privacy, basic human rights, and social justice issues.

APPENDIX B
PROCESS OBSERVATION FORM FOR DIVERSE SETTINGS©

Farah A. Ibrahim (2008)

This is an outline of variables that are critical in understanding group process.

Overview: Explain what the group you were observing was working on (brief synopsis):

1. Number of individuals in the group being observed:
2. Ethnic-cultural-gender-class, etc., identification of group members:
   List

3. What were the stated goals and objectives of the group activity? Were these accomplished? If yes, how did you assess this, by what outcomes? If not why did the group not achieve its goals?
4. Type of group:
   (a) Task ___ (b) Psychoeducational___ (c) Counseling___
   (d) Therapy___ (e) Brief___
5. Climate
   (a) Level of cultural empathy: (i) High___ (ii) Neutral___ (iii) Low___
   (b) Emotional climate: (i) Warm___ (ii) Neutral___ (iii) Cold___
   (c) Identification of positive resources of group members brought out in narratives (positive asset search): (i) High___ (ii) Low___
   (d) Activity level (movement toward resolution/achievement of group goals/tasks): (i) High___ (ii) Low___
   (e) Directionality of communication: One to One____ One to Leader____ One to group____
6. Leadership/membership roles and attending behaviors (list group member names):
   (a) Listening:
   (b) Observation:
   (c) Focusing:
   (d) Open-ended questions
   (e) Encouraging
   (f) Paraphrasing
   (g) Reflecting
   (h) Summarizing
   (i) Reframing
   (j) Interpreting
   (k) Linking
   (l) Self-disclosure
   (m) Feedback
   (n) Eliciting meaning
   (o) Reflecting meaning
   (p) Blocking
   (q) Assessing
   (r) Modeling
   (s) Offering information
   (t) Initiating
   (u) Evaluating
   (v) Terminating
7. Cultural intentionality (displayed by. . .):
8. Conflict resolution offered by:
9. Problem resolution efforts by:
10. Overall, how did you think the group was doing on all the various process dimensions?
    (a) Were all the members engaged and active? Yes___ No___
    (b) Was the energy level in the group high___ or low___?

(c) Were the members getting enough air time? Yes___ No___
(d) Which members were taking leadership and facilitative roles (list)?
(e) Which members were not engaged (list):

11. Was there a critical incident in this meeting?

    Yes___ No___

12. What is the stage/phase of development of this group?
    (a) Initial
    (b) Transition
    (c) Working
    (d) Closure and Termination
    (e) A combination of__________

13. How did the observation affect you personally?

APPENDIX C
GROUP COUNSELING TRAINING: SESSION FEEDBACK FORM©

Farah A. Ibrahim (2007b)

Please provide feedback on today's session, this will help me provide information, techniques, and skills in a manner that will be more meaningful for you.

Date: ____________

1. My goals for today's session were (please list, you can also use the back of this sheet):
2. I read the chapters assigned for this session, and I was prepared for the session:

   Yes____ No____
3. I experienced cognitive change today Yes___ No___
4. I experienced an affective change today Yes___ No___
5. I learned new skills today Yes___ No___
6. The group members that influenced my learning the most today were:
7. I would have preferred to work on ____________ today
8. My recommendation for future sessions is that we focus on:

   (a) Additional information on today's topic or on____________________
   (b) Additional practice on the following skill(s)____________________
   (c) I would like my peers/instructor to _________ make this course more meaningful

9. I was able to connect theory with practice during processing sessions:
   Yes____ No____

10. Overall today's session was (please circle one):
    Excellent Good Okay Not useful Not useful

11. In future sessions I will be: More active___ More prepared ___ Share my thoughts ____

Additional comments:

Thank you for taking the time to complete this anonymous feedback form!

A Grounded Theory of Western-Trained Asian Group Leaders Leading Groups in Asia

Nattasuda Taephant
Chulalongkorn University

Deborah Rubel
Oregon State University

Julia Champe
Southern Illinois University

This grounded theory research explored the experiences of Western-trained Asian group leaders leading groups in Asia. A total of 6 participants from Japan, Taiwan, and Thailand were interviewed 3 times over 9 months. The recursive process of data collection and analysis yielded substantive theory describing the participants' process of reconciling Western training with the Asian, international context in which they were leading groups. The concepts and process comprising this theory illustrate how participants engaged in reflective experimentation to integrate personal experience, Western training, and emic knowledge of cultures to develop culturally appropriate group interventions. Implications for group work practice, training, and research are discussed.

Interest in and use of group work is expanding internationally, including into the countries comprising Asia (McWhirter, McWhirter, McWhirter, & McWhirter, 2010). Leong and Leach (2007) suggested that researchers should increase efforts towards studying international applications of counseling to increase the quality of mental health services. Research efforts in the area of group work in Asian countries have been focused largely on group member variables including outcome and perceptions (e.g., Coven, 2004; e.g., Pan, Deng, Tsai, & Chang, 2011), with no systematic focus on leader variables or experiences.

This study aims to increase understanding of group leader experiences leading groups within an Asian international context.

Group work has been cited as a potentially effective mental health intervention for clients from various Asian cultures (Chung, 2004; Conyne, Wilson, Tang, & Shi, 1999; Coven, 2004; Leong, Wagner, & Kim, 1995; Pope, 1999). The literature has presented Asian people's attitudes toward seeking Western forms of psychological help as unfavorable (Kuo, 2004; Ringle, 2005; Yeh & Inose, 2002; Zhang & Dixon, 2003). This attitude has been attributed to the typically collectivistic orientation of Asian cultures and the tendency for helping theories to be based upon individualistic Western values and principles (Bemak & Chung, 2004). It is within this context that some suggest the collaborative environment of group work may be more comfortable for clients from collectivistic Asian cultures. Yet, even within group work, counselors who are unaware of cultural differences may provide ineffective or damaging treatment (Bemak & Chung, 2004).

For this discussion, the term "Western" refers to broadly defined cultural, political, and philosophical systems dominant in geographic regions such as the United States and Canada. The term "Eastern" broadly refers to the cultural, political, and philosophical systems common to Asian countries such as Japan and China (East Asian), Thailand and Vietnam (South East Asian), and India and Bangladesh (South Asian). Chung (2004), in writing about group work with Asian-American members, associates Western group work practice with a valuing of individualism, open conflict, egalitarian leadership, self-disclosure, and emotional expressiveness. She presents Asian-American group members, depending on factors such as acculturation, as valuing collectivism, harmony, authoritative leadership, and, potentially, less self-disclosure and emotional expressiveness. While her comments are focused on Asian-Americans, parallels with many Asian international populations are safe to assume.

Given the differences between Eastern and Western perspectives, culturally competent psychotherapy and group work requires "technical adjustments, theoretical modifications and philosophical reorientation" (Bemak & Chung, 2004, p. 18). Group leaders play a critical role in creating a therapeutic environment for group members (DeLucia-Waack & Donigian, 2004; Yalom, 1975), and group leaders who are not culturally sensitive may struggle with the task of balancing approaches grounded in the West, the process of adaptation, and safety. Understanding what group leaders experience and how they function when leading groups in Asian international contexts seems vital.

To date, the literature on group work with Asian populations provides evidence of some useful alterations to Western group work practice, but little focus on its application in an international context or on group leaders' experience of this process. There is a substantial body of literature describing culturally sensitive *theoretical* approaches to group work with Asian group members, primarily within the United States and, to a limited extent, within Asia. Examples within the United States include Chen and Han (2001) who provide a stage-specific model for enhancing Asian group members' integration into Western culture and Queener and Kenyon (2001) who describe a group-based prevention program for Southeast Asian adolescent girls. Similar articles describe group work approaches with specific populations throughout Asia, including high school students (Chong, 2005) and delinquent adolescents (Kit & Teo, 2012) in Singapore, college students in Taiwan (Pan, Chang, & Yu, 2006), and women in Burma (Norsworthy & Khuankaew, 2004).

Despite the availability of theoretical and practice literature in this area, *empirical research* on the use of group work with clients from Asian cultures addresses a limited number of areas. These areas include the effectiveness of specific group formats for treating clients from Asian cultures both within the United States and in Asia (e.g., Coven, 2004; Pope, 1999; Singh & Hays, 2008), Asian group members' perceptions or experiences of group work (e.g., Pan et al., 2011), and development of culturally sensitive group interventions for clients from Asian cultures (e.g., Rungreangkulkij, Wongtakee, & Thongyot, 2011).

Additionally, some authors and researchers have written about group leaders' experiences with Asian populations (e.g., Chang, 2005; Conyne, Wilson, & Tang, 2000; Conyne et al., 1999; Coven, 2004; Pope, 1999). However, this literature describes the experiences of Western group workers leading groups in Asia (Conyne et al., 2000; Pope, 1999) or Western group workers leading groups for immigrant or displaced persons within the United States (e.g., Singh & Hays, 2008). What is missing from this writing and research are holistic, in-depth descriptions of emic leader perspectives of group work processes within an Asian international context.

The impact of the limited nature of research in the area of emic group leader perceptions within an Asian international context cannot be underestimated. In 2000, Fuertes and Gretchen suggested that studying counselors from ethnic minority or indigenous groups who adapted counseling theory in their practice with culturally similar clients might provide valuable insight into the translation of traditional counseling into more culturally congruent interventions. The value of this type of exploration is demonstrated by Fernando (2009). Writing one of the few articles of its kind, Fernando (2009) provides a first-hand account of her leader experiences in a support group for female tsunami survivors in Sri Lanka. A Sri Lankan who was trained and currently practices in the United States, Fernando describes the challenge of reconciling her Western leader role with cultural expectations regarding authority and status and reveals some of her process of adaptation. This description provides useful insight into the complex interplay of an individual group worker's culture and training when leading groups in a challenging setting.

Despite the value of Fernando's (2009) account, it stands as a lone example of an account of a Western-trained Asian group leader's experience of leading groups in Asia and is not based on systematic study procedures. Clearly a need exists for exploratory research in the area of Asian group leaders' perceptions and experiences about the process of leading groups in Asia. This research attempted to fill this gap. The purpose of this study was to holitistically describe the experiences and perceptions of Western-trained Asian group leaders, in part to better understand how they applied or adapted principles of group work while leading groups in an Asian context, and to generate theory from these experiences. Given the exploratory nature of the research, a qualitative methodology, grounded theory, was used. The grand research question of this study was, "How do Western-trained Asian group leaders experience group leadership in an Asian international context?"

METHOD

For this study, the nature of the research question guided selection of the research method. Qualitative methods were suited to the exploratory purposes of this study in that Creswell (1998) stated that qualitative research is particularly appropriate to answer questions of "How" or "What." Additionally, Strauss and Corbin (1998) stated "Qualitative methods may be used to obtain the intricate details about phenomena such as feelings, thought processes, and emotions that are difficult to extract or learn about through more conventional research methods" (p. 11). Since the focus of this study is the group leader's complex interplay of feelings, thoughts, and actions in the environment of the group and culture, qualitative research is an appropriate choice. Further, grounded theory approaches, in particular, are appropriate for studying experiences over time, processes, and complex systems (Strauss & Corbin, 1998). Additionally, Fassinger (2005) describes the aim of grounded theory as producing, " . . . innovative theory that is 'grounded' in data collected from participants on the basis of the complexities of their lived experiences in a social context." (p. 157) Since the intent of this study was to explore a complex personal experience of group leadership in the particular social context of practicing group work in various Asian countries, a grounded theory approach seemed ideal. The grounded theory approach for this study was heavily influenced by constructivism where the theory that emerges during the study depicts an interpretation of the world, not an absolute truth, and represents knowledge constructed through interaction between researchers and participants (Charmaz, 2006).

Participants and Setting

This research utilized purposive selection where researchers select participants who are likely to provide information useful to answering the research questions (Patton, 2002). In this case, the researcher recruited master's or doctoral level group leaders from Thailand, Japan, and Taiwan who met the criteria of currently leading counseling or psychotherapy groups in their native country. These countries were selected due to the first author's familiarity with Thailand, their relatively high usage of counseling, and relative cultural heterogeneity (Barnes, 1996; Lin, 2004). The criterion of fluency in English was essential so that researchers and participants had a shared language. The criterion of master's or doctoral level training was essential to ensure a baseline of training and competence. The criterion of currently leading a counseling or psychotherapy group was also essential as this ensured a strong connection between the participant and recent, easily recalled experiences leading groups. Originally, training in the United States or Canada was not a criterion, but as recruitment went on it became apparent that all potential participants were from this demographic. This resulted in a slight shift in the focus of this qualitative study. Design flexibility is a hallmark of qualitative research design. Specifically, Hays and Singh (2012) indicate that, because of the non-linear nature of qualitative research, initial research questions should be broad and then may be refined as more information is gathered. After IRB approval, the first author began recruitment through emails sent to four counseling listservs (CESNET, COUNSGRAD, IAGP:TRANS, and DIVERSEGRAD) asking for volunteers and further asking that study information be passed on to potential volunteers who fit study criteria. The first author, who knew many counseling professionals in Asia, also contacted individuals to request that they pass on study information to potential volunteers. The researcher started data collection when 6 participants were located and remained open to recruiting more to achieve thick description and saturation.

The participants were diverse geographically and in gender. They were from three countries in Asia—Thailand, Japan, and Taiwan—and included 3 women and 3 men. Two of the participants held doctoral degrees in psychology and two held doctoral degrees in counselor education or counseling. The final two participants held master's degrees, one in expressive arts therapy and the other in social administration (equivalent to social work). Five participants graduated from institutions of higher education in the United States and one graduated from

Table 1 Participant Information

Participant Number	*Gender*	*Degree Type*	*Degree Location*	*Years of Group Work Practice*	*Country of Origin and Practice*	*Group Member Nationality*
1	M	Doctorate in Counselor Education	United States	30	Thailand	Thailand
2	F	Master's in Expressive Arts Therapy	United States	18	Thailand	Thailand, Australia, Europe
3	M	Master's in Social Administ-ration	United States	7	Japan	Japan
4	F	Doctorate in Counseling	United States	2	Taiwan	Taiwan
5	M	Doctorate in Psychology	Canada	12	Thailand	Thailand
6	F	Doctorate in Counseling Psychology	United States	2	Thailand	Thailand

a university in Canada. The sample of participants represented a broad range of experience. The length of time participants had been leading groups in Asia ranged from 1.5 years to 30 years. They were leading psychoeducation groups, personal growth groups, and therapy groups. See Table 1 for a graphic depiction of participant information.

Data Collection

The first author collected data about the participants' experiences of leading groups in Asia through audiotaped, semi-structured interviews using carefully developed interview questions. Interview questions reflected general ideas garnered from the literature and experience, and were constructed to be sufficiently focused to direct participants to talk about relevant experiences, yet broad enough to allow participants to express the uniqueness of their individual experiences (Strauss & Corbin, 1998). The researcher conducted the interviews through internet telephone and telephone. Semi-structured interviews were used to balance the researcher's experiences, the nature of phone interviews, the nature of naturalistic inquiry, and the nature of counseling research (Suzuki, Ahluwala, Arora, & Mattis, 2007). The initial interview questions were: (a) What influenced you as you lead this group? (b) How do you know what to do in your group? (c) What are you aware of, in yourself and your group members, while you are leading your group? (d) How does your awareness of culture impact you when you lead this group?

To focus the interviews, participants were asked to think about one of the groups they were currently leading and to use personal experiences from that group to answer the questions. The interviews lasted 30–45 min for each participant. After the data were transcribed verbatim, de-identified, and coded with a participant number to protect anonymity, they were analyzed. Subsequent recursive interviews of similar length were conducted using questions constructed to further clarify concepts and relationships that emerged from earlier rounds through the process of theoretical sampling (Strauss & Corbin, 1998).

For example, during first round analysis a tentative category was identified that described participants' experiences of experimenting with interventions within their groups. This eventually was conceptualized as "engaging in reflective experimentation." After the first round of interviews and analysis, however, it was not apparent how this process occurred, so several questions were constructed to allow participants to express more deeply how they experienced engaging in reflective experimentation. An example question was, "You've expressed that sometimes what you try in your groups works and sometimes it does not. How do you know if what you've tried in group has worked or not?" Three rounds of interviews utilizing this type of theoretical sampling to fill in gaps in understanding achieved saturation, where no new experiences or concepts were revealed by participants (Strauss & Corbin, 1998).

Data Analysis

Data analysis was guided by Strauss and Corbin's (1998) instructions for grounded theory data analysis. The first author first analyzed the transcripts using open coding and axial coding procedures. Open and axial coding were used concurrently to break apart text data to identify, combine, differentiate, and sort initial concepts into broad concepts describing major aspects of the participants' experience (categories), and more narrow concepts that described or specified categories (properties; Strauss & Corbin, 1998). During this process the researchers used constant comparison, where characteristics of emerging concepts are compared and, if necessary, reconceptualized to ensure that there was no overlap in concept definitions (Strauss & Corbin, 1998).

For example, during open coding the researchers found a group of codes or concepts related to participants' experiences of developing effective ways to work with their groups. These were grouped into a more abstract category called engaging in reflective experimentation. Further analysis of the data, via axial coding, led to identification of tentative properties of engaging in reflective experimentation related to motivation, personal development, and basic personal beliefs: *being motivated, developing a personal style*, and *believing in their philosophies*. Constant comparison of each of these properties with each other, the category *engaging in reflective experimentation, and other categories that had emerged, resulted in the reconceptualization of the properties being motivated and believing in their philosophies* as part of another category, *drawing upon inner resources*. This process of open and axial coding continued throughout the three rounds of interviews and theoretical sampling and was followed by selective coding. During selective coding all categories are connected into a larger schema based on their relationship to a central category (Strauss & Corbin, 1998). The central category is identified by its overall prominence, direct relationship to all other categories, and centrality in explanations of variability in the theory (Strauss & Corbin, 1998). In this study, the central category appeared to be related to participants' experiences of a trial and error-like process that was informed by knowledge, experience, and engagement with their groups. This central category was engaging in reflective experimentation. Subsequently, theory was developed around this central category by writing a storyline that incorporated all concepts, related them to the central category, and richly described participants' experiences of leading groups in Asian international contexts (Strauss & Corbin, 1998). Throughout the process, all concepts were constantly checked against the data to ensure that all participant experiences were represented by the major categories and properties (Strauss & Corbin, 1998).

The researchers have chosen to include brief verbatim passages from transcribed participant interviews to provide illustrative examples of categories and variations within categories. In addition to enhancing description, including representative participant quotes gives support to the emerging theory (Strauss & Corbin, 1998), and "exposes data to the reader" (Seale, 1999, p.157). All interviews were conducted in English, which was not the first language for the primary researcher or the participants. Minor edits were made for clarity, but any non-standard grammar or sentence construction remains intact. These quotes may enable research users to gain deeper insight into participants' conceptualizations as well as any "underlying assumptions, ambivalence, and uncertainties" (Corden & Sainsbury, 2006, p. 11) about their experiences.

Researchers' Disclosure and Trustworthiness

To ensure that the products of this research matched participants' experiences and provided the details necessary for readers to evaluate its usefulness to their contexts, the researcher followed Lincoln and Guba's (1985) criteria for trustworthiness. One important method to enhance the trustworthiness was controlling researcher bias (Creswell, 1998; Lincoln & Guba, 1985). First, providing a description of researcher roles is essential to better understanding the context of the study and the researchers' potential influences. The study was the first author's dissertation research. She led study design efforts, recruited, and interviewed all participants, and conducted data analysis. The second author consulted with and debriefed the first author frequently during the design, data collection, and analysis processes. The third author consulted with and provided feedback to the first two authors in the later stages of theorizing. All authors participated in the complex process of communicating the participants' experiences accurately in writing.

At the time of the research, the first author was a doctoral student in a counselor education program in the United States. She is Thai and received her master's degree in counseling psychology from a university in Thailand. She had run many groups in Thailand with predominantly Thai group members. The second author was an assistant professor of counselor education at a university in the United States. She is biracial—Japanese-American—and received her master's and doctoral degrees in counseling in the United States. She had led numerous groups with group members being predominantly Euro-American. The third author was an assistant professor of counselor education at a university in the United States. She is Euro-American and received her master's and doctoral degrees in the United States. She had run numerous groups with predominantly Euro-American group members.

The authors explored and described their experiences and assumptions related to the study questions. These assumptions included (1) that participants should try to adjust knowledge and experiences gained in the West to fit with their own and clients' cultural context, with the goal of providing culturally sensitive interventions, (2) that participants' understanding of Western and Eastern culture would assist them in some way while engaging in group work in their country of origin, and (3) that participants' experience of group work in their country of origin would have challenging aspects. During the entire research process, the first author journaled and debriefed frequently with the second author to clarify how her experiences might influence the process. The third author provided another perspective on potential biases through consultation during later stages of theorizing.

In addition to the above, prolonged engagement was used to increase trustworthiness. According to Lincoln and Guba (1985), prolonged engagement is spending adequate time to learn the culture, check for misinformation, and build trust. The first author, who conducted all interviews, shared varying levels of culture, including the cultures of counseling and group work, with participants. She interacted with participants multiple times including three individual interviews of approximately 30–45 min apiece and a fourth, member checking interview, over a 9-month period. During open-ended questioning, the participants shared increasingly personal information, indicating increased trust. When participants brought up their or group members' culture, she would encourage them to describe this more fully to increase her knowledge of the specific cultural contexts.

Triangulation was also used to increase the trustworthiness of this study. Triangulation is a strategy where multiple sources and methods of data collection are used to reduce the chance that research conclusions reflect systemic biases (Lincoln & Guba, 1985). The study utilized different data sources including phone interviews and the first author's journal and also employed literature triangulation, where research results are checked against concepts in the extant literature. Additionally, the research design incorporated member checking to enhance trustworthiness by minimizing the possibility of misinterpretation (Lincoln & Guba, 1985). Member checking consisted of sending tentative results to participants near the end of the analysis process and interviewing the participants to gain feedback about how the interpretations fit with their experiences.

Finally, trustworthiness was further promoted through measures that assisted others in assessing the applicability of the research conclusions to other settings (Lincoln & Guba, 1985). For this purpose, the researcher documented detailed descriptions of the context of the study, the study procedures, and the participants. Additionally, information needed for a confirmability audit was recorded and retained (Lincoln & Guba, 1985).

RESULTS

This study resulted in a multilevel descriptive model of Western-trained Asian group leaders' experiences of leading groups in Asia. In this section the major categories of that model are reported along with concepts that describe significant relationships between categories. Three rounds of interviews and data analysis produced three major categories describing participants' experiences including *working within Asian culturally influenced systems, drawing upon inner resources*, and the central category, *engaging in reflective experimentation*.

The category of working within Asian culturally influenced systems described participants' experience of running groups and advocating for group work within systems shaped by a set of cultural values, knowledge, and history. The category of drawing upon inner resources described these Western-trained Asian group leaders' use of their basic characteristics, beliefs, life experiences and accumulated knowledge during group work practice. The central category, engaging in reflective experimentation described the participants' process of boldly but mindfully integrating Eastern and Western knowledge and experiences into group work interventions, practice, and principles useful to their group members, groups, and communities. Engaging in reflective experimentation was a process that connected and interacted with the other two major categories, and these concepts became the basis of this emerging theory. In the following sections we further describe the categories and their interaction. Although engaging in reflective experimentation is the central category the other two categories are described first because they are components essential to the understanding of engaging in reflective experimentation.

Working Within an Asian Culturally Influenced System

The category of *working within Asian culturally influenced systems* described participants' experiences of forming and running groups within systems influenced by specific cultural values, knowledge, and history. They perceived the culturally influenced systems as having both supportive and challenging elements that impacted the systems' and individuals within the systems' openness to group work. Despite reporting challenges, the participants largely focused on the benefits they perceived they received from sharing part of the culture and from having relatively high levels of power within the systems.

The participants perceived several systemic factors that hindered their group work, and these factors varied from those that seemed very culturally influenced to those that seemed very similar to the challenges faced by group work practitioners in the West. Some of the challenges stemmed from lack of familiarity and congruence between the culturally influenced system and counseling or group work. Participant 3 shares

> I think the first thing that people told me when I came to Japan and started work is that "you know, Japanese people aren't used to counseling and they are not used to telling their feeling."

Participant 4 shares further about a similar challenge:

> Some of those kids . . . have been required to visit the counseling room quite often . . . (so) that they may build up (a) wall to anyone who wants to talk to them. so, that part is still hard . . . not just because of this population, but also in (this) culture we are not . . . used to talk someone about what we really think. . . .

And from participant 2:

> . . . If you are to go to somebody outside the family to share the family problem, it's to betray the family because it's bringing the inside or personal information of the family be told to the outside. . . .

Other challenges from the cultural systems stemmed from misperceptions caused by poor past experiences with counseling or group work. For instance Participant 2 shares:

> Some members had previously attend other group therapy before with different group therapist and . . . over time learn that one of the most important group rule regarding confidentiality was not be(ing) follow(ed).

And, Participant 2 also talks more about misperceptions that may have led to negative experiences with group:

> . . . they just put everybody in one group because they feel like . . . group leader is a baby sitter. . . . So (then) the nurse can have the patient out of their ward and do some activity. But when you don't separate and try to screen and put them in appropriate level . . .

Participants also perceived support and openness from their culturally influenced systems. Some of the reasons they received support from the systems surrounding them sound strikingly universal. The participants perceived that their systems supported group work due to budgetary reasons. Participant 3 shares, " . . . a lot of administrator here hear about group therapy and decide they want a group therapy in their agency . . . for a cost benefit." Participant 4 adds:

> . . . the boss of the agency didn't really want (me) to run the group. (But) one of the personnel in that agency . . . does really want me to run the group. So the . . . the boss of the agency are kind of like, "I don't really care, just finish that group, I can have some money to run the agency" since this is non-profit agency. They (are) . . . funded by the project they . . . developed and they got the budget from the government.

Participants also perceived their systems as becoming increasingly open. Participants had ways to deal with the challenges. They worked with their respective communities in order to continue their group work practice. They provided communities with positive experiences, knowledge, and information about their practice. As Participant 1 stated:

> During my 30 years period, people gain more . . . understanding of our work because our work is not very easy to communicate. It's more experiential, it's more abstract, it's not concrete . . . but if we have a chance to work with them directly . . . they learn and they see what we can do for them. So to understand . . . people must have a chance to participate . . . directly because this thing is experiential, not by word of explanation . . .

Additionally, most of the participants also taught at the university level. They not only facilitated groups but also taught students about group work practice. Therefore, they also had some impact in the communities and systems by training group leaders to work in the community. Here participant 2 relates her perception of this:

> Another thing would be supervision and teaching for students who are in training and students who come to observe and during follow up discussing. They learn something from it. It's always some good feeling to see that students are learning and changing also.

The motivation to begin and to continue group work practice was critical for these Asian group leaders. Their cultures and communities sustained their motivation to begin and to continue practicing group work in Asia. Spurred by their motivations, they perceived the challenge of leading groups in their cultural system as a resource. Participant 5 shares his overall perspective on this:

> A lot of people often consider culture to be an obstacle. I think it's actually helping factor. You always need some point of reference in your therapy or intervention or relation with people in the culture. And knowing what the limit is in term of culture is, help you get somewhere. Without it you don't have a guiding principle. But the problem is the guiding principle is not crystal clear. It's the gray one. That's why you have to fit in with it to see where the lines are really drawn . . .

Drawing Upon Inner Resources

Drawing upon inner resources described Western-trained Asian group leaders' experience of relying upon their basic characteristics, beliefs, and life experiences during group work practice. These characteristics, values, beliefs, and experiences acted as inner resources that the participants drew upon as they worked to lead groups and promote group work in Asia. At the foundation of these inner resources were the Western-trained Asian group leaders' individual characteristics, which were instrumental in beginning and continuing their group work practice in Asia. On this foundation lay a core set of beliefs and a set of experiences representing both Western and Eastern contexts. These beliefs and experiences related to group work and supported the participants as they promoted group work and led groups in Asia. Their motivation to practice group work was pivotal as they faced this challenge of developing ways of working that were suitable for their groups and group members.

Participants shared a common perception that their personal characteristics allowed them to do pioneering group work in Asia. Here Participant 1 describes a deep sense of caring and obligation that moved him to engage in group work:

> It's something inside. It's something inside our guts. It's not just being a counselor or counseling psychologist by training but we must have that thing in our mind to serve all human being as much as we can.

In addition to compassion and a helper identity, participants also indicated that they were people who found the challenge stimulating. Here Participant 2 discusses this:

> . . . Second, it's interesting for me, a challenge. If you look at it as challenges is always motivating to try. Healthy way of approaching things in life. . . .

Similarly, Participant 3 talked about how the element of trying something new was appealing to him:

> . . . The thing that I can add is when you have opportunity to try something new and you really have nothing to lose. You know, nothing to lose, you will gain. The opposite of nothing to lose is to gain something. You try what you can. But also it uses a lot of motivation. It's an opportunity . . .

These personal characteristics were in some ways inseparable from a set of beliefs held by participants that both guided their group work and motivated it. The beliefs integrated varying levels of Eastern and Western perspectives and were grounded by a strong belief in the power of group work to help people. Believing in group work was part of all of the participants' core belief systems. This belief developed from direct experiences as group members and also from working in groups. Here Participant 1 describes his trust in group work that gradually developed from his experiences as a group leader.

> . . . It's from my heart, from my senses, from my effort. It's from what I have put into groups with my whole heart . . . It's valuable. It's sacred. It's the place that make unreal person to become a real person. It's place that people can change from the worst to the best.

Participant 2 adds:

> . . . I think the part that I value it so much . . . when I was a student and when I worked here in United States professionally . . . is really encouraging me to be a group participant . . . I really value in those experience because having the direct experience of what it was like to go through the most painful part of your life and to see yourself go through that. So it's kind of confirmed your belief because, yes you gone through that before. And it's nothing that can be described in the textbook.

These Western-trained Asian group leaders also perceived the universal effect of group work. They perceived that the positive effect of their group work practice on group members was in part due to the common nature of human beings. This quote from Participant 5 illustrates this belief:

> . . . there are certain aspect of life that can be universal which is transcendent culture boundary and I think leading the group is one of them. You can be in any culture and you can lead group and may be some minor variation according to specific culture but in general I think its universal process. In a group you need to have a leader, group dynamic is similar. . . .

Yet, as much as they perceived the universality of human experiences and the value of group work, participants also reported differing affinities for Eastern and Western philosophies in their own lives and as the foundation of their group work. Here Participant 1 describes relying largely on an Eastern philosophy after training in the west and practicing in Asia for many years:

> I have an experience in what Buddha taught for quite sometimes. And I think now I know of what it is and where it is. So now I'm kind of lead a group by using Buddhist teaching as a guideline. The main teaching that I use, like a theme for practicing group counseling and psychotherapy . . . is four noble truths. This law covers all of phenomenal of the universe.

In contrast, Participant 2 describes discovering during her training that she related more to Western philosophy despite her upbringing and return to her country of origin:

> . . . the part of the counseling values . . . which is rooted in Western culture, I think that really matches what I think, what I believe. . . . Whether this is truly who I am and I just found the Western value that matches what I think. . . . I found it and. . . . I prefer that much more than Chinese value. . . . So I don't know which one happen first but either way . . . a lot of the values or the concepts that counseling have about human nature, I really believe. . . . So that's part of me that goes beyond the culture part. I mean that's really me. . . . I'm bringing that . . . that part of me into session.

Participants also shared perceptions that their experiences in both Eastern and Western contexts were valuable to group leadership in Asia. The benefits ranged from having an emic perspective and experience of leading groups in their own culture to personal growth as a part of Western training programs to learning about Western counseling and group work theories to gaining insight about the role of culture in human life.

Here Participant 3 talks about the invaluable nature of emic cultural knowledge in the group work process;

> . . . I think if the person who is completely alien to Japanese culture comes and tries this thing, it probably wouldn't work. You have to have some knowledge of the Japanese culture to be able to push the limits and that's what is. Pushing the limit of what someone will feel if Japanese. . . .

In contrast, Participant 2 gives an example of Western training being valuable in an Asian context:

> We are helping them to go to one therapeutic factor. . . . Yalom's recapitulation of family process. I help them to go back and try to understand what's going on. After they complete that theme then we bring them back to the here and now scene. They will experience that right now (when) they are in adult world. They are not in the childhood. So they have a power to change. . . .

In addition, participants reported inner resources that developed during Western training. Participant 2 here talks about personal growth as part of her Western training:

> . . . my sense of assertiveness is not (from) the way I been here. It's kind of gradually happened but more so after I went to the group therapy part. In my college year and graduate first year I barely spoke up in class. But then after going through the group therapy process and beginning work as a professional, then I need to speak up.

Participant 1 talks about how time in the United States shaped his identity, "To have a chance to study in the States, I think that's good time for me to see myself more clearly as an Eastern helper." Participant 3 talks about how the perspective gained from experiencing multiple cultures aided him in transcending specific cultures:

> . . . I compare three cultures that I know, the Latin culture, the Japanese culture, and American. And constantly, I'm kind of functionalizing in term of culture. I believe that culture is developed to response to some kind of necessary. So you have to see the function . . . of the culture and see what they are trying to do by maintaining culture norms and beliefs. And so when you know what that culture is trying to do . . . then for the first time, you can manipulate it, you can use it, you can change it, you

> can do all kinds of things with it. But you really need to see that culture (is) not just alone. . . .

These Western-trained Asian group leaders had many inner resources to draw upon during the process of developing personally and culturally appropriate styles of group leadership. They utilized their training experiences in the West and emic cultural understanding to develop ways to work with their groups. Their experiences in the West, emic cultural understanding, personal characteristics, and beliefs about group work combined to create a powerful set of resources with which to face the challenge of leading groups in their respective contexts. As part of this pool of resources, participants related that they found culturally appropriate ways to prepare group members for new experiences, working with their own authority status in varying ways to help group members feel safe to share in group. They related that they waited for indications that group members felt safe before making changes or introducing more culturally challenging interactions.

Engaging in Reflective Experimentation

While working within their cultural systems and relying upon their inner resources, these Western-trained Asian group leaders faced the challenge of working in the Asian context through a process of engaging in reflective experimentation. This process began with a sense of need. They perceived a need to transfer or translate what they had learned to their home context in a workable way. Here Participant 1 describes this sense:

> If we talk like a metaphor, it might be like I was a seed that look for a good place to be planted. So I had a chance to study in the West and as Thai, you know, I feel deeply those theory didn't fit my way of life here.

While engaging in reflective experimentation, participants felt motivated. They felt that this challenging process was the right thing to do, but they also felt vulnerable and anxious. Participant 3 expressed the feelings he had while engaging in reflective experimentation. He also reveals something about the "trial and error" nature of the process.

> . . . at a personal level you feel anxious. Because there's nobody that's going to sit there and tell you what's right and what's wrong and I don't think you can look at things as what's right and what's wrong. . . . But you look at things and it's kind of trial and error thing. You try it, maybe it's good, maybe it's bad and then you try it again. So you live through a lot of discomfort, a lot of feeling of anxiety. . . .

Participant 6 adds:

> Sometime I feel frustrate with it because it isn't like what I expected. Like I was trained in this way and I tried to mix it in another culture and I'm still new to adjust(ing) it to the new culture.

The "trial and error" nature of the reflective experimentation process was experienced by all participants. Here Participant 5 uses a metaphor to convey his perceptions of the process:

> . . . then you're going back to cook again. You serve a dish to your customer and then you watch their reaction. If they are really happy with the dish, then you make the right decision. If they cannot finish the dish, then you have to think again.

The participants' reflective experimentation or "trial and error" process contained two components that interacted continuously while they attempted to develop group interventions that worked. One component, developing awareness within the group, related to how they stayed aware of group member and group reactions. The other component, transferring, related to the participants' experience of translating and synthesizing group work knowledge and emic knowledge into useable forms. Their process of reflective experimentation resulted in both personal and professional growth, which increased their inner resources and contributed to further reflective experimentation processes.

Developing awareness within the group. Developing awareness described Western-trained Asian group leaders' process of attaining awareness of current dynamics of their groups and of individual group members while attempting to develop appropriate interventions. Developing awareness was critical for the participant's group work practice. They utilized awareness in the moment to assist them in responding appropriately and they also maintained awareness over time to monitor groups and individuals and to crystallize general ways to work with groups in their Asian context.

These Western-trained Asian group leaders used both universal and culturally unique ways to describe how they attained awareness within the group. Participant 1 describes the state he seeks during group leadership:

> Our mind has to be quiet when we lead group. This quietness allows us to see clearly into their stories. And within that story we can see the structure in their story.

Here, participant 5 relates an analogy that helps describe his experience of developing his awareness in group.

> I also teach martial art, it calls Aikido. For Aikido practice in the advance level, we have might be 3 or 4 people attacking you at the same time. So you are standing alone and you have to deal with all of them, all at once, trying not to be hit. And working in the group is like that. You have to be alert. Everything is going on at the same time around you.

Beyond describing how they placed themselves in a receptive state for awareness, participants also described in universal and culturally specific ways how they could tell their interventions were working. Here Participant 6 describes this feeling as "flow," " . . . one thing that Thai client and my Western client have when I conduct the group I can feel the flow of the group." She later adds, "I think as a group leader, we can feel that. It's (whether) the group flow or not. And the energy too, when the group (is) success. You can feel the energy is the positive energy." Participant 3 share similarly:

> a lot of times that thing that I look at is I'm looking for the expression. A lot of times when people are, you get the nail on the head. You know when you get the exact sentence, they all be surprised after that they all talk.

Conversely, Participant 6 describes becoming aware that the group is not responding well:

> . . . It works when I ask them to do breathing exercise or stay in the peaceful mind for very brief that work. . . . And the part that ask the participant to discuss about the content or discuss about. . . . CBT skills that we teach. So far I don't think it works. Because Thai student, they don't like to talk. . . .

Transferring. The process of *transferring* knowledge and experiences from training in the West to practice in Asia was also part of participants' experiences of reflective experimentation. They integrated their knowledge and experiences gained during their Western training with their emic cultural knowledge to respond to their groups and group members. The process of transferring began when they were trained. Participant 1 describes how he began questioning and searching during his Western training:

> . . . So I had a question. I think this question I have had it for a long time I think since I studied in a college. A question was "why must I study just Freudian or Rogerian or Jungian, you know. Was there a Thai psychologist in town, practice from our own viewpoint? But I found no one then.

Participant 4 describes:

> . . . My master and doctoral training is started in American. It's mean I get intensive and deepen training in American. That's truly seriously

> I would greatly affected by American culture, in training styles and in counseling styles. And so that's one part of me, pretty Westernize as far as profession is counselor. However, there's another part of me which is Taiwanese-oriented, which is my culture part. And how these two parts could be in conflict, may be, could be work together, maybe.

The process of transferring continued when they returned to their home countries to practice. Some strategies seemed a natural fit and the process went smoothly. Here Participant 3 describes not encountering culturally influenced barriers where others might think he might:

> The funny thing is interesting that I never had trouble about somebody talking about themselves when they're in trouble. That's contrary to the belief of what people believe about Japanese people because most people think that Japanese people are . . . are not open about their feelings.

In other cases, participants experienced tension between Western elements of their approach to group work and how these approaches were received by group members. Participants experienced that tension as difficult to resolve. Here Participant 2 describes the essence of this tension:

> . . . Let's say if you disagree with something . . . the culture of Eastern world expect you to be quiet about it . . . because argument is being view as disrespect. From the Western culture, it is encouraged because you are standing up for your right. . . . So this is something that you have to . . . try to blend in . . . because in the culture of psychotherapy we would like a person to be aware of their own feeling as well as to be able to verbalize it. So how can you integrate that into Eastern culture?

As part of reflective experimentation, Participant 2 continues to talk about the outcome of her reflective experimentation being something that bridges Eastern and Western expectations:

> . . . I try to use the technique of reframing and put into a dilemma . . . They have to solve their dilemma themselves. I reframed it in a way they see both sides as positive. You know, they may speak up even though in Asian culture, but the intention is good so they should do it. Because if they don't speak up then is them join in the problem. You are not helping but you are hurting. . . .

In summary, for these Western-trained Asian group leaders *engaging in reflective experimentation* meant practicing with the dual foundations of Western group leadership skills and emic cultural knowledge. With these foundations they adapted their in-the-moment interventions and broader style to varying degrees to suit the context. They perceived their practice as in some ways similar and other ways different from traditional group practice.

Interaction of Categories

Although the interactions between the major categories above were subtle and complex, this section will describe the two major interactions that seemed to affect participants' overall experience of leading groups in Asia. The first major interaction was participants' use of inner resources, particularly personal attitudes and beliefs, to deal with the challenges of working within an Asian culturally influenced system and engaging in reflective experimentation. Secondly, engaging in reflective experimentation contributed to participants' personal and professional growth and thereby added to the inner resources they drew upon during reflective experimentation.

Participants' reliance on inner resources, particularly their attitudes and beliefs, allowed them to persist during challenging times that were associated with working within an Asian culturally influenced system and engaging in reflective experimentation. When the participants felt frustrated or vulnerable in either the external system or within the groups they were leading, their desire to help, belief in group work, and enjoyment of challenge provided motivation. Here Participant 3 description illustrates how the interaction of his own nature and belief in group work allow him to prosper as a group worker both systemically and in his groups.

> I think what . . . the full motivation is that people . . . would think that groups don't work in Asia. But beyond being Asian . . . people are human and . . . humans regardless of where they are on the planet are social being and therefore the group is gonna work. And so while I'm doing a group I always think of that. That we are doing something that at first people would wonder "Is that really gonna go well in Japan, well and the other part of Asia?" Well, at the same time we're trying to prove something, right? . . . I think that's bringing a lot of motivation.

The second major interaction experienced by participants occurred in the recursive relationship between engaging in reflective experimentation and relying upon inner resources. Both parts of reflective experimentation, developing awareness of group interaction and transferring, required reliance upon knowledge as a part of inner resources. In particular, developing awareness of when group members were not responding well to their interventions required emic understanding about what might turn group members off and how group members might express their disengagement. Transferring, the process of integrating Western knowledge to the Eastern context, relied heavily upon knowledge of both contexts as well as more nuanced experience and understanding of how the leaders themselves had integrated those perspectives together.

Additionally, reflective experimentation fed back into inner resources in two ways. One was the storing of successful and unsuccessful experiences for use in future group leadership. More experienced participants thus had larger and more varied stores of experiences and knowledge specific to group leadership in Asia upon which to draw, while less experienced participants, while effective and engaged, were more actively experimental.

Another way reflective experimentation fed back into inner resources was in terms of personal and professional growth. Successful experiences leading groups in Asia fed participants' belief in group work and themselves as group leaders. Participants who had high experience levels expressed high confidence while participants who had less group work experiences indicated that they might question their practice. Additionally, they all perceived that their efforts to lead groups in Asia contributed to personal growth. As Participant 6 reflected,

> . . . lately I just lost a significant person. And after I lead the group, it really helps me too. . . . I find myself peaceful. I have some joy after the lost I have found recently. I'm still sad but some moment, somehow in the group I feel like . . . the suffering is . . . in Thai we called Anicca, like not permanent. At the moment I learn that another side of the coin, you have some happiness.

In summary, Asian group leaders created their interventions and developed their growth by integrating their Western group work training, cultural understandings, their core beliefs, and their awareness. Their awareness in group provided the basis to understand the results from group interventions and the transferring processes. They used inner resources and understanding of their cultural system to inform their process of reflective experimentation. Challenges during their practice were overcome through strong motivation fueled in part by their belief in group work and their resilient personal natures. The results of their process of reflective experimentation impacted them in terms of both personal and professional growth. Then their growth and their developed interventions impacted their awareness, their basic self, and their cultural system.

DISCUSSION

This study employed a constructivist grounded theory methodology to generate, clarify, and validate concepts describing Asian group leaders, specifically Thai, Taiwanese, and Japanese clinicians, who were trained in the West and practiced in Asia. The major findings of this research were concepts related to working within Asian culturally influenced systems, relying upon inner resources and engaging in reflective experimentation. These concepts and their subordinate concepts share similarities and differences with concepts in the extant literature.

The challenging experiences, such as systemic mistrust, related by participants that informed the theme of working within Asian culturally influenced systems have striking parallels to older, anecdotal descriptions provided in the literature of implementing group work within Western-influenced systems (e.g., Posthuma, 1999). This highlights and normalizes a potentially universal difficulty with misperceptions about group work based on poor practice within systems. Similarly, the positive aspects of working within the system, such as the systems' valuing of group work's efficiency and cost effectiveness, tend to mirror accounts that remain prevalent in the literature (e.g., Kalodner & Hanus, 2010). The participants' sharing, however, adds description of how Asian culture may uniquely shape this experience, particularly the unique position university educators may have within Asian countries and their potential contributions to advocating for increased or better quality group work.

The category of relying upon inner resources also shares similarities and difference with extant research and writing. Rubel and Kline (2008) described leader resources in their qualitative study of expert group leaders. In that study, leader resources represented accumulated experience, personality characteristics, and theoretical knowledge of experts trained in the west practicing in the west that, in a general sense, support the concept of relying upon inner resources. Relying upon inner resources, however, provides detailed description of several unique facets of Western-trained group leaders experiences of leading groups in Asia such as the interplay of Western training with Eastern culture and how participants own grounding in Eastern culture served as a resource. Participants' experiences parallel Fernando's (2009) report that while leading support groups with Sri Lankan tsunami survivors her cultural upbringing, ". . . made it possible for me to easily understand the member's daily life experiences, challenges, world-views, rituals, habits, and lifestyles, and what was considered 'correct behavior'" (p. 12). This illustrates the value of emic cultural knowledge or when attempting to lead groups in an Asian or other international setting.

The category of engaging in reflective experimentation, with its subordinate processes of developing awareness and transferring, evidences strong support by existing concepts in the extant literature as well as providing novel contributions. Accounts of reflective learning are common in the counseling and group work literature (e.g., Okech, 2008), as is the idea that leaders experience personal openness and presence as essential to fully understanding group interaction (e.g., Rubel & Kline, 2008). Additionally, the concept of transferring, as a part of engaging in reflective experimentation, shares commonalities with the process of bicultural skills development as described by authors such as LaFromboise, Coleman, and Gerton (1993). The results of this study, however, offer novel descriptions of how participants negotiated these experiences using both Western-training and their emic understanding of the Asian cultural context. This is reflected also in Fernando's (2009) sharing about remaining in contact with her groups' needs as a part of adapting, "I learned the meaning of 'going with the flow' and how important it is for a group worker to be flexible and spontaneous" (p. 18) and her deliberations regarding use of authority and structure in her role as group leader.

Limitations

This study contained several potential limitations related to subjectivity, language differences, and transferability. With regard to subjectivity, the primary researcher had led groups and trained group workers in both Asia and the United States and held a primarily Eastern perspective, while the second and third authors both had led groups and trained group workers only in the United States and held more Western perspectives. All received substantial group work training in the United States. As such they had assumptions that undoubtedly affected data collection and analysis. However, they remained reflexive with regard to these potential biases throughout the process, and member checking allowed participants to counteract any misinterpretations.

With regard to limitations due to language differences, all interviews were conducted in English by the first author, but English was not her or the participants' first language. Sometimes, the participants had difficulty conveying feelings and thoughts in English. When this occurred, the primary researcher allowed participants time to choose their words and to clarify meanings. The primary researcher also utilized relevant consultants, including the second author, to assist during data analysis. Again, member checking also reduced the possibility of misunderstanding. Additionally, the interviews were conducted via telephone and internet phone (Skype) which may have affected the ability to see body language, communication, and trust.

Relevance of these results to other contexts may also be limited. This research explored group leader experiences in a limited number of Asian countries, including Thailand, Taiwan, and Japan. The study was also specific to Western-trained clinicians and did not reflect the experiences of those trained in Asia. This potential limitation is, to a degree, counteracted by thick description of the research context, which may allow readers to make decisions about how applicable the results are to their own contexts.

Implications

The results of this study provide descriptions that may be beneficial to counselor educators, group leaders in training, and future research on group leadership. Counselor educators might utilize the descriptions to develop their own awareness of Asian international counseling students' process of making decisions about the applicability of Western and Eastern beliefs to group work practice. Counselor educators might encourage Asian international counseling students to understand and develop their transferring process through exploration of their culture of origin while they are training in the West.

This theory also illuminated some of the challenges to group work practice within Asian cultural systems, as well as the universal systemic challenges facing many group workers. Counselor educators might apply this information to the training and preparation of international counseling students who are planning on returning to their home countries to practice. Additionally, descriptions of Western-trained Asian group leaders practicing in Asia as they integrated and reconciled different cultural perspectives and expectations related to group work, may provide counselor educators with information useful to their teaching in the area of group work in multicultural contexts.

The study's findings related to group leaders' actions, thoughts, and feelings during the process of reflective experimentation provide valuable information for Asian international group leaders who are receiving training in the West. Participants emphasized risk-taking and responsiveness to the group during the reflective experimentation process. These descriptions may assist Asian international group leaders in training as they prepare themselves to lead groups and transfer knowledge gained in the West. The results may focus group leaders in training on the role of motivation, trust in group work, and willingness to take risks and be flexible in successfully adapting to leading groups in the Asian context. Additionally, participants' descriptions of their enthusiasm and success in the process may serve as inspiration to those just beginning.

This study also hints at future research that may prove useful. Future research might include a focus on developing deeper understanding of Asian group leaders' transferring processes, beyond the general descriptions provided here, or developing more detailed descriptions of specific interventions. Future studies might also include or focus on group leaders who are trained in institutions where English is not the predominant language or that are within the Asian cultural context.

FUNDING

This research was completed as part of Dr. Taephant's dissertation research at Oregon State University and was supported, in part, by a grant from the Association for Specialists in Group Work.

REFERENCES

Barnes, D. M. (1996). An analysis of the grounded theory method and the concept of culture. *Qualitative Health Research, 6*, 429–441. doi:10.1177/104973239600600309

Bemak, F., & Chung, R. (2004). Teaching multicultural group counseling: Perspective for a new era. *The Journal for Specialists in Group Work, 29*, 31–41. doi:10.1080/01933920490275349

Chang, S. C. (2005). An Asian way of healing: The psychology of meditation. In W. S. Tseng, S. C. Chang, & A. Nishizomo (Eds.), *Asian culture and psychotherapy implication for east and west* (pp. 212–222). Honolulu: University of Hawaii.

Charmaz, K. (2006). Constructing grounded theory: A practical guide through qualitative analysis. Los Angeles, CA: Sage.

Chen, M., & Han, Y. S. (2001). Cross-cultural group counseling with Asians: A stage-specific interactive approach. *The Journal for Specialists in Group Work, 26*, 111–128. doi:10.1080/01933920108415732

Chong, W. H. (2005). The role of self-regulation and personal agency beliefs: A psychoeducational approach with Asian high school students in Singapore. *The Journal for Specialists in Group Work, 30*, 343–361. doi:10.1080/01933920500184964

Chung, R. (2004). Group counseling with Asians. In J. DeLucia-Waackk, D. A. Gerrity, C. R. Kalodner, & M. T. Riva (Eds.), *Handbook of group counseling and psychotherapy* (pp. 200–212). Thousand Oaks, CA: Sage

Conyne, R. K., Wilson, F. R., & Tang, M. (2000). Evolving lessons from group work involvement in China. *The Journal for Specialists in Group Work, 25*, 252–268. doi:10.1080/01933920008411466

Conyne, R. K., Wilson, F. R., Tang, M., & Shi, K. (1999). Cultural similarities and difference in group work: Pilot study in a U.S.–Chinese task group comparison. *Group Dynamics: Theory, Research, and Practice, 3*, 40–50. doi:10.1037/10892699.3.1.40

Corden, A., & Sainsbury, R. (2006). *Using verbatim quotations in reporting qualitative social research: Researchers' views*. University of York, Social Policy Research Unit. Retrieved from http://www.york.ac.uk/inst/spru/pubs/pdf/verbusers.pdf

Coven, A. B. (2004). Gestalt group dreamwork demonstrations in Taiwan. *The Journal for Specialists in Group Work, 29*, 175–184. doi:10.1080/01933920490439329

Creswell, J. W. (1998). *Qualitative inquiry and research design: Choosing among five traditions*. Thousand Oaks, CA: Sage.

DeLucia-Waack, J. L., & Donigian, J. (2004). *The practice of multicultural group work*. Belmont, CA: ThompsonBrook/Cole.

Fassinger, R. E. (2005). Paradigms, praxis, problems, and promise: Grounded theory in counseling psychology research. *Journal of Counseling Psychology, 52*, 156–166. doi:10.1037/0022-0167.52.2.156

Fernando, D. M. (2009). Group work with survivors of the 2004 Asian tsunami: Reflections of an American-trained counselor. *The Journal for Specialist in Group Work, 34*, 4–23. doi:10.1080/01933920802600816

Fuertes, J. N., & Gretchen, D. (2000). Emerging theories of multicultural counseling. In J. G. Ponterotto, J. M. Casas, L. A. Suzuki, & C. M. Alexander (Eds.), *Handbook of multicultural counseling* (pp. 509–541). Thousand Oak, CA: Sage.

Hays, D. G., & Singh, A. A. (2012). *Qualitative inquiry in clinical and educational settings*. New York, NY: Guilford.

Kalodner, C. R., & Hanus, A. E. (2010). Groups across settings. In R. Conyne (Ed.), *The Oxford handbook of group counseling* (pp. 399–415). New York, NY: Oxford University Press.

Kit, P. L., & Teo, L. (2012). Quit Now! A psychoeducational expressive therapy group work approach for at-risk and delinquent adolescent smokers in Singapore. *The Journal for Specialists in Group Work, 37*, 2–28. doi:10.1080/01933922.2011.606557

Kuo, B. C. H. (2004). Interdependent and relational tendencies among Asian clients: Infusing collectivistic strategies into counseling. *Guidance & Counseling, 19*, 158–162.

LaFramboise, T., Coleman, H. L. K., and Gerton, J. (1993). Psychological impact of biculturalism: Evidence and theory. *Psychological Bulletin, 113*, 395–412. doi:10.1037/00332909.114.3.395

Leong, F. T. L., & Leach, M. M. (2007). International counseling psychology in United States: A SWOT analysis. *Applied Psychology, 56*, 165–181. doi:10.1111/j.14640597.2007.00283.x

Leong, F. T., Wagner, N., & Kim, H. L. (1995). Group counseling expectations among Asian American students: The role of culture specific factors. *Journal of Counseling Psychology, 42*, 217–222. doi:10.1037/00220167.42.2.217

Lin, Y. N. (2004). The application of converged counseling themes with Taiwanese clients. *Counseling Psychology Quarterly, 17*, 209–222. doi:10.1080/09515070410001728271

Lincoln, Y. S., & Guba, E. G. (1985). *Naturalistic inquiry*. Beverly Hills, CA: Sage.

McWhirter, J. J., McWhirter, P. T., McWhirter, B. T., & McWhirter, E. H. (2010). International group counseling. In R. Conyne (Ed.), *The Oxford handbook of group counseling* (pp. 469–486). New York, NY: Oxford University Press.

Norsworthy, K. L., & Khuankaew, O. (2004). Women of Burma speak out: Workshops to deconstruct gender-based violence and build systems of peace and justice. *The Journal for Specialists in Group Work, 29*, 259–283. doi:10.1080/01933920490477011

Okech, J. E. A. (2008). Reflective practice in group co-leadership. *The Journal for Specialists in Group Work, 33*, 236–252.

Pan, P. J. D., Chang, S., & Yu, Y. (2006). A support group for home-quarantined college students exposed to SARS: Learning from practice. *The Journal for Specialists in Group Work, 30*, 363–374. doi:10.1080/01933920500186951

Pan, J. D. P., Deng, L. Y., Tsai, S. L., & Chang, S. H. S. (2011). Taiwanese members' report of verbal interactions and their relations to demographic variables in the group counseling process. *Psychological Reports, 108*, 779–790. doi:10.2466/02.09.15.28.PR0.108.3.779790

Patton, M. Q. (2002). *Qualitative research and evaluation methods* (3rd ed.). Thousand Oaks, CA: Sage.

Pope, M. (1999). Applications of group career counseling techniques in Asian cultures. *Journal of Multicultural Counseling & Development, 27*, 18–30. doi:10.1007/s1056000525544

Posthuma, B. W. (1999). *Small groups in counseling and therapy* (3rd ed.). Needham Heights, MA: Allyn & Bacon.

Queener, J. E., & Kenyon, C. B. (2001). Providing mental health services to Southeast Asian adolescent girls: Integration of a primary prevention paradigm and group counseling. *The Journal for Specialists in Group Work, 26*, 350–367. doi:10.1080/01933920108413784

Ringel, S. (2005). Therapeutic dilemmas in cross-cultural practice with Asian American adolescents. *Child and Adolescent Social Work Journal, 22*, 57–69. doi:10.1007/s1056000525544

Rubel, D., & Kline, W. B. (2008). An exploratory study of expert group leadership. *The Journal for Specialists in Group Work, 33*, 138–160. doi:10.1080/01933920801977363

Rungreangkulkij, S., Wongtakee, W., & Thongyot, S. (2011). Buddhist group therapy for diabetes patients with depressive symptoms. *Archives of Psychiatric Nursing, 25*, 195–205. doi:10.1016/j.apnu.2010.08.007

Seale, C. (1999). *The quality of qualitative research*. London, England: Sage.

Singh, A. A., & Hays. D. G. (2008). Feminist group counseling with South Asian women who have survived intimate partner violence. *The Journal for Specialists in Group Work, 33*, 84–102. doi:10.1080/01933920701798588

Strauss, A., & Corbin, J. (1998). *Basics of qualitative research* (2nd ed.). Thousand Oaks, CA: Sage.

Suzuki, L. A., Ahluwala, M. K., Arora, A. K., & Mattis, J. S. (2007). The pond you fish in determines the fish you catch: Exploring strategies for qualitative data collection. *The Counseling Psychologist, 35*, 295–327. doi:10.1177/0011000006290983

Yalom, I. D. (1975). *The theory and practice of group psychotherapy* (2nd ed.). New York, NY: Basic Books.

Yeh, C.,& Inose, M. (2002). Difficulties and coping strategies of Chinese, Japanese and Korean immigrant students. *Adolescence, 37*, 69–82.

Zhang, N., & Dixon, D. N. (2003). Acculturation and attitudes of Asian international students toward seeking psychological health. *Journal of Multicultural Counseling and Development. 21*, 205–22. doi:10.1002/j.21611912.2003.tb00544.x

Teaching Group Counseling in Botswana: Two U.S.-Trained Counselors Discuss Experiences and Share Cultural Considerations for Practice

Angela D. Coker
University of Missouri–St. Louis
Aaron R. Majuta
University of Botswana

There is a paucity of research in the area of teaching group counseling within an African context. In this article we describe and reflect on our experiences teaching group counseling at an institution of higher learning in the country of Botswana. We discuss cultural traditions and strengths that support an environment of group work in Botswana, describe cross-cultural challenges we experienced along the way as we implemented Western-derived didactic and experiential components of group counseling training, and discuss the ways in which we addressed the cultural differences we encountered. Implications for future cross-cultural research and training are discussed.

There has been a growing interest in the internationalization of counseling (Gerstein, Heppner, Stockton, Leong, & Ægisdóttir, 2009) yielding increased faculty transcontinental exchanges and scholarly activity. More and more scholars from diverse backgrounds are able to seize opportunities to teach, conduct research, and participate in community outreach on a global scale. Such opportunities are often sought due to professional interests (Tang et al., 2012), and/or a desire to grow in the area of developing multicultural competencies (Coker, 2011; West-Olatunji, Goodman, Mehta, & Templeton, 2011). To this end, we see a steady growth of literature in the area of exploring the nature of counseling in various parts of the world (e.g., Hohenshil, 2010), but there still remains, with a few exceptions (e.g., Okech & Kimemia,

2012; Okocha & Alika; 2012; Richards, Zivave, Govere, Mphande, & Dupwa, 2012; Stockton, Nitza, & Bhusuman, 2010), a dearth of literature published in the area of counseling in Africa. This is particularly glaring when Africa is a vast diverse continent comprised of 55 separate nations whose collective population totals over one billion people (Briney, 2010).

In the area of group work, there is an even greater paucity of scholarship focused on training and practice in Africa. However, some recent publications have emerged that highlight group therapy in the country of Botswana. Such publications discuss benefits and outcomes using group work with special populations in the fight against HIV/AIDS (e.g., Nitza, Chilisa, & Makwinja-Morara, 2010; Stockton et al., 2012), and research with group counseling students in Botswana (e.g., Nitza, 2011). In fact Nitza (2011) was the first study designed to explore group climate and therapeutic factors present in group training classes in Botswana. The purpose of this paper is to share our experiences as two United States trained counselor educators teaching a graduate group counseling course at an institution of higher education in Botswana. We reflect and discuss cultural values and strengths that support an environment of group work in Botswana, describe cultural challenges we encountered as we implemented Western-derived experiential and didactic components of group counseling training, and discuss the ways in which we addressed specific cross-cultural challenges. For the purposes of this discussion, we use the terms "Western-derived" and "U.S. trained" interchangeably.

THE COUNTRY OF BOTSWANA

Botswana is a country located in southern Africa, neighboring the countries of South Africa, Namibia, and Zimbabwe. Botswana has a population of about two million people and is a member of the Southern African Developing Community (SADC). This means that Botswana is part of a regional cluster of countries that have a history of fighting against colonial rule and are working toward political and economic empowerment. Over the years Botswana has enjoyed tremendous economic and political growth and democratic governance since it gained independence from Great Britain in 1966. However, as with many developing countries, Botswana has had to grapple with a changing social landscape brought on by modernization and urbanization. Many social challenges have resulted from these factors including increased rates of changing immigration patterns, unemployment, poverty, increased incidents of crime, substance abuse, gender violence against women, teen pregnancy, and motor vehicle accidents and fatalities. In addition, Botswana has the second highest rate of the HIV/AIDS reported cases on the continent of Africa with 23% of Botswana's population being affected (National AIDS Coordinating Agency, 2010). The government of Botswana has declared HIV/AIDS a national emergency and is working aggressively to address this national health crisis. Their goal is to eradicate HIV/AIDS by the year 2016 (National AIDS Coordinating Agency, 2010). Although there have a been a number of continued challenges that predate the onset of Botswana's HIV/AIDS epidemic, this national health crisis has spurred an increased need for mental health professionals who are trained to serve individuals with a wide range of health, emotional, rehabilitation, and educational needs. Some of the most common mental health challenges that individuals living with HIV/AIDS face include feelings of personal sadness, social stigma, and community isolation, thus, requiring some to seek counseling support for anger management, depression, and anxiety (Stockton et al., 2012). Another significant mental health challenge that many individuals living with HIV/AIDS confront is financial stress. There is concern for having access to adequate health care and being able to afford the medications to manage their health. Second, they may worry about long-term care of their children, elderly parents, or other financially dependent extended family members. Many school counselors assert that the HIV/AIDS pandemic has sparked an increase in the rate of orphanhood and child neglect cases in Botswana. Many children and teens are left to assume adult responsibilities and roles due to the absence of a parental figure or supervising adult who may be critically ill or dying of HIV/AIDS. Psychologically many children often experience grief and loss, trauma, and educational disruptions triggered by the unexpected or anticipatory death of a parent (D. Mabiletsa, personal communication, June 12, 2013).

Education and Counseling in Botswana

According to Index Mundi (2013), the Gross Domestic Product (GDP), or the total financial expenditure allocated to education by the Botswana government in 2009 was 8.9%. Public education is open to all students on the primary and secondary level, but comparable to the United States, there has been an increase in the number of middle-class parents who opt to enroll their children in private schools with the belief that private schools offer their children a better quality education. Students at the post-secondary level who score well enough on their college entrance exams are eligible to receive free tuition paid by the Botswana government, in addition to a monthly stipend to help with their college expenses. Further, all public school instruction from primary levels through university post-secondary education is mandated to be delivered in the country's official language of English rather than in the native language of *Setswana* (Botswana Government, 1994). However, there is often a difference between what is mandated and what is customarily practiced in educational settings. Many educators and school counselors often use their professional judgment and will switch between English and Setswana when they are teaching a lesson that they want to make sure students understand. There have been vigorous thought-provoking debates on both sides of the post-colonial line regarding the long term effectiveness of this method, but some scholars working with school counselors on the primary and secondary level (e.g., Onyewadume, 2008) believe it is important and practical to allow students to speak in their native tongue when they need to convey thoughts and feelings about sensitive or difficult life situations—in this way they might be able to share their thoughts in a more accurate manner.

The advent and development of Western counseling practices in Botswana is a relatively recent phenomenon (Stockton et al., 2010). In order to meet the psychosocial needs of its citizens, the Republic of Botswana's Ministry of Education (1996) made provisions and began training school teachers to provide career and emotional support to students needing assistance. School teachers were the first ones trained because of their "frontline" status of interacting directly with students who would often be presented with difficult life challenges such as parental neglect, physical abuse, or orphanhood. In the beginning many of these schoolteachers were trained to handle such student concerns through professional development opportunities like workshops, seminars, and coursework. After their training, these teacher/counselors were called *paraprofessionals*—individuals who did not possess a master's degree, but who had at least a certificate or bachelor's degree in the area of education and had received specialized training in issues of counseling youth. However, in 1994 the University of Botswana began to train school counselors through the Postgraduate Diploma in Counselor Education (PGDCE) program which was later phased out for the master's degree in Counselling and Human Services which was introduced in 2001. The Department of Educational Foundations at the University of Botswana currently offers B.Ed.s, M.Ed.s, and Ph.Ds. in the area of counseling. Since that time, several other colleges have implemented counseling courses into their curricula. Counselors in Botswana established the Botswana Counselling Association in 2010, an organization dedicated to the professional advancement of counseling in Botswana. Currently the organization is advocating for the installation and implementation of credentialing standards and licensure requirements for counselors and paraprofessionals' training, practice, and supervision in Botswana (J.A. Muchado, personal communication, July 10, 2013).

Cultural Traditions and Strengths of Botswana

There are many cultural traditions and strengths that support formal and informal collective group work in Botswana. The Batswana people (a plural term used to describe people born in Botswana collectively) have a rich tradition of caring for humanity, collectivism, hard work, and creativity. First, within Botswana culture, there is a strong cultural tradition of spirituality (Amanze, 2002) that is very group-oriented and collectivist in nature. We believed this cultural value promoted a welcoming attitude and openness toward group counseling work. Furthermore, a general core value system of spirituality can be found in most African communities (Mbiti, 1989) and often provides the basis for much of Africa's counseling service delivery (Mwiti, 2006). This holds true in Botswana as over 71% of its citizens claim membership in the Christian faith, with smaller numbers reported following Catholicism, Islam, or a traditional indigenous religion. Second, there is a genuine concern and respect for others which supports many of the curative factors (Yalom, 2005) associated with participating in group therapy. Third, Batswana people have a rich tradition of personal and community development. They are very hardworking, generous, proud, and future-oriented citizens. Botswana's youth are especially creative, energetic, and enthusiastic about coming up with new ways of thinking and approaching life. Many of these cultural values can be observed in Batswana daily work habits and social interactions, in addition to citizens' pursuit of all levels of personal development including vocational and post-secondary education. In order to maintain a strong sense of development among its citizens, the government of Botswana has been a model country in allocating economic provisions that encourage and support individual and community development (Index Mundi, 2013).

THE GROUP COUNSELING COURSE

As stated earlier, the advent of counselor education in Botswana is a relatively recent phenomenon with much of the country's concentration on mental health services focused on training future school counselors. Although there are no current licensure requirements for counselors in Botswana, individuals pursuing a graduate degree in counseling at the University where group training is offered are required to successfully complete a semester-long course in order to graduate. The group counseling course we taught was structured in a weekly 2-hr format and divided into two parts. It consisted of a didactic lecture-oriented segment and an experiential learning component. The group course was taught at a public university that had an enrollment of about 15, 000 students representing both full-time and part-time learners. The university is located in a mid-size metropolitan setting boasting the largest concentration of ethnic, racial, and religious diversity in the country of Botswana.

About the Group Members

There were 20 graduate students enrolled in the group counseling course. Specific demographics included 17 women and 3 males. Every student was above the age of 25 and all were adult learners managing full-time jobs and full-time life responsibilities. Geographically, all were born in Africa and had a keen understanding of the cultural mores and values of Botswana life. Most had been at least mid-way through their 2-year graduate program and had been routinely assigned to read Western counseling textbooks and theories as part of their training. In terms of counseling focus, some students were studying to become community or pastoral counselors, but most had an interest in school counseling.

About the Authors

The first author (ADC) is an African American woman who has over 15 years of experience as a counselor educator. She was born and raised in the United States and was educated in a CACREP graduate program in counselor education. Areas of research include multicultural counseling and the internationalization of counseling. She has experience teaching group work, in addition to practicum, career, and multicultural counseling courses. She also has international experiences including professional travel to Brazil, Ghana, Nigeria, Namibia, South Africa, and Botswana.

The second author (ARM) is a *Motswana* man (a term used to describe someone born and raised in Botswana). He has 14 years of experience as a counselor educator, in addition to leading groups. He received both his M.A. and Ph.D. training in counselor education from institutions in the United States. It is important to note that although the second author is a Motswana, he encountered similar cultural challenges to those the first author experienced because he had been away from Botswana for several years and was going through his own re-acculturation process.

During the teaching of the course each author took weekly turns leading the didactic portion of the course and was responsible for leading their assigned experiential group for the entire duration of the semester. The syllabus developed for the course was heavily influenced by the authors' own counseling training in the United States. Further, even though both authors have extensive training and experience leading groups (and one author is Motswana), it became obvious that there were some transnational cultural issues that presented themselves in our work as instructors and group facilitators of the course. After each individual group session both group facilitators would process their experiences with each other. Below are some cross-cultural challenges we observed leading our individual groups.

Botho. Botho is the Setswana word for respect. The concept of "Botho" according to Amanze (2002), refers to the moral concept of personhood.

> [Botho] implies a person who is well behaved. . . . somebody who is able to maintain his dignity, that of his family and the community at large. It means someone who is able to discriminate between bad and good, right and wrong. It means someone that is humane—someone who thinks about other people. A person who is neither selfish or (sic) egotistical. At a higher level of abstraction the word *botho* means loving another person in the community as one loves oneself. (p. 125)

Translated into the context of group work, *Botho* can also mean "wait your turn," or "don't interrupt." It can also mean showing respect for others in a group by not cutting them off or even correcting another member if their assessment of the group's dynamics or content is not accurate. It can also mean waiting until the other group member has finished sharing their statements. While on the surface this is considered a culturally appropriate and polite thing to do, it may produce alternative group process dynamics or consequences. Alternative outcomes may occur as other group members who may be at varying levels of cultural adherence may want to contribute, but hesitate for fear of appearing disrespectful. Further, giving a group member too much time to speak may curtail the group facilitator's ability to "draw in" and engage other group members into the discussion within a limited and structured amount of time. Clearly the culturally bound western valued skill of *cutting off* (Coker, 2004) group members was not appropriate here. Both authors had internal conflict about how to resolve this issue given the limited amount of time we had to demonstrate group facilitation skills.

Age difference as a factor. Because Botswana's culture supports a structure of respect for elders, some group members appeared reluctant to confront older group participants during group sessions. This may have diminished some of the "power-sharing" in the group where certain group members were afforded more respect and deemed more "important" than others solely based on age. This is a very common cultural value in Botswana and throughout Africa where collectivist societies pay respect and deference to individuals based on age. According to (Amanze, 2002),

> Respect for one's elders was extended beyond the family to the tribe as a whole. In general young people were expected to respect and obey all those older than themselves to whom they addressed as "father" (rre, ntate) or "mother" (mme). Breaking this rule was considered as a penal offence in tribal law. (p. 161)

Collectivism and advice-giving. In the spirit of naturally operationalizing the value system of collectivism, *Botho,* and concern for others, many group members were very caring and would often give lots of advice and directives to other group participants. It was not uncommon for group members to suggest culturally tangible ways to deal with a life challenge. Often this advice-giving would translate into group members pointing out specific strategies on what others should do. As group facilitators we found tenets of this group dynamic consistent with Yalom's (2005) curative factors of imparting information and altruism. However, again this may have looked good on the surface, but it may have also undermined and impeded the individual who was receiving the advice the ability to develop coping strategies on their own. Secondly, we wondered if such advice-giving in this context worked to impede the exploration of feelings.

Understanding verbal and non-verbal communication. One of the challenges the first author had was in understanding some of the verbal communication of the students when they would switch from English to Setswana in order to convey a thought or emotion. Also, it was not uncommon for group members to be reluctant about identifying personal strengths or demonstrating self-praise. There is a Botswana proverb that says, "You cannot be the dancer and the drummer too." In other words it is considered culturally inappropriate for a person (the dancer) to point out their own personal accomplishments or positive attributes. It is considered much more appropriate if another person (the drummer) announces the person's good deeds or accomplishments. This is not to say that it is critical that group members boast about their positive attributes regularly, but we believe the identification of client/member strengths is an important centerpiece for group facilitators to build upon as they promote group member growth and development. With respect to non-verbal communication, both authors occasionally had difficulty reading group dynamics and understanding the underlying emotions of some group members. It was sometimes difficult to interpret the non-verbal facial expressions of some members. For example, many group members would wear a smile on their face to show a sign of respect or illustrate that they were cognitively present in the room, but the smile would not necessarily mean they were happy or agreed with what was happening or shared in the group.

Building rapport and connecting with group members. Being able to pronounce and remember students/group participants' Setswana names was a challenge for the first author (ADC). Although the pronunciation of Setswana names was not such a difficult issue for the second author (ARM), the pronunciation of student names who were from different ethnic groups within the diverse cultural landscape of Botswana did occasionally present an issue for (ARM).

Group facilitation and teaching. Although the majority of cultural challenges we encountered as instructors in class manifested themselves during the experiential portion of the group counseling class, there were a few that revealed themselves during the didactic portion of the class. In Botswana culture, students are often not socialized to actively engage verbally with instructors. They are taught to show respect for authority. Often they do not ask a lot of questions in class and note-taking and silence are customary. Unlike students in the States where interaction and verbal class participation is highly encouraged, we found many students in our class were accustomed to the traditional Botswana mode of teaching, which often meant straight lecturing by the instructor. During the experiential portion of the group class, often students would look to the group facilitators to provide structure, advice, and reassurance that they were doing things the "right" way. Many Batswana view teachers and instructors as highly respected individuals. We wondered if perhaps too much deference was afforded to us as instructors, which may have curtailed some group members' personal ownership of the group experience. Perhaps some of the deference could be attributed to traditional cultural values and behaviors that honor and respect persons of authority, but we believe it was probably a combination of both traditional values and students' desires to learn Western group techniques from Western-trained counselor educators. To this end, as we wrestled with the appropriateness of adapting Western group practices in Botswana, we believe the solution was not a dichotomous yes or no response. Rather, group practice and training in Botswana at best could be viewed as a potential marriage between traditional cultural practices, Western group work approaches, and an openness and integration of group practices from other cultures and ethnic groups yet to be explored. It is important to remember that there isn't just one culture in Botswana, but a variety of interwoven cultural groups comprised of individuals at varying levels of ethnic, cultural, and racial identity development and awareness.

DISCUSSION

As previously stated, the purpose of this article was to explore the cross-cultural experiences of two counselor educators trained in the United States who taught a group counseling course in the country of Botswana. Several cross-cultural issues manifested themselves that caused us to view the way we ultimately conceptualized group work in this particular cultural setting. Gerstein and Ægisdóttir (2007) remind counselor educators about the importance of respecting the cultural landscape and social values of host countries. Chilisa (2012) also warned researchers about the dangers of scientific colonization and the tendency of some Western-oriented scholars to suppress or ignore the indigenous knowledge systems of communities they collect data from. The globalization of counseling can be positive when operationalized with the use of true cultural understanding when counselors view resident citizens as subjects of cultural inquiry and not as objects. Chilisa (2012) also noted that "globalization is an extension of colonization" (p. 10), and that scholars must be careful not to reinforce a continued system of oppression by misapplying a foreign value system and knowledge base to evaluate the behavior of other cultures. Intellectual colonization can be defined as the oppression of one group by another (Chilisa, 2012), either in the ways researchers make selections in theory usage, methodology, or analysis of human behavior and social interaction. Taking our understanding of this definition of intellectual colonization, we realize that we may have unknowingly been guilty of this very mistake in our own assessment of our group facilitation experiences.

In order to truly interpret and understand the group dynamics we described, first we needed to rid ourselves of as much of our Western cultural filter as possible. For example, rather than analyze the impact of *Botho* as a cultural departure from the way we have been educated to understand how groups "should" be run (e.g., advocating for the use of cutting off techniques in order to interrupt a long-winded group member), we should use the cultural principle of *Botho* as a framework to understand appropriate group dynamics within a Botswana setting. *Botho* should be positively interpreted to mean: everyone is important and deserves to be heard. Further, if a group member does not demonstrate *Botho* they may be seen as potentially lacking in an essential Botswana core value. Second, as we consider the issue of ageism and our interpretation about the negative impact we believe ageism could have had on group dynamics, we failed to examine the potential positive benefits. We should have interpreted the inclusion of older group members as an asset and increased opportunity for group members to receive mature feedback, social support, and guidance. Further, the presence of older group members may offer opportunities for the dissemination of knowledge and wisdom in a group. Older group members or elders who participate in groups can add cultural value and credibility to the group. For example, if one were to develop a couples' group for individuals dealing with relationship conflict, it might be perceived as a culturally appropriate strategy to employ a group facilitator who appears to be mature and have life experience. Third, the value system of collectivism and advice giving is a central theme in many African communities. In a group context, it can be used as a framework for expecting and encouraging group cohesion and mutual support. Fourth, illuminating our understanding of the proverb "You cannot be the dancer and the drummer too" can be an opportunity to encourage group members to identify positive strengths and attributes in each other, and employ the skill of giving and receiving feedback. Finally, when it comes to teaching the didactic portion of group courses, the textbook selection is critical. Counselor educators working abroad need to work hard to find books written by authors who develop counseling theories specific to its indigenous country and its cultural values. It is important to decolonize the notion that only Western-thinkers have something to contribute to counseling. If we truly want to be multicultural as an academic field, we must be informed by the works of counseling scholars living in different parts of the globe (Gerstein & Ægisdóttir, 2007).

IMPLICATIONS FOR COUNSELORS CONDUCTING CROSS-CULTURAL TRAINING IN GROUP WORK

First, as group facilitators we responded to these cross-cultural challenges by debriefing with each other regularly after each experiential group counseling session. This became an important time for us to share our concerns and highlight successes. We also kept separate group counseling journals that documented our experiences each week so that we could log our journey as counselor educators. Lastly, we used peer supervision with other counselor educators to involve them in the process and to explore if they had any helpful suggestions for addressing some of the challenges.

We were careful not to share our cross-cultural observations with group members until we had debriefed with each other because we wanted to attend to our own internal issues before and not make them group issues. In the cases when we did share our challenges in leading our groups (e.g., the first author's difficulty in pronouncing Setswana names or understanding a group member who would refer to an incident in Setswana), we would invite students to consider how this group dynamic might have been different if we were in another cultural context. For any counselor interested in conducting cross-cultural training we believe it is important to learn as much about their host country as they can, including learning any indigenous languages and customs. Such a skill may increase counselors' effectiveness in understanding group members and their natural tendency to switch in and out of their native language. Counselors should also elicit the support and help of any available clinical supervision (Levers, 2013), both traditional (e.g., consultation with other counseling professionals) and non-traditional forms (e.g., consultation with community elders who are knowledgeable about cultural traditions). Counselors working with diverse cross-cultural populations are strongly cautioned not to use their own cultural values as a litmus test or filter for what is deemed correct behavior (Leong & Santiago-Rivera, 1999; Nitza, 2011). Other suggestions include:

- Group instructors/facilitators should process class/group experience immediately after each group and engage in peer supervision.
- Honor traditional Botswana culture. Honoring tradition is important yet group facilitators should find ways to integrate diverse strategies (where appropriate) that train students on how to conduct group work in a variety of settings. When teaching counseling students, be sure to remind them of the cultural differences that exist globally.
- Invite indigenous members of the community to speak to group classes and discuss the various ways in which traditional group interactions are expressed socially.
- Group facilitators should use name tags to remember group participant names. Caution should be given to making sure group facilitators use the name the group member feels the most comfortable using, For example many Batswana prefer to use their Christian names as opposed to their native or traditional one. It is important not to assume cultural identity preference.
- Be open to the process of cross-cultural learning and understand that the development of multicultural competence is an active, dynamic, and ongoing continuum.

Recommendations for Future Work

More research needs to be conducted in the area of group cross-cultural training, particularly in Africa. Currently the International Registry of Counsellor Education Programs (IRCEP) is an initiative designed to promote excellence in counselor education globally

(Stanard, 2013). They should expand teaching resources for educators to assist in dealing with any cross-cultural training, clinical, or research concerns that may arise. Further, there are several research questions that could be explored relative to examining counselors' experiences around developing cultural competencies with diverse groups. For example, it would be interesting to examine what impact an instructor's cultural background might have on the learning process of counselors-in-training who are culturally different in terms of nationality or race. Further, it would be important to explore culturally appropriate indigenous research methods (Chilisa, 2012) designed to examine issues in group counseling practice. Furthermore, research needs to be done to examine the re-acculturation process of native-born counselor educators who train in the United States and then return to their native country to teach. What cultural transitions and adjustment do they make in order to fit back into their native-born society, while at the same time attend to their professional identities as U.S. trained professional counselors and educators? These we see as beginning questions in the emerging and exciting field of international multicultural group work.

FUNDING

Partial funding for this research was obtained from International Studies and Programs at the University of Missouri–St. Louis.

REFERENCES

Amanze, J. N. (2002). *African traditional religions and culture in Botswana*. Gaborone, Botswana: Pula.

Botswana Government. (1994). *Revised national policy on education (RNPE)*. Gaborone, Botswana: Government Printers.

Briney, A. (2010, December 26). Geography of the countries of Africa: List of Africa's countries based on land area. *About.com Geography*. Retrieved from http://geography.about.com/od/africamaps/a/countriesofafrica.htm

Chilisa, B (2012). *Indigenous research methods*. Thousand Oaks, CA: Sage.

Coker, A. D. (2004). In response to a critical incident in group work—cutting off: It just feels impolite. In L. E. Tyson, J. Whitledge, & R. Perusse (Eds.), *Critical incidents in group counseling* (pp. 261–263). Alexandria, VA: American Counseling Association.

Coker, A. D. (2011). *Using a Fulbright-Hays Travel Abroad Grant to enhance cultural competence and professional identity as a counselor educator*. Nashville, TN: Association for Counselor Education and Supervision.

Gerstein, L. H., & Ægisdóttir, S. (2007). Training international social justice change agents: Transcending a U.S. counseling paradigm. *Counselor Education & Supervision, 47*, 123–139.

Gerstein, L. H., Heppner, P. P., Stockton, R., Leong, F. T. L., & Ægisdóttir, S. (2009). The counseling profession in- and outside the United States. In L. H. Gerstein, P. P. Heppner, S. Ægisdóttir, A. S-M. Leung, & K. L. Norsworthy (Eds.), *International handbook of cross-cultural counseling: Cultural assumptions and practices worldwide* (pp. 53–67). Thousand Oaks, CA: Sage.

Hohensil, T. H. (Ed.) (2010). International counseling [special section]. *Journal of Counseling & Development, 11.*

Index Mundi (2013). Retrieved from http://www.indexmundi.com/botswana/demographics_profile.html

Leong, F. T. L., & Santiago-Rivera, A. L. (1999). Climbing the multiculturalism summit: Challenges and pitfalls. In P. Pedersen (Ed.) *Multiculturalism as a fourth force* (pp. 61–74). Philadelphia, PA: Brunner/Mazel.

Levers, L. L (2013, April). *Supervision: An ethical issues*. Presented at New Perspectives Conference, Gaborone, Botswana.

Mbiti. (1989). *African religions and philosophy*. Portsmouth, NH: Heinemann.

Mwiti, G. K. (2006). *Christian counseling: An African indigenous perspective*. Pasadena, CA: Fuller Seminary.

National AIDS Coordinating Agency (2010). *Factsheet on statistical data of young people (10–29 yrs) on HIV and AIDS and sexual reproductive health in Botswana*. Gaborone, Botswana. Author.

Nitza, A. (2011). Group processes in experiential training groups in Botswana. *The Journal for Specialists in Group Work, 36*, 222–242. doi:10.1080/01933922.2011.578116.

Nitza, A., Chilisa, B., Makwinja-Morara, V. (2010). Mbizi: Empowerment and HIV/AIDS prevention for adolescent girls in Botswana. *The Journal for Specialists in Group Work, 35*, 105–114.

Okech, J. E. A., & Kimemia, M. (2012), Professional counseling in Kenya: History, current status, and future trends. *Journal of Counseling & Development, 90* 1,07–112. doi:10.1111/j.1556-6676.2012.00015.

Okocha, A. A. G., & Alika, I. H. (2012), Professional counseling in Nigeria: Past, present, and future. *Journal of Counseling & Development, 90*, 362–366. doi:10.1002/j.1556-6676.2012.00045.

Onyewadume, M. A. (2008). Vernacular as a resource for the implementation of guidance & counselling curriculum in Botswana. *The African Symposium, 8*, 175–181.

Republic of Botswana Ministry of Education. (1996). *Policy guidelines on the implementation of guidance and counselling in Botswana's education system*. Gaborone, Botswana: Botswana Government Printers.

Richards, K. A. M., Zivave, A. T., Govere, S. M., Mphande, J. & Dupwa, B. (2012). Counseling in Zimbabwe: History, current status, and future trends. *Journal of Counseling & Development, 90*,102–106. doi:10.1111/j.1556-6676.2012.00014.x

Stanard, R. P. (2013). International registry of counsellor education programs: CACREP's contribution to the development of counseling as a global profession. *Journal of Counseling & Development, 91*, 55–60. doi:10.1002/j.1556-6676.2013.00071

Stockton, R., Nitza, A., & Bhusumane, D. (2010). The development of professional counseling in Botswana. *Journal of Counseling & Development, 88*, 9–12.

Stockton, R., Paul, T., Morran, D. K., Yebei, P. K., Chang, S-H, & Voils-Levenda, A. (2012). A survey of HIV/AIDS counselors in Botswana: Satisfaction with training and supervision, self-perceived effectiveness and reactions to counseling HIV-positive clients. *Journal of HIV/AIDS & Social Services, 11*, 424–446.

Tang, M., Conyne, R., Heppner, P. P., Horne, S., Norsworthy, K., Romano, J. L., . . . Merchant, N. (2012). Implications of the international counseling experiences of pioneering US professionals considered from an ecological perspective. *International Journal for the Advancement of Counselling, 34*, 242–258. doi:10.1007/s10447-012-9154-8

West-Olatunji, C., Goodman, R. D., Mehta, S., & Templeton, L. (2011). Creating cultural competence: An outreach immersion experience in southern Africa. *International Journal for the Advancement of Counselling, 33*, 335–346. doi:10.1007/s10447-011-9138-0.

Yalom, I. D. (2005). *The theory and practice of group psychotherapy*. New York, NY: Basic Books.

International Cultural Immersion: Assessing the Influence of a Group Intervention on Intercultural Sensitivity for Counselor Trainees

Sejal M. Barden
University of Central Florida

Laura Shannonhouse
University of Maine

Keith Mobley
University of North Carolina at Greensboro

Scholars (e.g., Bemak & Chung, 2004) underscore the need for group workers to be culturally sensitive. One group training strategy, cultural immersion, is often employed to develop cultural sensitivity. However, no studies have utilized quasi-experimental methodologies to assess differences in cultural sensitivity between trainees that immerse compared to those that do not immerse. To this end, this article provides an overview of the Developmental Model of Intercultural Sensitivity, description of an international cultural immersion experience and quasi-experimental research design, analysis of data, discussion of results, implications for group facilitators and counselor educators, and suggestions for future research.

Awareness of cultural differences and the ability to respond to client needs appropriately is critical for the effective practice of counselors (Burnett, Hamel, & Long, 2004; Sue & Sue, 2012). Although scholars have argued for increased cultural competence for more than 30 years (Burnett et al., 2004; Lee, 2013; Pedersen, 1991; Reynolds, 2001; Sue et al., 1982; Worthington, Soth-McNett, & Moreno, 2007), counselor trainees remain unprepared to respond to the needs of minority populations (Ancis & Sanchez-Hucles, 2000; Sue & Sue, 2012), including immigrants of foreign countries (Chung & Grabosky, 2011). Based on self-reports, trainees feel underprepared to work with minorities (Kim & Lyons, 2003; Lee, 2013) and external measures indicate that beginning counselors continue to possess racial and gender biases upon conclusion of their training programs (Holcomb-McCoy & Myers, 1999; Ponterotto, Fuertes, & Chen, 2000; Sue & Sue, 2012). In addition to being culturally competent when conducting individual counseling, recent attention has highlighted the paucity in literature and need for counselor trainees to be culturally competent when facilitating groups.

While racial, ethnic, and multicultural dynamics are discussed in the group literature within the context of cultural competence (Bieschke, Gehlert, Wilson, Matthews, & Wade, 2003), it is generally agreed that the literature addressing multicultural and diversity issues in group work is in the preliminary stages (Bemak & Chung, 2004; Corey, 2004). In 1998, the Association for Specialists in Group Work (ASGW) established the Principles for Diversity-Competent Group Workers (PDCGW) to standardize and guide group workers in developing cultural competence (Haley, Brown, & Molina, 1998). In 2012, the PDCGW were revised and updated, currently titled "The Multicultural and Social Justice Competence Principles for Group Workers" (Singh, Merchant, Skudrzyk, & Ingene, 2012). The revised competency principles encourage counselors to be aware of their own biases and cultural identities, highlighting the need to understand how they may influence group processes and dynamics. In support of multicultural group competencies, Bemak and Chung (2004) assert that counselor trainees must develop self-awareness and cultural knowledge as a necessary foundation to effectively facilitate groups. Although dialogue on the necessity for multicultural group workers is prevalent, little has been done to integrate this need in current training practices (Smith & Shin, 2008). Therefore, gaps in effective pedagogical practices remain.

As such, recent reviews (e.g., Priester et al., 2008) have identified an absence of skills-oriented, experiential, multicultural training interventions in counselor preparation programs. Cultural immersion (CI), "direct, prolonged, *in vivo* contact with a culture different from that of the counselor trainee" (Pope-Davis & Coleman, 1997, p. 232), has been found effective at increasing cultural competence (Pedersen & Leong, 1997; West-Olatunji, Goodman, Mehta, & Templeton, 2011). Trainees process and debrief their field experiences in group, which is argued to be a critical component of CI (Lassiter, Napolitano, Culbreth, & Ng, 2008; Ribeiro, 2004; Shannonhouse, 2013) and the vehicle whereby trainees increase cultural competence (Abreu, Gim Chung, & Atkinson,

2000; Alexander, Kruczek, & Ponterotto, 2005). Debriefing in a group format is vital to process the strong emotions triggered by CI (Chung & Bemak, 2002). Without effective group process, trainees may retreat to previously held ethnocentric views to make sense of new ideas and feelings (Chung & Bemak, 2002; Goodman & West-Olatunji, 2009; Ishii, Gilbride, & Stensrud, 2009) which can negatively impact trainees and their interactions with community members (Hui, 2009).

While group process differs for every CI experience, there is agreement that reflection must be intentionally structured to explore personal biases and assumptions (Ginwright & Cammarota, 2002; Hernández, Almeida, & Dolan-Del Vecchio, 2005; Sakamoto & Pitner, 2005). By engaging in self-reflection and inner dialogue, individuals begin to think about their existence and identity "in-relation," affording them a greater awareness of another's context (Clark, 1993). Sensitivity in working with culturally diverse persons is argued to increase as understanding of cultural differences becomes more complex. *Intercultural sensitivity* is considered to be the attitudinal forerunner to cultural competence, defined by Hammer, Bennett and Wiseman (2003) as "attaining the ability to construe and experience cultural differences in more complex ways" (p. 421). Bennett (1986) posited a model of intercultural sensitivity, the Developmental Model of Intercultural Sensitivity (DMIS), that is based on concepts from cognitive psychology and constructivism, and operates on the assumption that individuals follow a predictable path as they gain experience with different cultures (Hammer et al., 2003).

Given the need to assess for effective pedagogical practices in increasing cultural sensitivity, conceptualizing counselor trainees' intercultural sensitivity in terms of developmental levels, and targeting pedagogical interventions based on developmental levels seems critical. Furthermore, limited scholarship has been grounded in strong theoretical models, focused on the efficacy of group interventions on increasing intercultural sensitivity, or has used quantitative research methodology. The purpose of this article is threefold. First, we provide an overview of the theoretical model, the DMIS that was used to conceptualize the cultural immersion experience. Next, results from a quasi-experimental pre/post comparison of students that participated in a group level international cultural immersion intervention compared to students that did not participate, as measured by the Intercultural Development Inventory (IDI; Hammer et al., 2003), an instrument grounded in the DMIS framework. Lastly, a discussion of results and implications for group facilitators and counselor educators will be provided. For the purpose of this article, intercultural sensitivity and cultural sensitivity will be used interchangeably. We begin with an overview of the DMIS.

DEVELOPMENTAL MODEL OF INTERCULTURAL SENSITIVITY

The DMIS focuses on change at the individual level through a developmental framework in which individuals advance through a series of stages in an effort to gain intercultural sensitivity. The six progressive stages are broken down into two groups; three ethnocentric stages (denial, polarization, and minimization), and three ethnorelative stages (acceptance, adaptation, and integration). The aim is to identify ethnocentric viewpoints and develop more ethnorelative perspectives (Hammer et al., 2003).

Individuals exhibiting characteristics in the ethnocentric stages of *denial, polarization*, and *minimization* avoid other cultures and experience their own culture as central to reality (Bennett, 1986). The denial stage is characterized by a rejection that cultural differences are present between groups and constitutes the ultimate ethnocentric position, where one's worldview is unchallenged and central to all reality. The next stage, polarization, includes both defense and reversal states. Defense is a state that involves recognizing differences and perceiving them as threatening, therefore engaging in defense strategies, whereas reversal is an overly critical orientation towards one's own culture. Because differences must be recognized in order to perceive them as either threatening or superior, this stage is seen as a progression from denying that there are differences. In the last ethnocentric stage, minimization, cultural differences are minimized under the weight of either cultural similarities or universalism. Minimization is viewed as development beyond denial and defense as cultural differences are overtly acknowledged and not negatively evaluated, yet persons in this stage fail to accept and understand the cultural context of others (Bennett, 1986; Paige, Fry, Stallman, Josic, & Jon, 2009).

Individuals exhibiting characteristics in the ethnorelative orientations of *acceptance, adaptation,* and *integration* value other cultures and experience their culture in the context of other cultures (Bennett, 1986). Acceptance is the state in which cultural differences are acknowledged and respected; one can see cultural values as relative and understands individuals through differences. The adaptation stage expands one's worldview, incorporating components of other worldviews, and involves a change in the organization of lived experience; one begins to form a bicultural identification. Lastly, integration involves a lack of strong cultural identification, in which one has the ability to be fluid, moving in and out of different cultural frameworks; thus the individual in this stage identifies as multicultural (Bennett, 1986; Paige et al., 2009). In sum, the more ethnocentric orientations in the DMIS can be seen as ways to avoid cultural differences by either denying the existence of difference, raising defenses, or minimizing the importance of them; while the more ethnorelative orientations are ways of seeking cultural differences by accepting the importance of difference, adapting perspectives, or integrating the concept of difference into one's identity (Bennett, 1986; Hammer et al., 2003).

Although the need for cultural sensitivity when working with individuals and groups has been the focus of scholarship and discourse, limited research exists focused on the efficacy of interventions targeting increased intercultural sensitivity. Counselor training programs need to assess the effectiveness of current training models in multiculturalism, highlighting how to teach counselor trainees to adapt and respond to the cultural differences when working with individuals and groups. Furthermore, the lack of empirical research focusing on changes in cultural sensitivity between experimental and comparison groups that participate in CI experiences highlights the need for scholars to investigate the influence of international cultural immersion using rigorous methodology such as experimental research designs.

CULTURAL IMMERSION

Several researchers (e.g., Arthur & Achenbach, 2002; DeRicco & Sciarra, 2005; Kim & Lyons, 2003; Rundstrom, 2005) examining the development of cultural sensitivity indicate that contact and exposure with people from diverse backgrounds develops higher degrees of cultural empathy, increased awareness, self-efficacy, and competence when compared to primarily didactic instruction. CI requires facilitators to create a safe environment in which counselors can challenge their existing worldviews and assumptions (Arthur & Achenbach, 2002; Barden & Cashwell, 2013; Paige et al., 2009). Group facilitators often engage trainees in educational group discussions regarding the larger socio-political-historical context of the communities in which trainees are immersed, and cultural values, beliefs, practices, and so on that individuals have encountered in the field (Alexander et al., 2005; Ishii et al., 2009), affording trainees a greater breadth and depth of understanding about the cultural context in which one is immersed. In addition to understanding content, CI positions trainees to experience being a culturally diverse "other," illustrating the struggles for minority clients and underscoring the influences of culture on behavior and the need for helping professionals to be culturally sensitive (Chung & Bemak, 2002). Processing a trainee's experience of being "other" is an example of a counseling group, often resulting in increased awareness. CI is intended to enhance the understanding of course content while moving beyond the narrow scope of knowledge acquisition (Pope-Davis & Coleman, 1997). In this way, immersion experiences provide a critical experience for counselor trainees that cannot be achieved solely by didactic instruction (Burnett et al., 2004).

NEED FOR THE STUDY

Limitations in empirical research supporting CI include instrumentation, sampling issues, and lack of rigorous methodology. The majority of multicultural counseling research has focused on self-report measures of cultural competence and sensitivity when assessing for the efficacy of various interventions. Additional limitations in the empirical foundation supporting cultural immersion include the limited reliability and validity of widely used multicultural assessments. For example, Constantine, Gloria, & Ladany (2002) asserted that three common multicultural measures do not support the factor structure that they purport to be grounded in. Additionally, Ladany, Constantine, Miller, Erikson, & Muse-Burke (2000) stated that current multicultural instruments may be actually measuring a form of multicultural self-efficacy, as measures tend to measure respondents beliefs about providing MCC services, rather than their actual abilities. A thorough critique of multicultural assessments is beyond the scope of this article; see Ponterotto, Rieger, Barrett, and Sparks (1994) for a detailed review of multicultural instrumentation and inherent limitations. Therefore, there is a need for CI research that utilizes psychometrically strong instruments grounded in clear theoretical underpinnings.

Few empirical investigations on CI have attempted to quantify changes with pre–post measurements (Anderson, Lawton, Rexeisen, & Hubbard, 2006). In our review of the literature, we found five empirical studies assessing for pre-post changes in intercultural sensitivity as a result of CI, although no studies sampled counselor trainees. Medina-López-Portillo (2004) measured the intercultural sensitivity of 28 American students who participated in (a) 7-week CI in Taxco, Mexico ($n = 18$), and (b) a 16-week CI in Mexico City ($n = 10$). Results indicated that intercultural sensitivity increased as a result of the CI, with students who spent more time in the field (i.e., 16 weeks) reporting higher gains in intercultural sensitivity. Similarly, Engle and Engle (2004) assessed the intercultural sensitivity of American students who took part in a CI in France for either one semester or a full year. Results indicated that duration of immersion was significant in predicting intercultural changes from pre- and post-immersion assessments. While spending more time immersed seems helpful to acquiring intercultural sensitivity, it is not clear how that time was spent, what mechanisms were utilized (i.e., selecting CI activities according to level of intercultural sensitivity), or if process groups were structured in a manner in which trainees where challenged to reflect about the host culture, or reflect upon their values, beliefs, and worldview, and the impact on their skills as a professional counselor. In another study, Pederson (2010) assessed three groups using pre- and post-IDI results: (a) a group of students ($n = 16$) that integrated diversity training pedagogy (e.g., guided reflection, group process, etc.), (b) a group of students ($n = 16$) in the same CI experience who did not have that diversity training, and (c) and a control group ($n = 13$) of students who stayed home. Pederson (2010) drew upon Vande Berg and colleagues (2004) and Lederman (2007) to argue that sending students to a location abroad for academic study is not sufficient toward increasing intercultural sensitivity, asserting that intentional guided reflection was needed to increase intercultural sensitivity. Similarly, Goodman and West-Olatunji (2009) claimed processing in group format is required during CI; they "engaged [students] in 3–4 hr of group process and reflection time daily" which "enabled them to engage in introspection and understanding" (Goodman & West-Olatunji, 2009, p. 461). In addition, Paige, Cohen, and Shively, (2004) reported overall increases in intercultural sensitivity as measured by the IDI, with significant declines in the reversal scores within the ethnocentric scales.

Only one of the aforementioned studies utilized a comparison group measure and none of them clarified the mechanisms whereby students acquired increased cultural sensitivity. A needed first step is a quasi-experimental research study with a comparison group to evaluate the impact on cultural sensitivity of an intentional CI (i.e., one that structured activities according to developmental level of intercultural sensitivity, and utilized both psycho-education and counseling process groups to debrief experiences in the field). Specifically, we postulated the following research questions: What differences exist in developmental levels of intercultural sensitivity for students who participated in an international immersion experience compared to students that did not participate? Do initial levels of intercultural sensitivity impact change in level of intercultural sensitivity as a result of participating in an international immersion?

METHODOLOGY

Participants

Participants for the current study included four groups of counselor trainees ($N = 37$) in a CACREP-accredited full-time counselor preparation program at a mid-sized University in the Southeast. Two groups (experimental) participated in a 3-week, 6 credit hr international cultural immersion course in Costa Rica either in the summer of 2011 or the summer of 2012, and two groups (comparison) did not participate in the immersion and were voluntary participants enrolled in courses either during the summer of 2011 or the summer of 2012. Comparison group participants engaged in coursework as usual according to their plans of study, without receiving any type of additional training or multicultural supplementation. Given the quasi-experimental design of this investigation with uncontrolled confounding variables (e.g., the specific courses enrolled in by comparison group participants), it is best to consider the non-experimental group as a comparison rather than control group (Creswell, 2008). A total of 19 participants contributed data from the experimental group (Male, $n = 3$; Female $n = 16$). Eighty-four percent ($n = 16$) of the participants identified as Caucasian, 10.5% ($n = 2$) as Asian-American, and 5.2% ($n = 1$) as Latino/Latina. Participants were doctoral ($n = 3$) and masters students ($n = 16$), with ages ranging from 23 to 32 years old ($M = 26.0$). Similarly, a total of 18 participants contributed data to the comparison groups (Male, $n = 4$; Female, $n = 14$). Seventy two percent ($n = 16$) of those participants identified as Caucasian and 9.1% ($n = 2$) identified as Black/African American. All comparison group participants were masters students ($n = 18$), with ages ranging from 23 to 45 years old ($M = 26.6$).

Experimental Group Intervention: International Cultural Immersion

The international immersion experience was primarily facilitated by a counselor education faculty member and co-facilitated by two doctoral teaching assistants with previous CI experience. Intervention activities for the international cultural immersion were selected based on the group's developmental level of cultural sensitivity as conceptualized by the DMIS. Given that the majority of participants were in ethnocentric stages of intercultural sensitivity development (see Results section for baseline data), primarily characterized as viewing their own culture as central to their reality, intervention activities were targeted to increase knowledge and awareness related to the existence of cultural differences, emphasizing different worldviews and perspectives based on cultural norms.

Preparation for the immersion. Examples of initial immersion activities included involving participants in monthly psycho-educational group meetings the semester prior to departure. Initial group meetings included ice breakers to build trust and group cohesion, such as having each student place a post-it note on their forehead with some stereotypical cultural identity (e.g., Christian, homeless, educated, etc.) and have students interact with them in a way that would illuminate the stereotype. Initial group meetings also focused on discussing fears, areas of anxiety, and other related questions that group members had pertaining to the upcoming immersion experience. During subsequent group meetings, each participant was responsible for presenting information about Costa Rica on specific topic areas (chosen by the group) and facilitating discussion within the group to encourage participation and leadership. Sample presentation topics included gender equality, impact of trauma on refugees, helping professions and heath care, the role of family, and indigenous ethnicities of Costa Rica. Group facilitators paid specific attention to group dynamics throughout pre-immersion psycho-educational groups and met frequently to share insights and areas of concern.

Prior to the immersion, partnerships were established with the Costa Rican Humanitarian Foundation (CRHF), a non-profit organization dedicated to solving social and economic issues for vulnerable populations in Costa Rica. The CRHF addresses needs identified by the communities it serves, focusing on education, preventative healthcare, and support for women, at risk youth, and indigenous populations. Establishing the partnership with the CRHF began with the primary group facilitator connecting the foundation liaison via phone and email to ascertain fit of immersion goals and the foundations mission. Next, the primary group facilitator traveled to Costa Rica and met with the foundation liaison several months before the immersion to establish connections and provide input into the immersion agenda, including goals and strategies for learning such as engaging in direct contact and working alongside community members during service projects.

Maurrasse (2003) emphasizes the need to build partnerships between the university and the community, emphasizing the importance of participants working alongside local community members in order to avoid feeling removed from the people impacted by their service and providing ample opportunities for cross-cultural understanding and cross-cultural challenges, both of which are areas rich in potential for individual processing. The partnership with CRHF enabled participants to immerse themselves in the local community and experience direct contact with individuals and organizations. Furthermore, the partnership benefited students by tailoring the experiences to best fit the purpose of enhancing cross cultural counseling. For example, given that the participants were in counselor training programs, a several-day workshop was created for participants to facilitate group activities and dialogue with a group of women that had experienced trauma and abuse. This interaction enabled students to increase their awareness, practice nonverbal counseling skills and learn firsthand of the universal experiences of pain and trauma.

Additional pre-immersion planning included group facilitators assigning participants to their host families and roommates prior to immersion. Roommate assignments were completed based on group facilitator observations of students' levels of anxiety, previous travel experience, personality characteristics, and familiarity with the language. Before departing, each student was given a course booklet including a detailed calendar for each day outlining what specific activities were, what time students needed to be ready and when group processing sessions would be held. Group facilitators attempted to find a balance between providing structured and free time (see Barden & Cashwell, 2013 for a detailed discussion of these recommendations). Additional resources in the course booklet included contact information, journaling templates, packing lists, detailed itineraries (available upon request), educational films, and other related information.

Experiences during immersion. During the immersion experience, students were exposed to a variety of cultural perspectives to expand their cultural knowledge, awareness, and sensitivity to the Costa Rican culture. American counselor-trainees became aware of how native Costa Ricans, commonly referred to as "Ticos," display pride in their country, its accomplishments, and remaining distinct from their geographic neighbors, and how they value their liberty. They also noted past virtues that have faltered as a result of foreign influence, modernity, and social change (e.g., drunkenness, drug abuse, theft, burglary, etc.). Most "ticos" remain strongly aligned with traditional values of respect and tolerance. Family and village community remain the cornerstone of society, as bonds are so strong that children often do not leave the home until they marry.

Each student participated in a variety of activities during the CI including homestays, cultural immersion tours, educational presentations, service work, and reflective processing. Each student had a home stay where they and their roommate lived with Costa Rican host families in a small suburban, middle class area during the 3 week immersion. Cultural immersion tours included visits to historic, cultural, and governmental sites where students learned more about current economic and political issues of Costa Rica and Central America. Specific examples of cultural tours included students visiting La Carpio, an impoverished township on the outskirts of San Jose that was primarily settled by Nicaraguan refugees and became the site of a massive landfill. Students visited the State of the Nation, a research and capacity building center focused on the promotion of sustainable human development, and engaged in seminars on the current state of education, literacy, and health in Costa Rica and indigenous villages to learn about medicinal healers. Through collaboration with the CRHF, students interacted with persons in an immigrant community and engaged Nicaraguan refugee survivors in creative activities such as drawing and storytelling related to their previous traumatic experiences and hopes for the future. Students were able to learn firsthand some of the challenges and losses faced by the refugee survivors and understand their current challenges related to child rearing, oppression, and intimate partner violence. Students were asked to facilitate small group activities, giving them first hand group facilitation experience. Additionally, students engaged in service work with the CRHF such as assisting in building bunk beds for local families and clearing rubble to enable the community in La Carpio to build a paved road. In sum, the selected activities were chosen by group facilitators to expose the students to a variety of cultural norms, traditions, challenges, and strengths based on their ethnocentric cultural developmental levels.

Group process. Each day, students participated in large group reflection sessions where they were encouraged to share their experiences for the day and discuss how the experience was impacting or challenging them. Facilitated by group leaders, group reflection sessions prompted students to reflect on their experiences broadly and also through specific salient experiences. Providing a safe, open, and non-judgmental environment was a primary goal of group facilitators. Given that group facilitators had participated in immersion experiences before, they used their own experiences of being challenged and model disclosure to create safety for the group. Group facilitators also participated in homestays and shared about the learning and challenges they were experiencing living within another culture. Facilitators were clear that although not each member had to share every day, processing in the large group was something they were expected to participate in.

Group members seemed to support one another through relating to each other's experiences and also challenge one another when conflict arose. One challenge some group members experienced were feelings of frustration based on the placement of their homestay. Although homestay families were given basic guidelines of how to interact with students, some families were naturally more engaged and welcoming than others. Additionally, some families were more fluent in English than others, allowing some participants to connect on deeper levels compared to participants whose families spoke no English. Through group process and reflection, facilitators acknowledged frustration and used experiences to deepen empathy for international learners in the United States and increase understanding of working with cross cultural populations.

In addition to large group reflections, students were instructed to set aside time daily to individually reflect on their experiences and write in their journal. Through both the group discussions and journaling, students were asked to link course content with their previous experiences and vice versa, evaluate their strengths and needs as a professional counselor, and deepen their understanding of the ethical and clinical implications of working with diverse groups in both national and international counseling populations. In the next sections, we describe the instrumentation that was used to assess differences within and between experimental and comparison groups.

Intercultural Development Inventory

For the current study, the Intercultural Development Inventory (IDI; Hammer et al., 2003), a 50-item instrument that assesses a person's dominant stage of intercultural development was used to assess for the impact of the immersion experience on developmental changes in intercultural sensitivity. The IDI is grounded in Bennett's (1986) DMIS theoretical framework and was developed in collaboration with Bennett and Wiseman (Hammer et al., 2003).

The IDI is formatted to provide participants with (a) a perceived orientation (PO) score (self-report of one's own capability in understanding and appropriately adapting to cultural differences), (b) a more objective developmental orientation (DO) score (indicative of a participant's actual orientation toward cultural differences), and (c) an in-depth textual profile of a respondents' predominant level of intercultural competence. The profile provides a detailed interpretation of the stage of intercultural development and transitional issues that accompany that stage (Hammer et al., 2003).

The IDI has undergone rigorous psychometric testing with more than 5,000 respondents during validation. A research team was trained in the DMIS and rated qualitative verbatim-transcribed interviews ($N = 25$) across the six DMIS orientations. Specific statements ($N = 200$) from an ethnically diverse sample of respondents were analyzed and clustered to develop a pilot version of the IDI with 239 sample items (Hammer et al., 2003). Based upon feedback from two pilot test respondent pools, the IDI was revised, undergoing a series of validation studies yielding a 50-item instrument. Confirmatory factor analyses, reliability analyses, and construct validity tests were then conducted on 4,763 individuals from 11 distinct, cross-cultural sample groups (Hammer, 2007). The final IDI revision, v.3, (Hammer,

2007) includes a total of five subscales: Denial, Polarization (defense and reversal as a combined orientation), Minimization, Acceptance, and Adaptation along a developmental continuum of intercultural sensitivity. The rigorous psychometric testing of the IDI supports the cross-cultural generalizability, validity, and reliability of an individual's core orientations toward cultural differences (Hammer, 1999, 2007; Hammer et al., 2003).

Procedure

This study implemented a quasi-experimental design with an experimental and comparison group of students in counselor education, with the international cultural immersion course considered the intervention or independent variable. Data collection occurred over a 2-year period, for four groups (i.e., two experimental groups and two comparison groups). Data collection for all groups occurred at similar time points; one semester prior to the departure for the international cultural immersion course and one semester after the students returned home from the immersion. All instruments were administered in paper pencil format on a University campus. Aims of the current research study were to investigate the impact of an international cultural immersion course for counselor trainees that immersed in Costa Rica when compared to their peer counterparts that did not immerse and to assess the extent to which the immersion expanded participants' intercultural sensitivity.

RESULTS

Preliminary Analyses

Results from the IDI instrument yielded individual profile reports for each participant regarding their (a) perceived orientation (PO), and (b) developmental orientation (DO) towards cultural difference and commonality. Before the immersion, a comparison of PO for immersed (M = 126.24, SD = 6.89) and non-immersed trainees (M = 123.22, SD = 5.85) revealed no significant difference between the groups t (37) = 1.48, p = .15. Likewise, a comparison of DO for immersed (M = 103.95, SD = 15.81) and non-immersed trainees (M = 98.24, SD = 13.43) also revealed no significant difference t (37) = 1.22, p = .23, suggesting that groups were similar prior to intervention.

Scores on the IDI prior to the immersion indicated that the majority of participants in the treatment groups favored an ethnocentric developmental orientation (n = 14). Specifically, participants were in the polarization ($n = 3$), minimization ($n = 11$), and acceptance stages ($n = 5$), indicated by group means as follows: Denial, $M = 4.68$, $SD = .29$; Defense, $M = 4.41$, $SD = .51$; Reversal, $M = 3.66$, $SD = .63$; Minimization, $M = 3.38$, $SD = .74$; Acceptance, $M = 3.87$, $SD = .67$; Adaptation, $M = 3.38$, $SD = .5$; and Cultural Disengagement, $M = 4.20$, $SD = .70$. Likewise, participants in the comparison groups also favored ethnocentric stages ($n = 17$). Specifically, participants were in the polarization ($n = 2$), minimization ($n = 15$), and acceptance ($n = 3$) stages, indicated by group means as follows: Denial, $M = 4.42$, $SD = .36$; Defense, $M = 4.44$, $SD = .55$; Reversal, $M = 3.63$, $SD = .66$; Minimization, $M = 3.06$, $SD = .63$; Acceptance, $M = 3.51$, $SD = .91$; Adaptation, $M = 3.19$, $SD = .60$; and Cultural Disengagement, $M = 3.55$, $SD = 1.29$.

Because polarization and minimization are ethnocentric stages in the DMIS, the majority of participants (in both comparison and treatment groups) ($n = 26$, 78.8%), seemed to make sense of cultural differences and commonalities based on their own cultural values, use broad stereotypes to identify cultural differences, and support less complex experiences of cultural difference and commonality (Hammer, 2007). There were seven participants (in both treatment and comparison groups) who were found to be in the acceptance stage, which falls within the ethnorelative developmental orientation. Participants in this stage are believed to make sense of cultural differences and commonalities based on one's own and other culture's values and practices, use cultural generalizations to recognize cultural differences, and support more complex experiences of cultural differences and commonality (Hammer, 2007).

At time two (i.e., post-immersion), participants in experimental ($n = 2$) and comparison ($n = 4$) groups experienced attrition or incomplete data for post-assessments. Results indicated that participants in the treatment groups were in the minimization ($n = 12$), and acceptance stages ($n = 5$). Participants in the comparison groups were found to be in the polarization ($n = 2$), minimization ($n = 11$), and acceptance ($n = 3$) stages. Therefore, developmental shifts in orientation remained largely unaffected for both experimental and comparison groups. Interestingly, participants in the experimental group who were previously in the polarization orientation seemed to shift into the minimization orientation, indicating developmental progression of cultural sensitivity. In addition, there were more changes in the students from the summer 2011 immersion as seven trainees advanced one developmental stage between the test administrations, whereas none of the students from the summer 2012 immersion advanced their developmental stage.

Main Analyses

To examine differences between participants in the treatment and comparison groups, repeated measures ANOVAs were conducted. Participation in the international cultural immersion experience (i.e., immersion or no immersion) served as the discrete within-subjects independent variable for both the treatment and comparison groups. Participants' observed DO and self-reported PO in intercultural sensitivity served as the continuous within-subjects dependent variables. Results indicated that participants who participated in the immersion experience did not have significantly different mean scores on DO than those who did not participate in immersion, $F(1, 31) = 2.07$, $p = .16$. Similarly, participants who were immersed did not have statistically significant different mean scores on self-reported PO than those who were not immersed, $F(1, 31) = 1.98$, $p = .17$. Examination of the simple effects indicated treatment group participants reported higher perceived intercultural sensitivity scores at post-assessment than comparison participants. The group means are shown in Table 1 and ANOVA results in Table 2.

A two-way ANOVA with repeated measures factor was conducted to examine the influence of a participant's initial developmental stage and participation in immersion on changes in intercultural sensitivity. Participation in the international cultural immersion experience (i.e., immersion or no immersion) served as the first discrete within-subjects independent variable while the participants' initially favored developmental stage (from the pre-immersion IDI administration) served as the second independent variable. Participants' observed developmental orientation (DO), and perceived orientation (PO) in intercultural sensitivity served as the continuous within-subjects dependent variables. For observed DO, neither immersion experience, $F(1, 27) = .91$, $p = .25$, nor initial developmental stage manifested a significant main

Table 1 Group Means of Intercultural Sensitivity by Time and Cultural Immersion

	DO		*PO*	
CI History	*Pre-treatment*	*Post-treatment*	*Pre-treatment*	*Post-treatment*
Immersed	102.15 (15.32)	107.85 (13.16)	125.43 (6.67)	127.80 (4.97)
Not Immersed	100.79 (13.06)	100.55 (13.68)	124.07 (5.93)	124.11 (5.48)

Note: Standard deviations appear in parentheses below group means.

Table 2 Change in Group Means of Intercultural Sensitivity by Time, Cultural Immersion, and Initial Developmental Stage

	Initial Developmental Stage		
Change in DO	*Polarization*	*Minimization*	*Acceptance*
Immersed	16.13	7.48	−6.61
	(14.77)	*(12.50)*	*(10.16)*
Not Immersed	6.00	.32	−4.59
	–	*(9.96)*	*(5.23)*

	Initial Developmental Stage		
Change in PO	*Polarization*	*Minimization*	*Acceptance*
Immersed	6.31	3.46	−3.35
	(6.01)	*(4.69)*	*(3.42)*
Not Immersed	1.46	.48	−2.17
	–	*(3.90)*	*(2.61)*

Note: Positive changes in means indicate growth in Intercultural Sensitivity. Standard deviations appear below group means in parentheses and italics.

effect, $F(2, 27) = 2.92$, $p = .07$, and no significant interaction was observed, $F(1, 27) = .52$, $p = .60$. For self-perceived PO, the immersion experience did not manifest a significant main effect, $F(1, 27) = 1.17$, $p = .29$, though initial developmental stage did, $F(2, 27) = 3.94$, $p = .03$. As with DO, no significant interaction was observed for PO, $F(2, 27) = .78$, $p = .47$. Examination of the simple effects indicated intervention group participants exhibited a greater change in both DO and PO intercultural sensitivity scores at post-assessment than comparison participants for all developmental stages. Additionally, participants tended to have an inverse relationship between initial developmental stage and intercultural sensitivity score growth for both intervention and comparison groups. Changes in group means are shown in Table 2 and ANOVA results in Table 3.

LIMITATIONS

The results of the current study may provide insight into the impact of an international cultural immersion group intervention on developing intercultural sensitivity for counselor trainees. Nevertheless, the results need to be interpreted within the context of study limitations. Sample size, social desirability, and differences between the two immersion experiences may be limitations impacting the generalizability

Table 3 2×2 Repeated Measures ANOVAs for Both DO and PO Between Counselor-Trainees Who Were and Were Not Immersed and Were at Different Developmental Stages

	Df	*F*	η^2	*Power*
DO				
Immersion	1	.91	.03	.15
Initial Developmental Stage	2	2.92	.18	.52
Interaction	2	.52	.04	.13
PO				
Immersion	1	1.17	.04	.18
Initial Developmental Stage	2	3.94	.23	.69
Interaction	2	.78	.06	.17

Note: Power computed at $a = .05$. Immersed $n = 17$, Not immersed $n = 16$

of the results. The sample in the current investigation consisted of relatively small groups and was limited in diversity as participants' predominately identified as Euro-American females sampled from one university. Although the sample was relatively homogenous, demographic data for participants in the sample were relatively representative to the population of counselor trainees. In addition there may have been a selection bias as participants chose to enroll in the international cultural immersion course as well as voluntary participation in comparison groups. Social desirability may also confound the results, as participants were volunteers responding to questions regarding their intercultural sensitivity, although the IDI instrument accounts for this by measuring both perceived and observed levels of intercultural sensitivity.

Furthermore, due to distinctions between the two groups of immersed trainees (i.e., the first group had seven members advance one developmental stage); there may have been differences between the first and second international immersion experiences. Examples of potential differences include the inclusion of four doctoral students in the first cohort, whereas the second cohort contained master's students alone. In addition, two teaching assistants worked with the instructor in the first cohort, assisting with the group process. Finally, although both groups completed journaling throughout immersion, a structured immersion journal template was utilized in the first year but not in the second year due to student feedback suggesting removing structured reflection. In sum, although the current investigation has limitations, we believe the findings from this study have several implications for group workers, and counselor educators.

DISCUSSION

Researchers (e.g., Alexander et al., 2005; Barden & Cashwell, 2014; Burnett et al., 2004; Canfield, Low, & Hovestadt, 2009; Tomlinson-Clarke & Clarke, 2010) have reported positive benefits of immersion experiences in developing helping professionals. However, results have been primarily qualitative and/or relied on anecdotal evidence such as participants' journals. This study provided the first known empirical exploration utilizing a quasi-experimental research design in conjunction with the Intercultural Development Inventory (IDI) with counselor trainees. Given that the IDI has been established as reliable, cross-culturally generalizable, and valid assessment of individuals and groups core orientations toward cultural differences, counselor educators may want to consider the utility of this instrument when assessing for cultural sensitivity over some of the more commonly used instruments in multicultural counseling research (Constantine et al., 2002; Hammer, 2007).

Results from the current study suggest that in comparison, participants in the current sample had lower scores for intercultural sensitivity than participants in previous studies (Altshuler, Sussman, & Kachur, 2003; Anderson et al., 2006). For example, Altshuler and colleagues (2003) reported that group mean IDI ratings for medical student study participants ($N = 24$) before a behavioral intervention were predominantly in the ethnorelative orientation of acceptance compared to participants in the current study who were largely represented in the ethnocentric orientations of defense and minimization. One explanation for differences in group means may be attributed to counselor trainees being less hindered by the tendency of social desirability than other helping professionals. Constantine and Ladany (2000) note that social desirability is a pattern of responding that reflects some individual's need to provide socially acceptable responses to questions rather than report their actual attitudes and feelings in order to present a favorable image.

Although we had expected to find more significant differences between experimental and comparison groups and/or between pre- and post-administrations of the IDI, the lack of significant changes in all four groups is interesting. Contrary to Andersen and colleagues (2006) and Paige et al. (2004) who report significant changes in overall developmental score, we did not find any significant changes on subscales or total scores. On the other hand, results from this study support findings from Andersen et al. (2006) on the lack of significance on specific subscales after a short term study abroad. Interestingly, we did see positive gains in group means for subscales that were categorized by ethnocentrism (i.e., defense and minimization). According to Bennett's DMIS, people develop sensitivity on each of the stages simultaneously, meaning they do not need to resolve the issues in one stage before moving on to the next stage (Bennett, 1993). Although the majority of changes were not significant to move students from one stage to the next, positive increases in mean scores suggest that students did increase cultural sensitivity within stages rather than between stages. It also noteworthy that the only students ($n = 7$) who increased intercultural sensitivity between stages were from the experimental condition.

Though main data analyses did not manifest significant findings, there are observable trends that are consistent with the general theme found in the literature on the effectiveness of cultural immersion on student development. When students are grouped by their initial favored DMIS orientation, those in the experimental groups displayed larger increases in their PO and DO scores. This trend is quite noticeable among students initially in the minimization stage (which also happens to account for the majority of students in the study). Also, the positive trend of immersion is greater on the measure of DO, rather than on that of PO. While perceived intercultural sensitivity and related measures of self-efficacy are important constructs for counselors, work with clients is more directly impacted by one's outward manifestation of intercultural sensitivity, or one's DO. Any training strategy that potentially can impact this external factor is of interest in the development of more culturally competent and effective counselors.

IMPLICATIONS FOR COUNSELOR EDUCATORS AND GROUP WORKERS

Bemak and Chung (2004) highlight the lack of systematic efforts in addressing the need for culturally sensitive group counselors to work across cultural boundaries, asserting that training and practice continues to be grounded in western-European models. The authors offer several steps for counselor educators to more effectively train graduate students to be prepared for facilitating multicultural group work, highlight the need to integrate current multicultural best practices and establish new standards for training using the multicultural and social justice competence principles for group workers. Therefore, building upon the support for integrating experiential education into multicultural group work seems clear. Specifically, encouraging group level cultural immersion experiences where students are exposed to being "other" seems appropriate in bridging the principles and competencies of group workers and actual pedagogical training practices. Given that the Multicultural and Social Justice Competence Principles for Group Workers calls for group facilitators to be aware of socio-political influence, differences in worldviews and cultures, and one's own values, biases, and limitations, it seems clear that training methods must focus on providing experiences for counselor trainees to be exposed and experience cultural differences (Singh et al., 2012). In a 2013 study, Barden and Cashwell identified critical factors to immersion experiences. Interestingly, the most commonly reported negative critical incident was related to group dynamics, with participants reporting feeling excluded from group, power dynamics with group facilitators and unsafe environments to openly process their experiences. Findings from this study support previous research regarding the need to attend to safety issues when facilitating multicultural experiential learning (Arthur & Achenbach, 2002). Although the current investigation did not specifically assess for safety within the group processing sessions, the facilitators followed recommendations from scholars (Arthur & Achenbach, 2002; Barden & Cashwell, 2014; Yalom & Leszcz, 2005) regarding integrating common group building strategies. Examples from the current investigation include using ice breakers to establish group cohesion, providing space prior to immersion and during immersion to discuss both positive and negative experiences, establishing group rules prior to immersion, and offering individual process sessions when needed, while immersed. Counselor educators are encouraged to keep group dynamics at the forefront when planning, implementing, and debriefing from cultural immersion experiences.

Another implication from the current study is the need for counselor educators to consider trainees' developmental levels of intercultural sensitivity when establishing interventions. For example, if trainees are primarily in ethnorelative orientations of cultural sensitivity, then it seems clear that decreased focus on exposure to different cultural norms and increased focus on integrating cultural differences into personal worldviews would be warranted. Although results did not indicate significant developmental changes for experimental group participants in the current study, more research is needed to understand why. For example, Tomlinson-Clarke and Clarke (2010) along with Ishii and colleagues (2009) contended that CI must be of sufficient duration for students to be confronted by and have to respond to the potential culture shock arising from being in another culture. Furthermore, group process and safety have been argued to be the conduit for trainees to work through cultural shock, resistance, and feelings that emerge as a result of being "other" (Barden & Cashwell, 2013; Chung & Bemak, 2002; West-Olatunji et al., 2011). Results from the current study suggest that the length of immersion along with opportunities to process CI experiences may have been factors given that scores in cultural sensitivity all increased but developmental levels did not change significantly. In summary, although results from this study have important implications for preparing future group workers in responding to diverse groups, several areas of future research remain.

RECOMMENDATIONS FOR FUTURE RESEARCH

As with all research, this study brought up more questions than it answered. Specifically, results from this study highlight the need to consider developmental levels of cultural sensitivity when developing interventions. Research that aims to assess developmental levels of intercultural sensitivity and adapts interventions such as immersion experiences based on developmental levels would substantially contribute to this body of research. Are certain interventions more effective for persons in ethnocentric orientations compared to persons in ethnorelative orientations? If students from mixed developmental orientations are all participating in the same immersion experience, are there ways to tailor process groups or journaling prompts to best facilitate developmental progression on a continuum of cultural sensitivity?

Future research on cultural immersion should continue the use of rigorous methodological designs. Examples may include quasi experimental designs and utilization of experimental and comparison groups to increase confidence that observed changes are a result of the immersion and no other external factors; qualitative designs to increase depth of understanding of how immersion experiences influence counselor trainees' development; or mixed method designs to complement and integrate findings from qualitative and quantitative data. Additionally, further research on the critical factors that increase or impede changes in cultural sensitivity is warranted. For example, research controlling for factors such as length of the immersion to better understand the minimum amount of time that students need to be immersed for significant change are encouraged. Additional factors that may increase or impede changes are related to group dynamics. Building upon the work of Barden and Cashwell (2013), research specifically investigating the influence of safety in group while immersed is warranted. Furthermore, given the call for counselor trainees to be culturally sensitive when facilitating groups, more research is needed on the translation between cultural immersion experiences and influence on group facilitation skills. In sum, while the body of literature on international cultural immersion is growing, ample opportunity remains for scholars to contribute and expand existing knowledge of the efficacy of immersion experiences.

CONCLUSION

In sum, results from the current study highlight the need to continue expanding and evaluating assessments and developmental levels of intercultural sensitivity for counselor trainees. Results from this study provide the first empirical quasi-experimental research design using the IDI instrument and DMIS theoretical framework to evaluate the efficacy of international cultural immersion experiences for counselor trainees. While the body of literature of cultural immersion as an effective pedagogical tool in increasing cultural sensitivity is promising (e.g., Arthur & Achenbach, 2002; Barden & Cashwell, 2014; DeRicco & Sciarra, 2005; Kim & Lyons, 2003; Paige et al., 2009), several areas of future research remain. As the endeavor to develop counselor trainees that are knowledgeable and skilled to work with groups from diverse backgrounds continues, counselor education programs have a responsibility to implement effective pedagogical approaches that enhance the development of cultural sensitivity.

REFERENCES

Abreu, J. M., Gim Chung, R. H., & Atkinson, D. R. (2000). Multicultural counselor training: Past, present, and future directions. *The Counseling Psychologist, 28*, 641–656.

Alexander, C. M., Kruczek, T., & Ponterotto, J. G. (2005). Building multicultural competencies in school counselor trainees: An international immersion experience. *Counselor Education and Supervision, 44*, 255–266.

Altschuler, L., Sussman, N. M., & Kachur, E. (2003). Assessing changes in intercultural sensitivity among physician trainees using the Intercultural Development Inventory. *International Journal of Intercultural Relations, 27*, 387–401.

Ancis, J. R., & Sanchez-Hucles, J. V. (2000). A preliminary analysis of counseling students' attitudes toward counseling women and women of color: Implications for cultural competency training. *Journal of Multicultural Counseling and Development, 28*, 16–31.

Anderson, P. H., Lawton, L., Rexeisen, R. J., & Hubbard, A. C. (2006). Short-term study abroad and intercultural sensitivity: A pilot study. *International Journal of Intercultural Relations, 30*, 457–469.

Arthur, N., & Achenbach, K. (2002). Developing multicultural counseling competencies through experiential learning. *Counselor Education and Supervision, 42*, 2–14.

Barden, S. M., & Cashwell, C. (2013). Critical factors in cultural immersion: A synthesis of relevant literature. *International Journal for the Advancement of Counseling, 35*, 286–297.

Barden, S. M., & Cashwell, C. (2014). International immersion: An exploratory study of critical factors and counselor development. *Journal of Multicultural Counseling and Development, 42*, 42–60.

Bemak, F., & Chung, R. Y. (2004). Teaching multicultural group counseling: Perspectives for a new era. *The Journal for Specialists in Group Work, 29*, 31–41. doi:10.1080/01933920490275349.

Bennett, M. J. (1986). A developmental approach to training for intercultural sensitivity. *International Journal of Intercultural Relations, 10*, 179–196.

Bennett, M. J. (1993). Towards ethnorelativism: A developmental model of intercultural sensitivity. In R. M. Paige (Ed.). *Education for the intercultural experience* (pp. 21–71). Yarmouth, ME: Intercultural.

Bieschke, K. J., Gehlert, K. M., Wilson, D., Matthews, C.R, & Wade, J. (2003). Qualitative analysis of multicultural awareness in training groups. *The Journal for Specialists in Group Work, 28*, 325–338.

Burnett, J., Hamel, D., & Long, L. (2004). Service learning in graduate counselor education: Developing multicultural counseling. *Journal of Multicultural Counseling and Development, 32*, 180–191.

Canfield, B. S., Low, L., & Hovestadt, A. (2009). Cultural immersion as a learning method for expanding intercultural competencies. *Family Journal, 17*, 318–322.

Chung, R. C., & Bemak, F. (2002). The relationship of culture and empathy in cross-cultural counseling. *Journal of Counseling and Development, 80*, 154–159.

Chung, R. C., & Grabosky, K. T. (2011). Multicultural-social justice leadership strategies: Counseling and advocacy with immigrants. *Journal for Social Action in Counseling and Psychology, 3*, 86–102.

Clark, M. C. (1993). Transformational learning. In S. B. Merriam (Ed.), *An update on adult learning theory* (pp. 47–56). San Francisco, CA: Jossey-Bass. (New Directions for Adult and Continuing Education. No. 57)

Constantine, M. G., Gloria, A. M., & Ladany, N. (2002). The factor structure underlying three self-report multicultural counseling competence scales. *Cultural Diversity & Ethnic Minority Psychology, 8*, 334–345.

Constantine, M. G., & Ladany, N. (2000). Self-report multicultural counseling competence scales: Their relation to social desirability attitudes and multicultural case conceptualization ability. *Journal of Counseling Psychology, 47*, 155.

Corey, G. (2004). *Theory and practice of group counseling* (6th ed.). Pacific Grove, CA: Brooks Cole.

Creswell, J. (2008). Educational research: Planning, conducting, and evaluating quantitative and qualitative research. Upper Saddle River, NJ: Pearson/Merrill Prentice Hall.

DeRicco, J. N., & Sciarra, D. T. (2005). The immersion experience in multicultural counselor training: Confronting covert racism. *Journal of Multicultural Counseling and Development, 33*, 2–16.

Engle L., & Engle, J. (2004). Assessing language acquisition and intercultural sensitivity development in relation to study abroad program design. *Frontiers: The Interdisciplinary Journal of Study Abroad*, 219–236.

Ginwright, S., & Cammarota, J. (2002). New terrain in youth development: The promise of a social justice approach. *Social Justice, 29*, 82–95.

Goodman, R. D., & West-Olatunji, C. (2009). Applying critical consciousness: Culturally competent disaster response outcomes. *Journal of Counseling & Development, 87*, 458–465.

Hammer, M. R. (1999). A measure of intercultural sensitivity: The Intercultural Development Inventory. In S. M. Fowler & M. G. Mumford (Eds.), *The intercultural sourcebook* (vol. 2, pp. 61–72). Yarmouth, ME: Intercultural.

Hammer, M. R. (2007). *The Intercultural Development Inventory manual* (vol. 3). Ocean Pines, MD: IDI, LLC.

Hammer, M. R., Bennett, M. J., & Wiseman, R. (2003). Measuring intercultural sensitivity: The Intercultural Development Inventory. *International Journal of Intercultural Relations, 27*, 421–443.

Hernández, P., Almeida, R., & Dolan-Del Vecchio, K. (2005). Critical consciousness, accountability, and empowerment: Key processes for helping families heal. *Family Process, 44*, 105–119.

Holcomb-McCoy, C. C., & Myers, J. E. (1999). Multicultural competence and counselor training: A national survey. *Journal of Counseling & Development, 77*, 294–302.

Hui, S. M. Y. (2009). Media montage: Difficult dialogues about service learning: Embrace the messiness, *About Campus, 14*, 22–26.

Ishii, H., Gilbride, D. D., & Stensrud, R. (2009). Students' internal reactions to a one-week cultural immersion trip: A qualitative analysis of student journals. *Journal of Multicultural Counseling and Development, 37*, 15–27.

Kim, B. S. K., & Lyons, H. Z. (2003). Experiential activities and multicultural counseling competence training. *Journal of Counseling and Development, 81*, 400–408.

Ladany, N., Constantine, M. G., Miller, K., Erickson, C., & Muse-Burke, J. (2000). Supervisor countertransference: A qualitative investigation into its identification and description, *Journal of Counseling Psychology, 47*, 102–115.

Lassiter, P. S., Napolitano, L., Culbreth, J. R., & Ng, K. M. (2008). Developing multicultural competence using the structured peer group supervision model. *Counselor Education & Supervision, 47*, 164–178.

Lederman, D. (2007). Quality vs. quantity in study abroad. *Inside Higher Ed*. Retrieved from http://www.insidehighered.com/news/2007/02/21/abroad

Lee, C. (Ed.). (2013). *Multicultural issues in counseling: New approaches to diversity* (4th ed). Alexandria, VA: American Counseling Association.

Maurrasse, D. J. (2003). Higher education/community partnerships: Assessing progress in the field. *Introduction to Service Learning Toolkit: Readings and resources for faculty*, second *edition*. Providence, RI: Campus Compact.

Medina-Lopez-Portillo, A. (2004). Intercultural learning assessment: The link between program duration and the development of intercultural sensitivity. *Frontiers: The Interdisciplinary Journal of Study Abroad*, 179–200.

Paige, R. M., Cohen, A. D., & Shively, R. L. (2004). Assessing the impact of a strategies-based curriculum on language and cultural learning abroad. *Frontiers: The Interdisciplinary Journal of Study Abroad*, 253–276.

Paige, R. M., Fry, G. W., Stallman, E. M., Josic, J., & Jon, J. E. (2009). Study abroad for global engagement: The long-term impact of mobility experiences. *Intercultural Education, 20*, 29–44. doi:10.1080/14675980903370847

Pedersen P. (1991). Special issue: Multiculturalism as a fourth force in counseling. *Journal of Counseling and Development, 70*, 4–251.

Pederson, P. J. (2010). Assessing intercultural effectiveness outcomes in a year-long study abroad program. *International Journal of Intercultural Relations, 34*, 70–80.

Pedersen P. J., & Leong, F. (1997). Counseling in an international context. *The Counseling Psychologist, 25*, 117–121.

Ponterotto, J. G., Fuertes, J. N., & Chen, E. C. (2000). Models of multicultural counseling. In S. D. Brown & R. W. Lent (Eds.), *Handbook of counseling psychology* (3rd ed., pp. 639–669). Hoboken, NJ: John Wiley & Sons.

Ponterotto, J. G., Rieger, B. P., Barrett, A., & Sparks, R. (1994). Assessing multicultural counseling competence: A review of instrumentation. *Journal of Counseling & Development, 72*, 316–322. doi:10.1002/j.1556-6676.1994.tb00941.x

Pope-Davis, D. B., & Coleman, H. L. (1997). *Multicultural counseling competencies: Assessment, education, and training, and supervision*. Thousand Oaks, CA: Sage.

Priester, P. E., Jones, J. E., Jackson-Bailey, C. M., Jana-Masri, A., Jordan, E. X., & Metz, A. J. (2008). An analysis of content and instructional strategies in multicultural counseling courses. *Journal of Multicultural Counseling & Development, 36*, 29–39.

Reynolds, A. L. (2001). Multidimensional cultural competence: Providing tools for transforming psychology. *The Counseling Psychologist, 29*, 833–841.

Ribeiro, M. (2004). A qualitative analysis of adult learners' immersion experiences to South Africa: Implications for multicultural training. In *VISTAS 2004, proceedings of American Counseling Association Annual Conference*. Retrieved from http://counselingoutfitters.com/vistas/vistas04/12.pdf

Rundstrom, T. W. (2005). Exploring the impact of study abroad on students' intercultural communication skills: Adaptability and sensitivity. *Journal of Studies in International Education, 9*, 356–371.

Sakamoto, I., & Pitner, R. O. (2005). Use of critical consciousness in anti-oppressive social work practice: Disentangling power dynamics at personal and structural level. *British Journal of Social Work, 35*, 435–452.

Shannonhouse, L. (2013). *The relationships between multicultural counseling competence, cultural immersion, & cognitive/emotional developmental styles: Implications for multicultural counseling training* (Unpublished doctoral dissertation). Retrieved from http://libres.uncg.edu/ir/uncg/listing.aspx?styp=ti&id=10151

Singh, A. A., Merchant, N., Skudrzyk, B., & Ingene, D. (2012). *Association for specialists in group work: Principles for diversity-competent group workers*. Retrieved from http://www.asgw.org/pdf/ASGW_MC_SJ_Priniciples_Final_ASGW.pdf

Smith, L. C., & Shin, R. Q. (2008). Social privilege, social justice, and group counseling: An inquiry. *The Journal for Specialists in Group Work, 33*, 351–366. doi:10.1080/01933920802424415

Sue, D. W., Bernier, J. E., Durran, A., Feinberg, L., Pedersen, P., & Smith, E. J. (1982). Position paper: Cross-cultural counseling competencies. *The Counseling Psychologist, 10*, 45–52.

Sue, D. W., & Sue, D. (2012). *Counseling the culturally diverse: Theory and practice* (6th ed.). New York, NY: John Wiley & Sons.

Tomlinson-Clarke, S. M., & Clarke, D. (2010). Culturally focused community-centered service learning: An international cultural immersion experience. *Journal of Multicultural Counseling & Development, 38*, 166–175.

Vande Berg, M. (Ed.). (2004). Special issue on the assessment of learning abroad. *Frontiers: The Interdisciplinary Journal of Study Abroad, 10*(1), 1–10.

West-Olatunji, C. A., Goodman, R. D., Mehta, S., & Templeton, L. (2011). Creating cultural competence: An outreach immersion experience in Southern Africa. *International Journal for the Advancement of Counseling, 33*, 335–346.

Worthington, R. L., Soth-McNett, A. M., & Moreno, M. V. (2007). Multicultural counseling competencies research: A 20-year content analysis. *Journal of Counseling Psychology, 54*, 351–361.

Yalom, I. D., & Leszcz, M. (2005). *The theory and practice of group psychotherapy* (5th ed.). New York, NY: Basic Books.

Group Counseling and *Satsang*: Learning From Indian Group Practices

Christopher Rybak
Bradley University

Deepa Sathaye
Pune, India

Megha Deuskar
Fergusson College

Group counseling is a highly complex process that has undergone continuous exploration to improve understanding and development to make it more effective. Learning how diverse cultures approach the leadership and interaction within small groups can provide additional insight and perspective to the commonalities and differences of varied groups. This article explores a diversity perspective offered through satsang. Satsang *is an ancient Asian Indian approach to personal and spiritual development within a group setting that includes a leader who has advanced knowledge and expertise related to leading the* satsang.

The diverse cultural perspectives of the world offer varied insights and perspectives on human self-understanding and relationships. Non-Western perspectives such as yoga psychology have undergone extensive reflection and application for millennia (Mishra, 1973). Exploring diverse perspectives can offer additional ways of understanding of how Western approaches to counseling are effective and ways in which these approaches might be enhanced and more deeply rooted by connecting them with diverse and indigenous traditions (Rybak, 2004).

In general, the level of self-understanding is fragmented as each of us has many aspects of ourselves of which we lack awareness (Perls, 2010). As a result, we are not able to see others or ourselves as whole beings. Group interaction increases self-understanding as it helps fill those gaps so that we can become more unified and better able to connect with others and ourselves (Chen & Rybak, 2004).

The confluence of Eastern and Western practices has significantly enriched our understanding of how the therapeutic processes involved with group counseling can enhance wellbeing (Rybak & Deuskar, 2010). Western practice has contributed research into the mechanisms, structure, and dynamics of effective group leadership while Eastern practices have contributed time-tested skills that include the mindfulness approaches involved in meditation and *satsang* (Singh, Jain, & Singh, 2014). This article will describe this confluence from the perspective of *satsang*.

SATSANG DESCRIBED

Satsang is an ancient Indian cultural process similar to group counseling. "Sat" means truth. "Sang" means in "company of" or "in association with" somebody who represents or who is a seeker of truth. The process involves three components. The first one being a presence of a leader who has attained high level of self-awareness. Next, individuals who are seeking the company of such a leader, and thirdly, a communication taking place among these individuals in various verbal and nonverbal forms (predominantly verbal). Traditionally in Indian culture this typically involves listening to or reading scriptures, reflecting on, discussing, and assimilating their meaning (Frisk, 2002). Additionally traditional to Indian culture are values that promote a collectivistic orientation and commitment to interpersonal harmony, both of which serve to promote a likely willingness of Indians to partake in group tasks (Kim, Atkenson, & Umemoto, 2001).

Traditionally, *satsang* is a slow, long, and continuous process that may have no time frame for the number of sessions, which is contrary to the counseling group sessions that are comparatively short termed with specific goals. At the same time, *satsang* can offer a setting that helps group members focus with firm intention on the present experience. Considering that human beings need repetition, and also that one who is seeking may not always be in the receiving mode, a seeker may sometimes withdraw from their efforts. The seeker, by definition, is on a path of self-discovery. *Sadhana*, or the process of self-improvement, is a long and slow process, requiring considerable and sustained effort to maintain a healthy body and a sharp mind. Constant exposure to the world outside, with its emphasis on materialism and striving may cause the seeker to lose focus. Especially in the early stages of self-transformation, a high risk is posed by tendencies in the seeker to get distracted by external forces that draw one away from careful self-examination and building deeper self-awareness. In order to counter such tendencies *satsang* emphasizes continuity and perseverance that keeps the individual seeker on the path of learning and constant appraisal with encouragement from peers with whom is developed a strong and positive bonding. Ideally *satsang* sets up conditions for the seeker to experience a feeling of deep caring and supportiveness from others in the *satsang* group. In terms attributed to Yalom and Leszcz (2005), *Satsang* promotes therapeutic factors including altruism and group cohesion.

Satsang shows similarity to the Socratic method where students seek truth by their own insights. They both function as a system, a spirit, a method, and a type of philosophical inquiry or an intellectual technique, all rolled into one. Groups can be a place where participants can learn to identify and speak their inner truths while having their experiences acknowledged and understood. In early life, people often experience the burden of presenting a persona that may be less than meaningful or expressive of their true inner life. It is important that groups create an environment that is truly respectful and accepting of individuals who will have characteristics that are different from others. Despite the shells of outer differences, members can develop an awareness of the core of being that is their true essence and unites all (Rybak, 2004). Groups can establish a rejuvenating setting where "The Self meets itself in the sacred mirror of satsang" (Krystal, 2003, p. 117). This is a powerful highlight of *satsang* groups: the mirroring of group member characteristics to one another, both the universal commonalities as well as the tendencies that stem from particular background experiences. Such mirroring offers the opportunity for members to honor the inner strengths that arise as well as develop greater understanding of challenges faced by each, ultimately in an effort to enhance skills of living and relating to others. Leadership fostering a group environment of acceptance and openness contributes to the ability of group members to activate the mirroring process that promotes the interplay of thoughtful focus on the inner experiences of each member along with their outer relationships.

SATSANG AND GROUP WORK SIMILARITIES

Like group counseling *satsang* also aims at preventive as well as remedial results, having specific focuses on educational, social, and personal growth while emphasizing discovering internal resources of strength by practicing yoga, music, different forms of meditation, and *pranayama* in which breathing patterns are used to manage one's energy (Rybak & Deuskar, 2004). Since ancient days in India, great leaders had the same mission of spreading awareness, empathy, and compassion, while helping the masses accept reality, reduce suffering, and create in them a feeling of peace. Such *satsang* leaders had no emotional turmoil in them and had a feeling of universality. Such feelings are comparable with the notion of *coherence* as described by McCraty (2010) that includes a unified, focused, and peaceful state.

Some of the common goals *satsang* seekers experience that are similar to group counseling members are to trust oneself and others, and to develop a sense of universality and compassion for others. The seekers increase self-awareness, self-acceptance, and self-confidence. This process is very similar to what happens in therapeutic groups. Shared experiences by group members can help other members to find different ways to deal with normal issues and resolve conflicts. *Satsang* helps seekers develop a clearer view of their inner self and their mission in life. As suggested by Yalom and Leszcz (2005), effective groups promote development of a sense of universality and compassion for others by each member.

INNER AND OUTER ASPECTS OF *SATSANG*

For each individual, one's personal, inner emotions affect the quality of one's interactions with others. At the same time, one's outer, interpersonal experiences often impact one's inner emotional life. An appropriately designed group promotes significant experiences in order to encourage awareness and added dimensions to one's emotional understanding through the meaningful interpersonal relationships that develop within a group (Rybak & Deuskar, 2004). The outer, interpersonal experiences of *satsang* can offer group members the opportunity to know others first in terms of external similarities and differences, but then begin to recognize more of one another's essence as the harmony of the group develops. Along with that recognition, a deeper awareness of one's own essence is often achieved. Eastern traditions such as Buddhism have identified methods of helping individuals nurture keys to relationship with self and others through mindfulness and compassion (Wang, 2005). Leaders who guide occasional shifts toward the contemplative and reflective aspects of experience can foster such relationship skills within a group.

Individual Level of *Satsang*

Satsang begins with oneself first; in complete noble silence as one individually looks deep inside and become more clearly aware of what is true for them. Through this process one would come across the flaws and weaknesses embedded deep inside. *Satsang* begins with the process of acceptance, and then continues building on self-awareness. The process may further take the individual towards self-development. Freedom of choice is present for each member so that each can conduct self-discovery of meaningful emotional experiences. Many times group members enter a group experience without having a clear sense of their own life experiences on cognitive, emotional, and behavioral levels (Cohen & Cantor, 2010). They also may tend to be unable to make effective interpretation and use of feedback provided by others in their lives. They may often misconstrue the responses of others around them (Cohen & Cantor, 2010), either being excessively reliant on such information or overly resistant to possible implications. Mindfulness offers a means of developing both the inner and outer awareness necessary for a group experience to be effective and successful for the group members and to find a way to effectively synthesize and integrate inner and outer information sources.

Mindfulness. Mindful attention to one's experiences and heightened awareness of others around one can play an important role in one's development during a group or *satsang*. As described by Brantley, Doucette, and Lindell (2008), "Mindfulness heightens the experience of inner life events of emotions, thoughts, and sensations. One can also bring mindful attention to the outer life, including relationships and social experiences" (p. 10). Participation in a healthy, functioning group raises one's sense of connection and aliveness. Hanson and Mendius (2009) noted: "Mindfulness involves the skillful use of attention to both inner and outer worlds" (p. 13).

Nurturing mindfulness can assist an individual in the development of self-compassion and in building an ability to observe one's self from a dispassionate yet compassionate perspective (Neff, 2009). Developing a capacity to consider oneself in an objective way allows for a place of greater understanding of oneself that is not fueled by either harsh self-derision or an excessive need to defend and protect oneself from real or perceived criticisms. Enhancing greater objectivity in viewing oneself and gaining release from one's potentially overbearing self-criticism allows an individual to also more objectively, openly, and compassionately understand the motivations and actions of others around them (Neff, 2009). Self-compassion increases the likelihood of emotionally connecting with fellow beings. As Neff (2009) described, "Self-compassion connects one's own flawed condition to the shared human condition, so that one's own characteristics and experiences are considered from a broad, inclusive perspective" (pp. 561–562).

Developing the capacity for mindful self-compassion leads toward a greater sense of wholeness, harmony, and coherence. Coherence encompasses emotional, cognitive, spiritual, as well as physiological dimensions such as heart rhythm and breath (McCraty, 2010). These functions contribute to greater efficiency of neural processing and allow one to shift more smoothly and appropriately from internal awareness to the external. In addition to increasing one's ability to navigate social relationships, greater individual coherence contributes to a positive energy field that can be sensed by others subconsciously if not consciously (McCraty, 2010). Group leaders who have been able to advance their own level of coherence through mindful compassion of self and others can use such awareness and experience in encouraging the growth of group members. Likewise, through the activation of therapeutic factors such as modeling and interpersonal learning (Yalom & Lesecz, 2005), group members can promote the development of greater coherence in others even as they build this ability in themselves. Recent powerful developments in neuroimaging research suggest that these kinds of positive behavioral, social, and emotional changes for group members are reflected by neuroplastic adaptation of brain functioning (Siegel, 2007, 2012). Developing mindfulness is one of the ways in which group members can learn to guide and promote their own growth (Siegel, 2007).

Mindfulness and neuroplasticity. Developing a practice of mindfulness contributes to the positive neuroplasticity of the brain. Neuroplasticity is the capacity of the brain to continue its development by forming and strengthening neural connections within the brain. The more practice, the stronger the connections become (Rybak, 2013; Siegel, 2007). Often mindfulness is developed through particular meditation practices such as vipassana that is typically taught in 10-day retreats that include about 10 hr of meditation per day (Goenka, 2013). Working with and enhancing the positive neuroplasticity of the brain allows each person to develop more fully toward their ultimate capabilities and increase their potential to become more effective in their daily actions as well as relationships. Mindful awareness of self and others within a group can help increase one's ability to manage relationships in more meaningful and productive ways even as one develops the inner neural connections that support increasingly effective outer behaviors that contribute to enhanced social interactions. Groups led by skilled leaders offer an ideal setting to connect individual mindfulness with more fulfilling group interaction.

Group Level of *Satsang*

People with varied mindsets and energy levels come together in *satsang* with a common motive or purpose. In olden days Rishis conducted *satsangs* for their disciples or followers. The Rishis were preachers of spirituality who taught the art of living (Bose, 1930). Traditionally devotees viewed the Rishis as saints who were blessed and possessed an extraordinary positive energy such that their words and actions tended to be highly influential to those in attendance. The preaching and thoughts were in the form of lectures (*pravachanas*), hymns, and devotional songs (*Abhangas* and *Kirtanas*). These lectures were often lucid and interspersed with short stories mainly aimed at clarifying the subtleties on the path of spirituality. Just as the nuances of interpersonal skills have to be explained in simple language to group members, the Rishis and saints clarified the path of spirituality outlined in ancient texts for the seekers, in as simplified a form as possible. Devotional songs and group chanting are primarily aimed at creating positive group energy, as well as getting the seeker disengaged from thoughts of the outside world (Singh et al., 2014).

The Rishis dealt with a diverse population with respect to age, socioeconomic status, level of education, sexual orientation, and other aspects of diversity. As the group is diverse it provides a microcosm of the external world to the member as well as the potential for rich feedback. It helps the people gain insight, know the hidden truth within them, reduce miseries, and make fundamental changes in their ways of thinking and ultimately aiming at forgetting oneself (Bose, 1930). Through cohesion the member develops a sense of belonging, as well as ways of being intimate and caring, and of challenging others in a positive manner. The result of this is therapeutic and educational. The group process is self-reflective in order that the experience is brought to awareness in a way that helps illuminate the experience more fully. The purpose of illumination is to bring greater awareness to the interpersonal dimensions of life and these in turn on the individual inner experiences (Rybak & Deuskar, 2004).

Group coherence: "Energetic field." The inner attunement of emotionally and socially intelligent members contributes to the harmonious interaction of other members. Those members who are still developing their social (Goleman, 2007) and emotional intelligence (Goleman, 2005) have the opportunity to observe and entrain their own reactions to others in the group who may have further developed their abilities to center themselves and to work with others in less conflicted ways. As members participate in the functioning of the group in healthy ways, they begin to assimilate those skills inwardly and outwardly to various degrees.

As group members spend time with one another and get to know one another, the members tend to become more open and accepting of one another (Uvnas-Moberg, 1998; Wang, 2005). The group develops a kind of emotional "energetic field" (McCraty, 2010, p. 20) within which the members interact and build upon the inner emotional states of one another. Research cited by McCraty (2010) suggests that humans and animals may have the ability to respond to the bioenergetics field being produced by others, particularly those who are close at hand and emotionally connected.

Harmonious group interactions are reflected in an efficient flow of energy and information among group members (McCraty, 2010). This is not a situation in which individual group members stifle significant concerns and questions about the functioning of the group. When group members hide their true thoughts and feelings, it results in group collusion rather than group coherence (Chen & Rybak, 2004). Coherent groups can bend and flex with diverse views and perspectives and come out stronger and even more effective. The diversity of perspectives can contribute to added energy and creativity within a group as the members learn to manage such differences in positive ways.

Findings from neuroscience using brain imaging suggest the presence of particular neurons that fire during an empathic reaction to others (Keysers, 2008; Rizzolatti & Fabbri-Destro, 2008; Rybak, 2013; Schulte-Ruther, Markowitsch, Fink, & Piefke, 2007). These brain cells have been called "mirror neurons" for they appear to indicate an internal representation of the experience of others who are being observed. Research suggests that mirror neurons are activated during empathic encounters with others—that mirror neurons enable us to empathically connect with others (Schulte-Ruther et al., 2007). As such, the social interactions within groups appear to be facilitated through mirror neurons connecting those engaged in interaction (Keysers, 2008). Mirror neurons develop and are modified through life experiences (Rizzolatti & Fabbri-Destro, 2008). Interactions within a group setting offer opportunities for members to both activate and develop their social and empathic skills, perhaps to build the capacity of their mirror neurons to function more fully and effectively.

Social interactions can be utilized in groups in differing ways according to the purpose and goals for the group. Some groups teach members specific coping skills such as assertion training and bereavement groups, or insight groups for personal growth and development. Other groups offer the possibility of remediating and managing significant personality-based issues (Chen & Rybak, 2004). The interactive skills and interpersonal learning that occurs can enhance the positive impact of each of these types of groups often seen in Western settings. *Satsang* groups share both commonalities and differences as described below.

PURPOSE-BASED *SATSANG* GROUPS

People with the same purpose and goals coming together share similar ideas. The degree of thought, assertiveness, motivation, and energies in them would vary, for example, in addiction treatment centers, for patients with various problems, for those who are about to leave the hospital and reenter the community and terminally ill patients. It is a common practice in India to have *satsang*s for these populations, to remotivate them, and help them with specific coping skills. Singing devotional songs and listening to spiritual scripts helps them divert their attention from their suffering toward a more hopeful experience of life. The *satsang* group provides empathy and the support necessary to create an atmosphere of trust that helps sharing and exploring similar concerns (Singh et al., 2014).

In crisis and calamities *satsang*s have always been of great source of remotivation and a feeling of togetherness in dealing with various crisis situations and even natural calamities in India. The Indian culture believes in "The Law of Karma" (Eswaran, 1975) that helps them accept reality from within at both conscious and subconscious levels, *satsang*s have helped people understand this concept. They believe that every situation is created to offer learning of some kind for one's own progress as an individual. This belief doesn't make those suffering feel like victims, but instead promotes a strong belief in positivity, and reduces their anxiety to some extent. The help and empathy extended to each other is with a feeling of extended family system that prevents the feeling of loneliness.

As an example, in Gujarat, India following a devastating earthquake that struck in 2002 where almost every person had lost family members or friends, *satsang* camps were established all over the country within 48 hr of the episode. Healing the sufferers and empathizing with them was the common goal of all the *satsang*s, promoting a feeling of oneness and bonding as if a large extended family. They included group activities such as prayers, community food dining areas, common shelter homes, medical aids, and other necessary supplies for many months (Bochasanwasi Shri Akshar Purushottam Swaminarayan Sanstha [BAPS] Charities, 2012). Efforts were made to insure that no person was left unattended. Children were taken care of by foster parents, aunts, uncles, and neighbors at the camps. *Satsang*s helped people get back to normalcy earlier than expected (Shaw, Gupta, & Sarma, 2003) and as a result the people of Gujarat are moving ahead with positivity and growth with *satsang*.

In addition to crises response, a number of ongoing *satsang* groups have been established to help with ongoing and everyday issues. These groups emphasize the aspects of altruism and universality (Yalom & Leszcz, 2005) and applying these factors to societal conditions. Specific examples of present day *satsang*s which have helped society follow. Branches of these India-based organizations can be found in the United States.

The Art of Living Foundation

The Art of Living Foundation (Pandya, 2014) is based in south India. Founded by Sri Sri Ravi Shankar, this organization has millions of seekers all around the world seeking spiritual progress through their *satsang*s (Singh et al., 2014). He aims at a violence-free and stress-free world. The Art of Living courses offer training in managing difficult emotions and improving relationships through Sudarshan Kriya yoga that includes special breathing techniques for reducing the effects of stress (Brown & Gerbarg, 2005).

Vipassana Meditation

Vipassana meditation (Goenka, 2013) is taught in group sessions by S. N. Goenka and has an international presence. Vipassana means to see things as they really are. It is one of India's most ancient techniques of meditation. It was taught in India more than 2500 years ago as a universal remedy for universal ills. Mindfulness training is a centerpiece of Vipassana meditation in which participants learn to observe their inner thoughts and awareness from an objective perspective without feeling compelled to react (Sulekha, Thennarasu, Vedamurthachar, Raju, & Kutty, 2006).

GROUP/*SATSANG* LEADER

From Indian tradition, the *satsang* group leader has usually undertaken a long process of self-development, whose character and behaviors are held up as an ideal for the members (Frisk, 2002). They bring to the *satsang* their personal qualities, values, and life experiences which promotes growth in the members' lives. The *satsang* leaders remain on the path of self-appraisal toward continued self-development, which fosters honest self-investigations in others.

The *satsang* group leader focuses on the needs of others which the group sees the leader demonstrate, and not just in the words they hear the leader say, which provides a model for effective group direction. *Satsang* leaders typically have developed strong group leadership skills. They use open-ended questioning effectively to promote self-investigation, and encourage members to become aware of their unused power, but not to foster dependency. They make the members aware of their cultural heritage and ethnic self-knowledge. They have great clarifying skills, and often take support of scriptures and mythological references. They show a sense of responsiveness and authenticity verbally and nonverbally. They bring the members great enthusiasm, and promote creativity. They are very active, sensitive listeners who can empathize with and are very compassionate towards members. They have sincere interest in the wellbeing and growth of the members. Such skills are equally applicable to leadership of Western groups (Chen & Rybak, 2004).

Group leadership requires that facilitators develop an ability to tune in to and manage the dynamic tensions that are a part of any group. From traditional Indian philosophy these dynamic forces are termed *gunas*. Gunas are of three types: *sattva, rajas,* and *tamas.* Respectively, they concern wise awareness, power, and maintaining a steady state. Effective group leaders learn to monitor and balance these forces in healthy ways for the group so members can build relationships with one another, learn new perspectives within the context of the group, and develop behaviors that better enable them to accomplish life goals (Ballantine, 1999; Mishra, 1973; Rybak & Deuskar, 2004, 2010). Such concepts drawn from Indian sources can provide added insight into the leadership process for groups in a Western setting.

Groups can provide a place for bringing together and directing the creative energies of the members in positive ways. Breath is a basic element of life that can bring energy or stifle it depending on whether breathing is done well or becomes too shallow. Group leaders can teach members breathing skills and remind members to be aware of the quality of their breathing at key moments within a group meeting such as at the very start and sometimes at the end. Encouraging members to take full diaphragmatic breaths may help set the stage metaphorically as well as physically for dealing with important issues fully, then letting these issue go once they have been addressed (Rybak & Deuskar, 2004, 2010).

Satsang leaders may conduct guided group meditation sessions. The leader usually gives instructions to maintain a relaxed but alert body posture, to focus on the breath, to be a passive onlooker of one's own mind and to not get carried away with any thoughts. The leader keeps the time, and takes responsibility for bringing the practitioners back to an awareness of their body after the session. Such guided meditation, practiced in groups, is very effective, as the group energy induces greater peace and better focus during the session. Versions of these skills can be used within Western counseling groups as well for general purposes of promoting calm but focused sessions or for specifically addressing particular symptomatic needs of clients such as those who are especially anxious or distracted.

Group Leadership and Mindfulness

A group leader typically sets the pace and structure for a group and has a major impact on the functioning and development of a group. The ability of the group leader to focus clearly and sensitively on group members while being mindful of the implications of member behaviors and interactions with one another is governed through the self-regulation of the group leader (Wang, 2005). The degree of self-compassion of a group leader and other group members is reflected through compassionate and flexible interaction and treatment of others in the group, as the group emotional environment acts as a kind of "sacred mirror" (Krystal, 2003) for each person in the group including the leader. As suggested above, the inner harmony and coherence of the group leader as well as other members contributes to the overall harmony of the group as a whole (McCraty, 2010).

Borrowing from ancient Eastern as well as more recent Western approaches, group leaders can encourage a mindfulness approach by group members by asking them to reflect on their inner cognitive and emotional reactions within the moment during group interactions and how these inner reactions may inform them of their relationships with others in the group (Cohen & Cantor, 2010). Asking group members to begin to describe their insights into the motivations and actions of others in the group (Cohen & Cantor, 2010) offers group members the opportunity to vicariously step out of their own worlds and into the experiences of others, thereby potentially enhancing the level of their social intelligence (Goleman, 2007) as group members learn to empathize and relate more effectively with their fellows.

Focus Group Research on *Satsang* Experience

Research on *satsang* groups in India based on focus group discussions found that *satsang* members experienced relief from daily stress, gained a sense of unity with less negativity, were more accepting of differences, and felt more altruistic. Overall, the experience of participation in a *satsang* group enhanced member wellbeing (Singh et al., 2014).

SUMMARY

The approach of *satsang* is embedded within a deep collectivistic tradition of cultures as in India, while the Western approaches to group counseling typically do not include such a high cultural context within the structure and process of group interaction. Eastern approaches to group work through such orientations as *satsang* can help augment and inform the traditional Western approaches to group counseling (Khanna, McDowell, Perumbilly, & Titus, 2009). In making decisions about the structure of various types of groups that they are facilitating, group leaders can consider the process and types of inner and outer connections made by group members within *satsang* groups. Then, the decision whether the level of personal development encouraged within *satsang* groups might be appropriate for other types of groups common to Western settings can be considered.

The model provided by *satsang* groups that focus on seeking truth in the companionship of fellow truth-seekers offers a particular context to gain additional understanding of the application of key group counseling skills identified by Lieberman, Yalom, and Miles (1973): emotional stimulation, caring, meaning attribution, and executive functions. With respect to emotional stimulation, while *satsang* groups have been traditionally formed around deeply held spiritual beliefs, Western groups can be developed around other types of commonly held values appropriate to the group being formed. Examples of these types of groups include recovery from domestic violence, divorce, and sexual abuse. Offering caring for one another within *satsang* groups is particularly emphasized and contributes considerably to the ongoing sense of cohesion and therapeutic impact of such groups. Meaning attribution is another hallmark of *satsang* groups as key values of the group members are explored and highlighted. The executive functions of *satsang* leaders are likewise prominent organizing aspects of *satsang* groups as the *satsang* leaders have advanced knowledge and skills that tend to be well known to and honored by the group participants.

While developed to meet the needs of Indian group members to best fit their traditional collectivistic cultural practices (Singh et al., 2014), particular aspects of *satsang* group leadership can be applied to Western groups including continuous self-development of group leaders and the use of mindfulness skills in utilizing the power of the present moment in the midst of group member interactions. Although these ideas are not entirely new to Western group leadership, the collective nature of Indian culture offers a particular lens with which to more sharply view these aspects and increase understanding of their place and potential. The combination of extended group leader self-development and mindful attention to the group offers the potential to enhance group leaders' skills in timing of key interventions such as knowing when to step in to share relevant information, promote group member relationship-building interaction, and when to encourage group member reflection in order to modulate the energy and learning potential within the group. In this way the leadership skills used in *satsang* groups can be applied to advance the interactive process of Western groups.

In conclusion, skills for effective *satsang* group leadership that have direct application with respect to the leadership of Western groups include being action oriented, compassionate, sensitive with empathic listening abilities, and skilled in appropriate confrontation. Other desired characteristics include a high degree of self-awareness, knowledge of cultures and ethnic backgrounds, responsiveness to group members, and ability to use power judiciously. Additional group leadership skills include the ability to be encouraging of others, creative, and oriented toward a strength-based stance toward members while attending to their wellbeing and positive growth. Ultimately, as with other group leadership skills, *satsang* group leaders promote clarity of understanding for group members without fostering dependency upon the *satsang* leader in order that members are empowered to implement learning that has occurred within the group in an intentional and mindful manner.

REFERENCES

Ballentine, R. (1999). *Radical healing: Integrating the world's great therapeutic traditions to creative a new transformative medicine*. New York, NY: Harmony Books.

BAPS Charities (2012). *Gujarat Earthquake rehabilitation and relief work report*. Retrieved from http://www.bapscharities.org/mediacenter/documents/images/guj_eq.pdf

Bose, G. (1930). The psychological outlook in Hindu philosophy. *Indian Journal of Psychology*, *5*, 119–146.

Brantley, J., Doucette, D., & Lindell, A. (2008). Mindfulness, meditation, and health. In A. L. Strozier & J. E. Carpenter (Eds.), *Introduction to alternative and complementary therapies* (pp. 9–29). New York, NY: Haworth.

Brown, R. P., & Gerbarg, P. L. (2005). *Sudarshan Kriya* Yogic breathing in the treatment of stress, anxiety, and depression: Part II—Clinical applications and guidelines. *The Journal of Alternative and Complementary Medicine*, *11*, 711–717.

Chen, M., & Rybak, C. (2004). *Group leadership skills: Interpersonal process in group counseling*. Belmont, CA: Brooks/Cole.

Cohen, M. A., & Cantor, D. (2010). Mindfulness in group psychotherapy. In S. Fehr (Ed.), *101 interventions in group therapy* (pp. 477–481). New York, NY: Routledge.

Easwaran, E. (1975). *The Bhagavad Gita for daily living volume 1: The end of sorrow*. Tomales, CA: Nilgiri.

Frisk, L. (2002). The satsang network: A growing post-Osho phenomenon. *Nova Religio: The Journal of Alternative and Emergent Religions*, *6*, 64–85. doi:10.1525/nr.2002.6.1.64

Goenka, S. N. (2013). *Vipassana meditation*. Retrieved from http://www.dhamma.org/en/qanda.shtml

Goleman, D. (2005). *Emotional intelligence*. New York, NY: Bantam.

Goleman, D. (2007). *Social intelligence: The new science of human relationship*. New York, NY: Bantam.

Hanson, R., & Mendius, R. (2009). *Buddha's brain: The practical neuroscience to happiness, love, and wisdom*. Oakland, CA: New Harbinger.

Keysers, C. (2008). The mirror neuron system: New frontiers. *Social Neuroscience, 3*, 193–198.

Khanna, A., McDowell, T., Perumbilly, S., & Titus, G. (2009). Working with Asian Indian American families: A Delphi study. *Journal of Systemic Therapies, 28*, 52–71.

Kim, B. S. K., Atkinson, D. R., & Umemoto, D. (2001). Asian cultural values and counseling process: Current knowledge and directions for future research. *The Counseling Psychologist, 29*, 570–603.

Krystal, S. (2003). A nondual approach to EMDR. In J. J. Prendergast, P. Fenner, & S. Krystal (Eds.), *The Sacred Mirror: Nondual wisdom and psychotherapy*. St. Paul, MN: Paragon House.

Lieberman, M. A., Yalom, I. V, & Miles, M. B. (1973). *Encounter groups: First facts*. New York, NY: Basic Books.

McCraty, R. (2010). Coherence: Bridging personal, social, and global health. *Alternative Therapies, 16*, 10–24.

Mishra, R. S. (1973). *Yoga sutras: The textbook of yoga psychology*. Garden City, NY: Anchor.

Neff, C. (2009). Self-compassion. In M. R. Leary & R. H. Hoyle (Eds.) *Handbook of individual differences in social behavior* (pp. 561–573). New York, NY: Guilford.

Pandya, S. P. (2014). Sudarshan Kriya and Pranayama: Insights into an Indic spiritual practice for promoting well-being. *Journal of Spirituality in Mental Health, 16*(1), 51–71. doi:10.1080/19349637.2014.864544

Perls, F. (2010). Coopers Union—Lecture Series: "The self. Finding the self through gestalt therapy" (from a talk delivered March 6, 1957). *International Journal for Gestalt Therapy, 33*, 27–51.

Rizzolatti, G., & Fabri-Destro, M. (2008). The mirror neuron system and its role in social cognition. *Current Opinion in Neurobiology, 18*, 179–184.

Rybak, C. (2004). Indigenous healing practices: Traditional forms from the core of being. In M. Blows, S. Srinivasan, J. Blows, P. Bankart, M. DelMonte, & Y. Haruki (Eds.), *The relevance of the wisdom traditions in contemporary society: The challenge to psychology* (pp. 125–138). Delft, The Netherlands: Eburon.

Rybak, C. (2013). Nurturing positive mental health: Mindfulness for wellbeing in counseling. *International Journal for the Advancement of Counseling, 35*, 110–119. doi:10.1007/s10447-012-9171-7

Rybak, C., & Deuskar, M. (2004). The yoga of group work: How a wisdom tradition illuminates current practice. *Group, 28*, 191–209. Retrieved from http://www.egps.org/

Rybak, C., & Deuskar, M. (2010). Enriching group counseling through integrating yoga concepts and practices. *Journal of Creativity in Mental Health, 5*, 3–14. doi:10.1080/15401381003626782

Schulte-Ruther, M. Markowitsch, H. J., Fink, G. R., & Piefke, M. (2007). Mirror neuron and theory of mind mechanisms involved in face-to-face interactions: A functional magnetic resonance imaging approach to empathy. *Journal of Cognitive Neuroscience, 19*, 1354–1372.

Shaw, R., Gupta, M., & Sarma, A. (2003). Community recovery and its sustainability: Lessons from Gujarat earthquake of India. *The Australian Journal of Emergency Management, 18*(2), 28–34.

Siegel, D. J. (2007). The mindful brain: Reflection and attunement in the cultivation of wellbeing. New York, NY: Norton

Siegel, D. J. (2012). *The developing mind: How relationships and the brain interact to shape who we are* (2nd ed.). New York, NY: Guilford.

Singh, K., Jain, A., & Singh, D. (2014). Satsang: A culture specific effective practice for well-being. In H. Águeda Marujo, L. M. Neto, (Eds.), *Positive nations and communities: Collective, qualitative and cultural-sensitive processes in positive psychology* (pp. 79–100). New York. NY: Springer.

Sulekha, S., Thennarasu, K., Vedamurthachar, A., Raju, T. R., & Kutty, B. M. (2006). Evaluation of sleep architecture in practitioners of Sudarshan Kriya Yoga and Vipassana meditation. *Sleep and Biological Rhythms*, *4*, 207–214.

Uvnas-Moberg, K. (1998). Oxytocin may mediate the benefits of positive social interaction and emotions. *Psychoneuroendocrinology*, *23*, 819–835.

Wang, S. (2005). A conceptual framework for integrating research related to the physiology of compassion and the wisdom of the Buddhist teachings. In P. Gilbert (Ed.), *Compassion: Conceptualization, research and use in psychotherapy* (pp. 75–120). New York, NY: Routledge.

Yalom, I., & Leszcz. M. (2005). *The theory and practice of group psychotherapy* (5th ed.). New York, NY: Basic Books.

Understanding the Islamic Concept of *Usrah* and Its Application to Group Work

Nabisah Ibrahim
Siti Rozaina Kamsani
University Utara Malaysia

Julia Champe
Southern Illinois University–Carbondale

With the significant growth of the Muslim population and the promotion of multicultural group work for diverse populations in the United States, there is an increased need to provide group approaches that are relevant to the concepts and spirituality of Islam. The Usrah *group, an Islamic group work approach commonly practiced by Asian Muslims, and its goals, history, and foundational principles are described. Comparisons with Western group work practice are made, and gender homogeneity, leader and members' roles, and group norms are discussed. Culturally relevant application issues, future research, and implications for group workers are included.*

Studies show that factors such as gender, religion, culture, and identity are important aspects of well being that influence interaction and outcomes of group process (M. S. Corey & Corey, 2006; Pederson, 2000; Sue & Sue, 2012). For group members to fully benefit from the group process, group workers need to move beyond traditional group practices, especially when working with group members from diverse religions and cultures, including the Muslim population.

Muslims represent approximately one-fifth of today's global population. It is estimated that there are seven to nine million Muslims in the United States (Abu-Ras & Abu-Bader, 2008; Smither & Khorsandi, 2009). In the United States, more attention has been given to Muslim cultures in the Middle East. However, there are large

Muslim populations located in the Asia Pacific region, including the Southeast Asian countries (Hall, Livingston, Brown, & Mohabir, 2011). While Muslims around the world share the same foundation of Islamic faith and beliefs, the implementation of Islam is largely influenced by cultural norms and practices (Baggerly & Abugidari, 2010; Banawi & Stockton, 1993). Discerning between culture and religion can be difficult for Westerners. An illustrative example: As followers of Islam, many (but not all) Muslim women cover their heads with the *Hijab* (head scarf) as dictated by their faith. What the *Hijab* looks like, however, varies by culture. In Southeast Asian countries, such as Malaysia, Indonesia, and Singapore, Muslim women typically wear colorful *Hijab* and clothing, while Muslim women in other cultures may wear only black.

Given the large size of the Muslim population and the current trend of Asian immigrants in the United States (Hall et al., 2011), it may be increasingly necessary and useful for American group workers to have more than a passing knowledge of Islam and the variety of cultures, which practice it. A small body of group work literature describes working with Muslim populations using traditional Western group approaches, such as psycho-educational (Chongruksa & Prinyapol, 2011), counseling (Shechtman & Tanus, 2006), and grief therapy (Baggerly & Abugidari, 2010). Other authors have argued that applying Islamic spirituality to traditional Western helping interventions is a necessity when working with Asian Muslims (Hall et al., 2011; Hodge, 2000). There is currently a gap in the group work literature on approaches that incorporate relevant concepts found in Muslim culture and Islamic spirituality. In fact, Islamic spiritual practice offers a rich tradition of a form of group work that has yet to be described in the group work literature.

The purpose of this article is to describe an Islamic group work approach commonly practiced by Asian Muslims known as an *Usrah* group. We will begin with an overview of the *Usrah* group, its goals, and history. Group structure, gender homogeneity, group leader and member roles, and norms are described. Included in the overview are brief descriptions of the foundational concepts or "pillars" underlying the practice of *Usrah*, and the Islamic concepts of family and universality that are shared by all Muslims across cultures and countries. Next, the principles of *Usrah* are applied to group work practice, and in the concluding section, implications for practice and directions for future research are presented.

Through the explication of its practice and concepts, the reader will understand how the *Usrah* group is unique, and in some ways similar, to group work practiced in the United States. Throughout this article, occasional parallels will be drawn between the *Usrah* group and

Western group work concepts and practice. However, drawing cross-cultural comparisons runs the risk of reinforcing an etic or cultural universality perspective where one may not exist (Draguns, 2003). The reader is encouraged to "hold lightly" the Western group work lens. For instance, while we discuss the practice of same-gender group composition, a deeper analysis of its effectiveness or of the social justice issues which are (from a Western perspective) inherent in gender-segregation will need to be addressed elsewhere. Instead, it is the authors' intention to describe a culturally specific phenomenon for a Western group work audience.

THE *USRAH* GROUP

Islam is a way of life for Muslims, and a group orientation is an integral part of daily life. From daily congregation prayers to annual religious feasts like *Eid-ul Fitri,* which celebrates the end of *Ramadan*, a sense of unity among Muslims is regularly reinforced. Every Muslim, for instance, is encouraged to perform the five daily formal prayers or *salat*. Congregational prayers held at a *mosque* are opportunities for Muslims to develop a sense of belonging and caring for one another. Even if a Muslim is alone or unable to attend a congregational prayer, he or she is assured of praying with others nearby; *salat* times are established by geographic location. This group orientation strengthens Muslims' faith as well as their relationships with one another (Banawi & Stockton, 1993) and is pervasive throughout the Muslim world. In a discussion on "generic" or transferrable workplace skills developed through Islamic religious and educational practices, S. Ahmad (2012) described the collectivist Muslim perspective at the heart of these practices, noting "It is almost impossible for someone to work toward a goal individually" (p. 46). One of the important Islamic values in developing a strong and harmonious society is the concept of unity. This concept of unity begins with the family.

Usrah is the Arabic word for family. Arabic connotations of the word include a protective shield, and individuals joined together for a common cause (www.masgreaterla.org). A religious educational activity, the *Usrah* group or "circle discussion," has been cited as an effective educational method (Baba, 1991; Tamuri, 2010) with deep roots in Islamic religious traditions (S. Ahmad, 2012). The term *Usrah* is interchangeable with "study circle," or *Halaqah*. The social definition of *Usrah* has expanded to mean supporting and helping the individual to develop a better life by understanding and practicing Islamic teachings and values (Hassan Al-Bana, 1985). In this regard, the *Usrah* group is formed through participation with a group of people who share common characteristics such as the faith, beliefs, and values of Islam (www.masgreaterla.org). The *Usrah* group provides support among members for righteousness and good deeds, and renews members' commitment to Islamic teachings and principles (Kamsani, 2013; Muslim American Society Greater LA, 2015).

Goals of *Usrah* Group

The *Usrah* group plays an important role in the social, educational, and spiritual aspects of Muslim society, which are reflected in its goals. The goals of the *Usrah* group are to (a) strengthen members' relationship with the Creator, (b) make Islam a way of life, (c) encourage the individual's personal and spiritual growth, (d) cultivate a sense of belonging, (e) practice teamwork, (f) instill a sense of unity among group members and all Muslims, and (g) enhance society as a whole.

The main objective of *Usrah* is to provide a space for Muslims to learn about God *(Allah)*, His religion (Islam), and His Prophet. In learning about *Allah* and Islam, there are two primary sources of knowledge; The *Quran* and the *Hadith* (Imam Nawawi, 2001). The *Quran* contains the words of *Allah* revealed in Arabic to the Prophet Muhammad. The *Hadith* contains the sayings and actions of the Prophet Muhammad, and explains the content of the *Quran*. The sayings and actions of the Prophet, guided by *Allah* through His *Quranic* verses, are the model for Muslims to follow as their way of life. In the *Usrah* group, the *Quranic* verses and the *Hadith* are discussed among group members to disseminate knowledge about *Allah,* His religion, and His Prophet, to meet the goals of strengthening members' relationship with The Creator *(Allah),* and to encourage daily living in accordance with Islam.

A related goal of the *Usrah* group is to help the individual achieve personal and spiritual growth. Islam emphasizes *Ummatan Wasata,* a balanced society that promotes overall well-being in terms of physical/material and spiritual growth (Imam Nawawi, 2001). Islam encourages Muslims to lead a balanced life for the purpose of achieving success in this world and the hereafter. In *Usrah* groups, the discussion not only focuses on Islamic spiritual teaching, but also covers a wide range of topics including social relationships, marriage, Islamic law, business transactions, daily prayer, interpersonal development, Muslim attributes, morality, family matters, individual rights, and social justice. In this way, the *Usrah* group provides an environment in which members can build a Muslim identity while strengthening spirituality. This in turn benefits the whole of Muslim society. Islam emphasizes the notion of brotherhood and sisterhood among Muslims, regardless of race, ethnicity, culture, and age. In order to achieve this vision, it is important to instill a sense of belonging in the hearts of all Muslims. A sense of belonging, a feeling of unity, and teamwork among members are further goals of the *Usrah* group.

History of *Usrah* Group

The *Usrah* group is an important component of life for many contemporary Muslims wherein Islamic spirituality and cultural values are reinforced. The objective of *Usrah* is to train and educate the broad spectrum of Muslim society about Islamic knowledge and way of life.

Practically, the *Usrah* group is implemented in many different contexts, including schools, nongovernmental organizations, government organizations, and informally among friends or neighbors out of personal interest (Kamsani, 2013).

The *Usrah* group functions as a mechanism to help join the hearts of its members by developing true brotherhood and sisterhood, trust and mutual understanding, loyalty, and a sense of belonging among Muslims (*Usrah*, 2003). In fact, the concept of brotherhood (*Al-Ikhwan*) means each individual Muslim is a brother to all other Muslims, an essential value that reinforces Islamic unity. The implementation of *Usrah* began when Prophet Muhammad used this approach as a method to deliver his message of Islam in Arab society. The Prophet Muhammad preached his message to his family members, relatives, and close friends.

Since the foundation of Islam, the implementation of *Usrah* has been practiced as one of the strategies of Islamic progress. In 1928, Al-Imam Hassan Al-Bana introduced the concept of *Usrah* as an educational training method among members of his organization, Al-Ikhwan Al-Muslimeen (Muslim Brotherhood). Al-Ikhwan Al-Muslimeen was the first Islamic political organization, and its objective is to understand modern Islamic radicalism. In this organization, *Usrah* is a monthly discussion among Al-Ikhwan's members for whom attendance is compulsory to strengthen the internal structure of the organization and address any external challenges (Aboul-Enein, 2003; Kamsani, 2013).

The *Usrah* group has become an important social medium for providing knowledge and information about Islamic teachings and practices among all Muslim followers (Kamsani, 2013). Especially in Malaysia, *Usrah* groups are an established and effective means for developing a good relationship with God (Allah), helping people to deal with life struggles, and encouraging self-improvement (Din, Mohamad Yusak, & Abd Manap, 2011) and future planning (Manuty, 1989). In an ethnographic study on the emerging Malaysian "study circle movement" of the 1980s, Baba (1991) identified several ways *Usrah* groups had positive effects on individuals and organizations, and on Malaysian educational development. While a review of the literature indicates little research exists on *Usrah* group dynamics or process, it is a well-established and effective *Tarbiyah* or education method.

Implementation of *Usrah* in Educational Settings

The *Usrah* group is a significant method for preparing Muslims to find and develop their intellectual and leadership abilities, and enhance quality of life based on Islamic principles. It is commonly used in Malaysian educational settings, including religious, government, and private schools, as well as in universities for *sahsiah* (self-development), *akhlaq* (moral development), and Muslim identity development. While the research is limited, *Usrah* groups have been identified as an effective educational approach for improving students' moral and identity development (Mustari & Mohd Salleh, 2010; Tamuri, 2007). A well-respected higher educational setting, the International Islamic University Malaysia (IIUM), has implemented *Usrah* group as a curricular activity that supports students' academics.

Established in 1983, IIUM aims to produce well-rounded professionals by emphasizing strong academic performance and good Islamic values and ethics (Mohd Amin, Yusuf, & Haneef, 2011). Each IIUM student is required to take credited courses, Study Circle (*Usrah*) I and II. For first year students, for instance, the *Usrah* group is offered in two different modules, each of which provides different content pertaining to students' values, behaviors, and spirituality. First semester *Usrah* group content focuses on strengthening and enhancing students' perception of Islam as a worldview for balanced civilization development. In the second semester, the *Usrah* group focuses on promoting a well-balanced personal and collectivistic life. This module helps students understand the concept of consistency *(Istiqamah)* and inculcates a strong sense of belonging among all Muslim students (Shuriye, 2011).

Pillars of *Usrah*

The spiritual and social purposes of the *Usrah* group are guided by three main principles or pillars; *Ta'aruf, Tafahhum*, and *Takaful* (Hassan Al-Bana, 1985). These principles, among others, are part of the philosophical and spiritual foundations of Islamic thought and practice, which provide "essential guidelines for Muslims' faith and conduct" (Banawi & Stockton, 1993). The pillars are descriptive of both the practice and process of *Usrah* groups. The terms are used to describe the group purpose, attitudes, and behaviors of group leaders and members, as well as the group processes and developmental stages of the *Usrah* group.

The first pillar of *Usrah* is *Ta'aruf,* or coming to know one another (I. Ahmad, 2005; Hassan Al-Bana, 1985). *Ta'aruf* is an action, a purposeful attempt to get to know another person's background, interests, hobbies, difficulties, customs, and culture (S. Ahmad, 2012). Members of an *Usrah* group must strive to come to know the behavior, self, and identity of the other members. It is through the intentional actions of *Ta'aruf* that the second pillar, *Tafahhum*, develops.

Tafahhum is mutual understanding or unity of thought, especially around Islamic religious beliefs, which helps individuals work together. "When everybody in a group understands their goal, objectives, and duties, they can generate ideas and act accordingly to achieve them" (S. Ahmad, 2012, p. 46). This second pillar requires group members to make efforts to understand each other by being open to differences in opinions and values. On its webpage for *Usrah* groups, the Muslim American Society of Greater L.A. describes *Tafahhum* as an intimate, understanding relationship: "It means that nuances are not always required, sentences often times do not need to be completed, and the bonds of friendship are very tight and solid" (Muslim American Society Greater LA, 2015).

The third principle of *Usrah* is *Takaful*, a solidarity and cooperation among Muslims based on shared responsibility for one another. The concept of *Takaful* denotes joint liability for the well-being of fellow Muslims, and empathy towards others (S. Ahmad, 2012). *Takaful* develops as a result of the previously mentioned pillars, actions, which engender feelings of brotherhood and sisterhood. Within a particular *Usrah, Takaful* may be most analogous to the concept of group cohesiveness (Yalom & Leszcz, 2005), yet it also has a broader meaning; *Takaful* means Muslims have a responsibility to carry the burdens of others.

An additional concept, sometimes described as the fourth pillar of *Usrah*, underscores the role and purpose that *Usrah* groups have for Muslims. *Tarbiyah* comes from the Arabic word for increase, growth, and loftiness (Muslim American Society Greater LA, 2015), and refers to a system of education or guidance. To be actively involved in an *Usrah* group is one way in which Muslims engage in *Tarbiyah*, or a continuous process of mental, physical, and spiritual development.

Structure of *Usrah* Group

The *Usrah* group shares some characteristics of Western group types, especially psychoeducational groups, and at the same time, it is unique. An *Usrah* group usually consists of between 6 and 10 members although the size varies depending on group objectives and age of members. *Usrah* groups for college students may be larger, with 8 to

12 members in a university setting. For older adults, *Usrah* groups are usually smaller, with 5 to 8 members. Literature on group work with older adults suggests smaller groups may be necessary due to members' physical and psychological needs (Henderson & Gladding, 2004). Furthermore, the elderly population in Malaysia is the smallest age group (Department of Statistics Malaysia, 2012); there are not many very old people. As the life expectancy of elderly people in Malaysia increases, the difference in group size may be eliminated.

Typically an *Usrah* group meets weekly, with different topics assigned each week. Depending on the setting, it may be time limited. For college students, an *Usrah* group may be conducted over two semesters as a 2-hr weekly group with specific learning modules. An *Usrah* group established by women in a neighborhood, on the other hand, may meet once a week for a year or more, as desired. *Usrah* groups can have an open or closed group membership. In a college setting, the format of *Usrah* may be a closed group, whereas in a community or work setting, it may have an open group membership. There is no requirement or restriction for attendance, yet it is encouraged in an open group membership.

Gender Homogeneity

One of the unique characteristics of the *Usrah* group is its homogeneity in terms of gender. The group composition can either be all male or all female. Gender separation in *Usrah* groups follows Islamic religious requirements. In Islam, *Haya* (modesty or shyness) is part of *Iman* (faith). It is important for both genders to be modest and maintain dignity. In addition, according to Islamic legislation, relationships between men and women are founded on a commandment in the *Al-Quran* (Holy Book). As stated in one *Quranic* verse (Surah Al-Ahzab: 53), "And when you ask the ladies for anything, ask them from before a screen. That makes for greater purity for your hearts and for theirs" (Ali, 1994). The separation of genders in *Usrah* groups provides both men and women with comfortable and safe environments in which to discuss personal issues that may not be appropriate to discuss in mixed company.

Group Leader Roles

The requirements for gender-separation apply to the group leaders for *Usrah* groups as well. Men's *Usrah* groups are led by a *Naqeeb* (male leader) and a *Naqeebah* (female leader) leads women's groups. To be qualified to be *Naqeeb* or *Naqeebah*, the leader must have basic knowledge of Islam. In some cases, the *Naqeeb* and *Naqeebah* receive specific training in the *Usrah* model or will be chosen based on previous experience. For instance, in educational settings where *Usrah* is a curricular experience, the *Naqeeb* and *Naqeebah* receive training to become *Usrah* educators, able to teach and guide group members as well as answer questions about Islam. The *Naqeeb* and *Naqeebah* also organize programs to enhance the *Ukhuwah* (brotherhood or sisterhood) relationships among members. For example, he or she may plan outside activities for group members such as home visits, picnics, or travel.

Regardless of setting, the *Naqeeb* and *Naqeebah* must be role models to the other members in the *Usrah* by demonstrating good behavior in speech and action. Leaving room for cultural variations, Muslims are expected to be nonconfrontational, show respect to elders, and be accepting of other's ideas and perspectives. Modeling positive attributes may encourage the group members to be positive examples for others. Muslims should avoid the hypocrisy of having high expectations of others without following suit. As mentioned in one of the *Quranic* verses (2:44) "Do you order righteousness of the people and forget yourselves while you recite the Scripture? Then will you not reason?" (Ali, 1994). This verse explains the importance of being congruent in one's good behavior and an example to others.

Member Roles and Group Norms

Certain roles and responsibilities are expected of *Usrah* group members in order to formulate an effective group that reaches its objectives. One of the most important member responsibilities is sincerity of intention. In Islamic faith, every deed begins with intention. Every person will get rewards, in this world and in the hereafter, for intentional good deeds.

This concept is applied in the development of each *Usrah* group where all members are encouraged to purify their intentions and willingness to join the groups (Din, Muhammad Yusak, & Abd Manap, 2011). The sincerity to join the *Usrah* group will determine the effectiveness of the group as well as the group dynamic (I. Ahmad, 2007). It is required for the *Naqeeb* or *Naqeebah* to emphasize the importance of sincerity of intention to all prospective group members so they can willingly decide to join the group and prepare to follow the group guidelines.

The second member responsibility for *Usrah* is preparation for participation. In an *Usrah* group, all group members are expected to prepare themselves for the *Usrah* sessions. They are expected to cognitively, physically, and spiritually prepare by attending all group sessions, preparing group materials, and participating in group discussion. The amount of preparation is different based on the types of *Usrah* group. For example, a woman who joins an *Usrah* group to develop a better Muslim identity may be encouraged to prepare herself with the knowledge on effective Muslim characteristics and share these with the group. The expectation of preparation helps establish a facilitative group norm that all group members will contribute to the group discussion. It can also instill feelings of empowerment and group ownership among members.

One expectation of group members and leaders in an *Usrah* group is avoidance of arguments and contentious debate. Islam does not encourage Muslims to use confrontation while dealing with defensive people, especially in the group setting. According to Islamic teachings and principles, the best way to deal with defensive people is through the policy of patience, tolerance, and avoidance. This may be considerably different from Western group practice. To Western group workers, avoidance of confrontation can negatively impact productive group work and inhibit effective interaction (G. Corey, Corey, Callanan, & Russell, 2004). However, from an Islamic perspective, avoiding confrontation is good behavior. It is not seen as a sign of a cowardice or weakness but as a sign of patience and tolerance. The noncontentious, collaborative atmosphere helps *Usrah* group members remain connected despite any differences of religious interpretation (Baba, 1991). This perspective provides Muslims with the opportunity to become stronger and demonstrate perseverance, rather than doing harm to other people by becoming defensive (Khan, 2005).

Practicing patience and tolerance in the group setting helps the individual contribute his or her opinion and demonstrate respect for others' opinions. By striving to uphold the principle of *Takaful* that promotes cooperation and the practice of patience and tolerance, each group member learns to contribute his or her opinion while demonstrating respect for others. This norm is important in developing and strengthening a positive group feeling among group members and leaders (I. Ahmad, 2005). In fact, individuals have cited the collaborative learning environment, discussion content, and mutually beneficial relationships among members as reasons for joining an *Usrah* group (Baba, 1991).

APPLICATION OF *USRAH* PRINCIPLES TO GROUP WORK PRACTICE

While commonly translated in English as "study group," the *Usrah* group has little in common with such a task-type group, particularly given its important place in the spiritual and social lives of its members. It is in some ways similar to a Western-style psychoeducational group, in that member learning is the focus and the leader is charged with presenting content and facilitating discussion. As noted earlier, while cross-cultural comparisons may result in oversimplification, there are interesting parallels and similarities between Western group models and *Usrah* group which are offered here for reflection and understanding. In this section, a comparison of *Usrah* and Western group work principles and practices is offered, framed by the principles of the *Usrah* group.

The three pillars of *Usrah* group provide guidance for group leaders and members, influence content and process, and shape structure. In following the principles of *Ta'aruf, Tafahhum*, and *Takaful*, leaders are helped in developing *Usrah* group content, facilitating group discussion, and encouraging member interaction (I. Ahmad, 2007). For members, these principles also provide direction and establish expectations for member attitude and behavior.

***Ta'aruf*: To Know One Another**

Ta'aruf is a principle, a practice and a process. The term refers to the code guiding Muslims' coming to know one another in an intimate, personal way, as well as the process of doing so. It is also a descriptor of a distinct introductory section that occurs during an *Usrah* group. Typically, the *Naqeeb* or *Naqeebah* begins the session by welcoming the group members, introducing themselves, and encouraging members to share as well. Leader self-disclosure is usually cautioned against in Western group work, and subject to much consideration and guidelines (M. S. Corey, Corey, & Corey, 2010) especially in beginning development stages. It is a common practice in the *Usrah* group. Leaders self-disclose as a model and encouragement for group members.

Through *Ta'aruf*, group members will get the opportunity to learn about each others' background, behaviors, personality, and identity (I. Ahmad, 2007). Members may share as much about themselves, their family, and background as is comfortable. Self-disclosure about the facts and details about members' lives "outside of the group" is often discouraged in Western group work, where it can be seen as distracting from the here-and-now focus (M. S. Corey et al., 2010; Gladding, 2008). In *Usrah*, such personal disclosures are seen as benefitting the development of rapport and brotherhood/sisterhood among members.

Members are encouraged to take time and effort to listen respectfully and accept one another unconditionally. By knowing and accepting one another, the group leader and members create a safe environment to share further experiences. The practice and process of *Ta'aruf* creates a productive group environment (Kamsani, 2013) in which members can develop socialization techniques and imitative behaviors

(Yalom & Leszcz, 2005). Through *Ta'aruf*, the *Usrah* group allows members to expand their personal knowledge and skills by observing others' behaviors. Although the *Ta'aruf* usually takes place in the beginning of an *Usrah* session, getting to know one another informally continues throughout the life of the group. Having *Ta'aruf* in the earliest stage of *Usrah* is important in determining the success of *Usrah* group later on. As Gladding (2008) notes, self-disclosure is a "multidimensional activity" that "involves listening and receiving feedback" (p. 152). The more effort the group members put into getting to know each other, the better chance they will have to reach the second principle of *Usrah* group, *Tafahhum* (Nordin, Ahmad, & Tamuri, 2011).

Tafahhum: Understanding One Another

Tafahhum refers to the development of mutual understanding among group members. Members actively engage in group discussion and share their personal experiences, problems, and life struggles while striving to develop empathy, love, and care towards each other. To achieve real understanding of each other, group members are encouraged to accept and acknowledge each other's weaknesses and strengths. Members who open up about themselves will be able to get to know more about each other and develop a sense of brotherhood/sisterhood. Group members are also encouraged to be nonjudgmental and to avoid confrontations that can lead to fights and unkind feelings. To enhance *Tafahhum*, the group leader provides feedback and support, motivation, and encouragement for group members (I. Ahmad, 2007).

The principle of *Tafahhum* is aided by searching for similarities between group members while respecting differences. For example, in an *Usrah* group for international students from different countries, the *Naqeeb or Naqeebah* encourages members to share their cultures through food, storytelling, personal cultural experiences, and cultural activities. Another way of developing understanding, as well as a sense of belonging, among group members is through teamwork and team-building. Often used in an *Usrah* group for teenagers and college students in educational settings, members are assigned responsibility for tasks such as leading group discussion or making presentations. Through these activities, group members learn the importance of shared responsibility and working out differences in order to achieve a sense of unity. Because all group members are encouraged to recognize and respect the similarities and differences in feelings, thought, and actions among members, practicing *Tafahhum* allows group members to gain insight into human interactions and relationships. Hence, it promotes the concept of universality and interpersonal learning among group members that are important in determining group success (Yalom & Leszcz, 2005).

Takaful: Mutual Support

The third pillar of *Usrah*, the principle of *Takaful* highlights the relationship between and the cohesiveness among group members (Kamsani, 2013). Through the implementation of *Takaful*, group members support and help each other in making life decisions, share difficulties and burdens, and support each other without expecting anything in return (I. Ahmad, 2007; Nordin et al., 2011). The principle of *Takaful* builds a therapeutic working alliance among group members because it encourages the development of patience and tolerance, especially when dealing with defensive people. In this regard, *Takaful* promotes group cohesiveness and altruism that is essential for group success (Yalom & Leszcz, 2005). Muslims may be unwilling to expose their own weaknesses to others, or confront others about theirs, a value based on a belief that God will be more willing to overlook one's weaknesses in the afterlife if one has been willing to overlook the weaknesses of others while on earth (Hodge & Nadir, 2008). A working alliance among group members is considered crucial in promoting group cohesiveness.

Therefore, typical Western group work interventions like confrontation, a challenging technique used to help members understand how others may perceive them (M. S. Corey & Corey, 2006), would be very discomforting to many Muslims.

Tarbiyah: Growth and Development

In its broadest sense, the *Usrah* group is a mechanism of *Tarbiyah*, or the process of educating and uplifting individuals by increasing their knowledge and understanding of Islam, their relationships with Allah, themselves, and others. In working toward *Tarbiyah*, group members encourage, teach, and guide one another in practicing good behavior and building character. The *Usrah* group often develops a lively culture of advice giving and receiving among group members. Advice-giving among members increases the opportunities for member growth and betterment, and the development of a stronger Muslim identity (I. Ahmad, 2007).

Through shared advice, members learn how to boost their commitment, build interpersonal and intrapersonal skills, and be disciplined to achieve success in life. This stands in contrast to Western ideas about advice-giving, especially in a therapeutic group setting, where it may be seen as evidence of stalled group development or even interpersonal pathology (Yalom & Leszcz, 2005). Western-trained leaders are often taught to block advice-giving interactions among members and to refrain from giving advice, being mindful of the leader's implicit authority and the weight advice may carry with members (N. Brown, 2009). In the context of *Usrah* groups and the guiding principle of *Tarbiyah*, however, it may be more accurate to understand member-to-member advice-giving as a characteristic and culturally based form of imparting information. Furthermore, advice-giving among *Usrah* group members may be understood as both a type and product of Yalom's (Yalom & Leszcz, 2005) concept of altruism, wherein members "receive through giving" (p. 12).

IMPLICATIONS FOR GROUP PRACTICE AND FUTURE RESEARCH

Given its religious and political history and importance, its prominent role in formal educational systems, and its place in the everyday lives of Muslims around the world, the *Usrah* group is unique as a widely implemented group type with a vital role in contemporary societies. The *Usrah* is an example of a group whose guiding principles, structure, and process may be usefully applied when working with Muslims in other contexts and modalities.

While a group's purpose and goals may not have the religious educational focus of a traditional *Usrah*, incorporating key concepts and structures can create a familiar format for Muslim group members. The core concepts of *Usrah* can be applied to different types of group work. For example, group counselors can promote the norms of brotherhood/sisterhood among their Muslim group members to develop a strong group dynamic. The orienting principles, group leader roles, and even the responsibilities of group members can be promoted in either homogeneous or heterogeneous groups with Muslim group members.

Groups With Muslim Members

An understanding of Muslim cultures and the Islamic faith is a necessity for counselors working with Muslim populations (Ibrahim & Dykeman, 2011), especially given the social stigma surrounding mental health issues and cultural mistrust experienced by Muslims in the United States (Amri & Bemak, 2012). While literature is sparse, there is some evidence to suggest that Muslims may be open to some types of group work interventions, such as parenting or 12-Step groups, and that these can be effective modalities perhaps because of the collectivist orientation of many Islamic cultures (Nassar-McMillan & Hakim-Larson, 2003). In addition to a group orientation and group support among Muslims, Banawi and Stockton (1993) identified several Islamic values likely to positively influence group work with Muslims including emotional expression, respect for leaders, a tradition of reflection and contemplation, and a *Quranic* emphasis on optimism and personal responsibility. The authors note, however, that some of these same values may also negatively affect group work. Respect for authority figures, for instance, "may get in the way of frank and open expression of opinions and feelings about leaders," while Muslims' strong group orientation is "usually based on family, tribe, or religious affiliation" (p. 153). As a result and perhaps further exacerbated by cultural mistrust and experiences of discrimination, Muslims may hesitate to participate in a group with non-Muslim group members (Nassar-McMillan & Hakim-Larson, 2003).

CASE EXAMPLE: ACCULTURATION GROUP FOR MUSLIM AND NON-MUSLIM STUDENTS

Incorporating tenets of Islamic faith may be helpful for group work with Muslims (Banawi & Stockton, 1993; Hodge & Nadir, 2008). Consider, for example, an acculturation program for international graduate students newly arrived at an American university. A comprehensive program can combine a variety of learning experiences, including psychoeducational group work for addressing acculturation issues, practicing conversational English, and navigating American university and community settings. Such groups can be excellent settings for cross-cultural understanding and the development of mutual support among Muslims and non-Muslims.

To promote sisterhood among Muslim and non-Muslim female group members, for instance, the group leader could also use a unique *Usrah* group practice that is widely used in Malaysia: conducting group at a group members' house. This home visit practice is usually done after the group has reached the stage of *Tafahhum*, where members understand each other at a deeper level and accept each other's strengths and weaknesses. It helps group members further develop rapport, share each other's burdens beyond the group circle, and it extends the notion of family.

Muslim and non-Muslim members may benefit from the application of key *Usrah* group concepts. For instance, the group facilitator could apply the principle of *Ta'aruf* to group practice and process. In an immigrant acculturation group, a structured introduction period can help members from diverse backgrounds and cultures come to understand one another. Prior to engaging members in *Ta'aruf*, it may be helpful to begin with a brief discussion of the purpose and its foundation in Islamic perspectives on how all Muslims are considered family where they are expected to protect, love, and accept each other nonjudgmentally. Both Muslim and non-Muslim group members may benefit from a discussion on shared humanity with an emphasis on members' accepting similarities while respecting differences. As *Ta'aruf* is practiced throughout every session, the leader can gradually pose questions that encourage deeper member disclosure, for instance, how adapting to a new culture affects members' interpersonal relationships, career, and daily life.

Minorities in *Usrah*

Ethnic or cultural diversity of membership in an *Usrah* group may more likely be a reflection of the context in which the group occurs. For instance, in a culturally diverse environment like a university in the United States, where Muslims from around the world join in worship, an ethnically diverse *Usrah* group may be the norm. In Muslim countries, however, due to sociocultural and political factors, ethnic minority membership in an *Usrah* group may be a rarity.

In ethnically diverse Malaysia, for example, "religion correlates strongly with ethnicity" (Williamson, 2006, paragraph 36), and most members of the Malay ethnic majority are Muslim (Hassan, 2007).The population is primarily divided among three ethnic groups: Malay (60%), Chinese (27%), and Indian (11%), with only 2% other ethnicities. There are some ethnically Chinese and Indian Muslims; the 2000 Census cited some 400,000 ethnic Chinese Muslims in Malaysia (Department of Statistics Malaysia, 2001). Although these ethnic groups have retained their distinct cultures, interaction in social and economic arenas is generally positive (Cultural Information-Malaysia, 2009). For example, all Malaysians regularly share in Malay, Chinese, and Indian national holidays.) Nevertheless, while the relative ethnic homogeneity of Muslims in Malaysia suggests ethnic diversity in *Usrah* groups to be rare; all *Usrah* members are guided by the common purpose of *Usrah* and its guiding principles. Despite cultural differences, members come together to share in their religious beliefs.

Sexual orientation is generally considered a taboo topic in the Muslim population, regardless of location. In Muslim countries like Malaysia, Saudi Arabia, Egypt, and Brunei Darul Salam, homosexuality is considered a crime, as stated in the *Sha'riah* laws (Islamic Laws; see Faruqi, 2011). Because Muslims are beholden to the *Sha'riah* laws in their respective countries, it is unlikely that a homosexual individual would disclose their orientation in an *Usrah* group. Windwalker (2013a, 2013b), in anonymous interviews with a gay man and a lesbian woman in Malaysia, both of whom were Muslim, found that his interviewees did not disclose their orientation in most spheres of their lives, fearing legal and social repercussions. At present, there is a dearth of literature on homosexuality in the Muslim world, and it appears that no research exists on the religious behaviors of Muslims whose sexual orientations are forbidden by religious law. Windwalker's interviewees reported that their Muslim faith was a source of comfort and support, and described gay and lesbian communities of practicing Muslims. Given such anecdotal reports, this is an area in need of future research.

Respecting *Haya* in Group Work

An understanding of the religious and cultural foundation for traditional gender boundaries is essential when working with Muslim clients. Gender homogeneity in group member composition and leader selection is important (Amri & Bemak, 2012; Hodge & Nadir, 2008). Membership in a mixed gender group is a "cultural violation" (Hays, Arredondo, Gladding, & Toporek, 2010) for Muslims, and would be very uncomfortable for many Muslims as it would affect their *Haya* (modesty or shyness). In Islam, *Haya* is an important virtue for Muslims as it is indication of faith (Nofal, 1993). Shyness here, however, does not mean timidity or lack of confidence but rather self-consciousness about one's actions and their consequences. *Haya* has been described as the "uneasy feeling accompanied by embarrassment, caused by one's fear of being exposed for unworthy or indecent conduct" (Haya [Shyness], 2014, p. 21). For Muslims, little distinction is made between private life, where religion is practiced, and public secular life (Hodge & Nadir, 2008). While the concept of *Haya* is embedded in Islamic teachings and morality around the world, the practice of *Haya* is still an individual choice, and is shaped by culture (Stuff, 2014).

Let us return to considering the implications for Muslims of participation in the acculturation program for international graduate students; suppose this semester-long program employs direct classroom instruction, field trips, and as described earlier, and short-term psychoeducational groups. Uninformed group workers may not be aware of the ways these activities can pose challenges for Muslims committed to living in accordance with Islam.

Generally speaking, Muslim men and women are comfortable in a mixed-gender classroom setting, where interactions are limited to traditional student roles. Field trips to public spaces can also be appropriate mixed-gender learning experiences, as long as unrelated men and women were not required to sit together during transportation.

However, a mixed gender small group, an intimate setting with potential for close psychological and physical proximity and direct interaction among men and women, would be most discomfiting. To be in such a setting would jeopardize one's *Haya*, while a homogeneous-gender group is both an appropriate and productive setting. Here, individuals can freely share their experiences with members of their own gender without compromising the tenets of Islam. Freedom of expression in same-gender small groups is not limited to Muslims.

The idea of same-gender group composition producing a safe and productive group is supported in group research. In same-sex groups, members feel more comfortable expressing their opinions, feelings, and emotions (Zinck & Littrell, 2000). Hospital-based support groups for women with breast cancer are often facilitated by female medical or counseling professionals, under the assumptions that an all-female group creates a safe place in which women can share common experiences without being embarrassed to talk about their body parts in the presence of men. While research has shown that female group members perceive male group leaders as understanding of women's issues, female group members may also feel it is inappropriate to discuss some personal concerns in the presence of male leaders (Friedman, 1998). Mixed-gender groups may take longer to develop group cohesiveness among members (Rosenthal, 1985) and it has been suggested that mixed-gender groups may provide an environment for unhealthy relationships between men and women, distracting from the group process (Draper, Ritter, & Willingham, 2003). Although the literature suggests several benefits of mixed-gender groups, Nahon and Lander (2010), in an empirical randomized study of male gender-based and non gender-based groups, found significant increases in members' ability to express feelings, understanding of self and others, and positive psychological well-being in all-men's groups.

Furthermore, the literature suggests that male and female leadership styles and power differentials may negatively impact mixed-gender groups. Both men and women expect men to take leadership roles in groups, and men may see women's concerns as unimportant (A. Brown & Mistry, 2005). Men's and women's power sharing and decision-making can differ greatly, affecting group dynamics in a way that suppresses women's voices. For Muslim women, being in mixed-gender groups may be particularly challenging; incorporating processes and principles undergirding *Usrah* group, as described above, may provide a familiar group structure in which they may feel freer to participate.

Regardless of the relative merits of same- or mixed-gender group composition, *Usrah* groups are gender homogenous, in alignment with Islamic principles and Muslim cultural expectations. A gender-mixed group would not be considered an *Usrah*. The principles and structure of *Usrah* group can still be used in mixed-gender groups for other purposes. In a university setting in the United States, for instance, a dissertation support group composed of American and International doctoral students may emphasize the group's *Tarbiyah* purpose, and encourage members to develop *Ta'aruf, Tafahhum*, and *Takaful* as they support one another in academic success

Limitations

One of the limitations of *Usrah* group is the lack of group work training among *Naqeeb/Naqeebah* (group leaders). As noted earlier, the minimum requirements for *Naqeeb/Naqeebah* are to have a basic knowledge of Islam, basic teaching skills, and good leadership characteristics. Because there is no requirement or standard for group work theory and skills, *Naqeeb/Naqeebah*, group facilitation may not be always effective or efficient.

Without group work training, for instance, *Naqeeb/Naqeebah* may be ineffective group facilitators by relying on teaching behaviors such as lecturing, or by engaging in unhelpful leader behaviors, such as not giving everyone a chance to talk, showing favoritism, or not redirecting a monopolizing member. All these actions can negatively affect group process and dynamics.

Another limitation of the *Usrah* group may lie in its specific purpose and the cultural context in which it occurs. For individuals with mental health issues, there are few available sources of support in many Muslim cultures. In Malaysia, for instance, depression is still taboo because of the fear of rejection. People with depression may choose not to seek treatment due to stigma. While *Usrah* is not designed to aid individuals with mental health issues, membership in such a group may provide regular, caring support in a cohesive environment. However, membership in an *Usrah* group may not provide adequate support for individuals with more serious mental health issues. Moreover, membership in *Usrah* group may mask the necessity of seeking specific treatment for those with more serious mental illness.

Future Research

Effectiveness. While the literature supports the use of the *Usrah* group in educational settings as an effective teaching/learning modality (S. Ahmad, 2012; Baba, 2002, 2005; Baggerly & Abugideiri, 2010; Tamuri, 2007), little research has been conducted on the effectiveness of *Usrah* in other settings. Exploratory research on the effectiveness of *Usrah* groups for different populations would also contribute to the literature. Some settings and populations for future research include correctional institutions, rehabilitation centers, and welfare institutions. Most effectiveness research has been on *Usrah* group work in Southeast Asian countries; expanding this to include descriptive and effectiveness research in other countries may broaden our understanding of how *Usrah* groups are used around the world. Effectiveness could also be measured through the inclusion of non-Muslim group members. Exploratory research on the group work models described earlier, in which *Usrah* structures and practices are incorporated into culturally diverse groups may illuminate any contributions the key principles make to developing effective group process and dynamics.

Group leader characteristics. While being knowledgeable about Islam and being of good character are often the main qualifiers required of *Naqeeb/Naqeebah*, research on other effective leader characteristics is lacking. In addition, investigations into leader qualities associated with effectiveness and group development have yet to be done. One avenue may be in exploring the degree to which *Naqeeb/Naqeebah* who lack training in group facilitation skills fare as compared to those who have received specific group work training. It may also be illuminating to explore the degree to which the leadership skills of pretrained *Usrah* group leaders match up with frequently noted leadership skill sets, like executive function, caring, emotional activation, and meaning attribution (Yalom & Leszcz, 2008).

Training and practice. Research on *Naqeeb/Naqeebah* training may be beneficial. Specific training in group leadership skills may be beneficial to group learning outcomes, especially in time-limited educational settings. Given that components are important in determining the content of *Usrah* discussion and interaction within the group, it is important that future research examine how and what type of facilitation training for *Naqeeb/Naqeebah* is beneficial. One possibility within an educational setting, such as a university, may be to require that the *Naqeeb/Naqeebah* take part in an *Usrah* group prior to becoming a group leader, with ancillary instruction in group work theory. Finally, the experiences of *Usrah* group members have yet to be documented in the literature. Exploratory or qualitative research in this area may provide *Usrah* group leaders and professional educators with important information on members' perceptions of the group experience.

Group dynamic and process. To date, there appears to be no literature on any interactions between the three pillars of *Usrah* and resulting group dynamic and process. Yet to be addressed are questions about how each pillar or principle contributes to and promotes group dynamics, nor have there been any systematic attempts to define and operationalize these principles in group terms. While research supports *Usrah* group principles in promoting a cooperative learning environment, it has yet to be determined if—and to what extent—these principles contribute to effective group dynamics. While the *Usrah* group is an established and frequently used group throughout the Muslim world, there remains much that is unknown about this unique group modality and its effects on its members.

REFERENCES

Aboul-Enein, Y. H. (2003). Al-Ikhwan Al-Muslimeen: Muslim Brotherhood. *Military Review, 83*(4), 26–31. Retrieved from http://oai.dtic.mil/oai/oai?verb=getRecord&metadataPrefix=html&identifier=ADA512326

Abu-Ras, W., & Abu-Bader, S. H. (2008). The impact of the September 11, 2001 attacks on the well-being of Arab Americans in New York City. *Journal of Muslim Mental Health, 3*, 217–239.

Ahmad, I. (2005). *Teks Usrah Peringkat Pengenalan*. Kuala Lumpur, Malaysia: Sarjana Media.

Ahmad, I. (2007). *Panduan Usrah dan Gerakan Islam*. Kuala Lumpur, Malaysia: Sarjana Media.

Ahmad, S. (2012). Generic skills from Qur'anic perspective. *International Journal of Islamic Thought, 1*, 43–53.

Ali, A. Y. (1994), *The holy Quran: Text & translation*. Kuala Lumpur, Malaysia: Islamic Book Trust.

Amri, S., & Bemak, F. (2013). Mental health help-seeking behaviors of Muslim immigrants in the United States: Overcoming social stigma and cultural mistrust. *Journal of Muslim Mental Health, 7*, 43–63. Retrieved from: http://quod.lib.umich.edu/j/jmmh/10381607.0007.104/–mental-health-help-seeking-behaviors-of-muslim-immigrants?rgn=main;view=fulltext

Baba, S. (1991). *The Malaysian study circle movement and some implications for educational development* (Unpublished doctoral dissertation). Northern Illinois University, DeKalb, IL:

Baba, S. (2002). The study-circle (*Usrah*) movement of Malaysia: A collaborative approach to Islamic learning. *Muslim Education Quarterly, 19*(2), 4–12.

Baba, S. (2005). *The dynamics of study circles: Some reflections on ABIM's collaborative learning system*. Kajang, Selangor: Academy for Civilizational Studies.

Baggerly, J., & Abugideiri, S. (2010). Grief counseling for Muslim preschool and elementary school children. *Journal of Multicultural Counseling & Development, 38*, 112–124. doi:10.1002/ss.307

Banawi, R., & Stockton, R. (1993). Islamic values relevant to group work, with practical applications for the group leader. *The Journal for Specialists In Group Work, 18*, 151–160. doi:10.1080/01933929308413749

Brown, A., & Mistry, T. (2005). Group work with "mixed membership" groups: Issues of race and gender. *Social Work with Groups, 17*, 133–148. Retrieved from http://www.haworthpress.com/web/SWG

Brown, N. (2009). *Becoming a group leader*. Upper Saddle River, NJ: Pearson.

Chongruksa, D., & Prinyapol, P. (2011). Efficacy of group counseling awareness and respect among Thai Buddhist and Thai Muslim students. *Counseling Pychology 24*, 181–193. doi:10.1080/09515070.2011.615135

Corey, G., Corey, M. S., Callanan, P., & Russell, J. M. (2004). *Group techniques*. Belmont, CA: Brooks/Cole.

Corey, M. S., & Corey, G. (2006). *Groups: Process and practice*. Belmont, CA: Thomson Brooks/Cole.

Corey, M. S., Corey, G, & Corey, C. (2010). *Groups: Process and Practice* (8th ed.). Belmont, CA: Thomson Brooks/Cole.

Cultural Information-Malaysia. (2009). *Centre for Intercultural Learning, Foreign Affairs and International Trade Canada*. Retrieved from: http://www.intercultures.ca/cil-cai/ci-ic-eng.asp?iso=my

Department of Statistics Malaysia. (2001). *Population and housing census of Malaysia 2000*. Kuala Lumpur, Malaysia: Department of Statistics Malaysia.

Department of Statistics Malaysia. (2012). *Malaysian census statistics yearbook Malaysia*. Retrieved from http://www.statistics.gov.my/portal/index

Din, N., Mohamad Yusak, Y., & Abd Manap, M. F. (n.d.). *Usrah Wadah Pendidikan: Pengaplikasiannya Melahirkan Insan Terpelajar Dan Terdidik*. Retrieved from http://www.ipislam.edu.my/uploaded/.pdf

Draguns, J. G. (2003). Universal and cultural aspects of counseling and psychotherapy. In P. B.Pedersen, J. G. Draguns, W. J. Lonner, & J. E. Trimble (Eds.), *Counseling across cultures* (5th ed., pp. 29–49). Thousand Oaks, CA: Sage.

Draper, K., Ritter, K. B., & Willingham, E. U. (2003). Sand tray group counseling with adolescents. *The Journal for Specialists in Group Work, 28*, 244–260. doi:10.1177/0193392203252030.

Faruqi, S. S. (2011, May). *The constitution of a Muslim majority state: The example of Malaysia*. Paper presented at Constitution-making Forum: A Government of Sudan Constitution, Khartoum, Sudan. Retrieved from http://unmis.unmissions.org/Portals/UNMIS/Constitution-making%20Symposium/2011-05_Faruqi_Malaysia.pdf

Friedman, S. S. (1998). Girls in the 90s: a gender-based model for eating disorder prevention. *Patient Education and Counseling, 33*, 217–224. Retrieved from http://www.ncbi.nlm.nih.gov/pubmed/9731159

Gladding, S. (2008). *Groups: A counseling specialty*. Upper Saddle River, NJ: Pearson.

Hall, R, Livingston, J. N., Brown, C., & Mohabir, J. (2011). Islam and Asia Pacific Muslims: The implications of spirituality for social work practice. *Journal of Social Work Practice, 25*, 205–215. Retrieved from doi:10.1080/02650533.2010.545484

Hassan Al–Bana. (1985). *Usrah dan dakwah*. Kuala Lumpur, Malaysia: Dewan Pustaka Fajar.

Hassan, M. (2007). Explaining Islam's special position and the politic of Islam in Malaysia. *Muslim World (Hartford, Conn.), 97*, 287–316.

Hays, D., Arredondo, P., Gladding, S. T., & Toporek, R. L. Integrating social justice in group work: The next decade. *The Journal for Specialists in Group Work, 35*, 177–206.

Henderson, D. A., & Gladding, S.T. (2004). Group counseling for older adults. In J. L. DeLucia-Waack, D.A. Gerrity, C.A. Kalodner, & M.T. Riva (Eds.), *Handbook of group counseling and psychotherapy* (pp. 469–478). Thousand Oaks, CA: Sage.

Hodge, D. (2000). The spiritually committed: An examination of the staff at faith-based substance abuse providers. *Social Work and Christianity, 27*, 150–167.

Hodge, D. R., & Nadir, A. (2008). Moving toward culturally competent practice with Muslims: Modifying cognitive therapy with Islamic tenets. *Social Work*, *53*(1), 31–41. doi:10.1093/sw/53.1.31

Ibrahim, F., & Dykeman, C. (2011). Counseling Muslim Americans: Cultural and spiritual assessments. *Journal of Counseling and Development*, *89*, 387–396.

Imam Nawawi (2001). *Imam Nawawi's collection of forty hadith: Text, translation and notes*. Kuala Lumpur, Malaysia: Islamic Book of Trust.

Islamic Community of Northern California. (2014). Haya (Shyness). *The Islamic Bulletin, 10*, 21–22. Retrieved from http://www.islamicbulletin.org/newsletters/issue_23/issue23.pdf

Kamsani, S. R. (2013). *Religious identity, self-concept, and resilience among female orphan adolescents in Malaysia: An evidence-based group intervention* (Unpublished doctoral dissertation). Southern Illinois University, Carbondale, IL.

Khan, M. A. (2005). *Islam does not teach confrontation*. Retrieved from http://www.cpsglobal.org/content/islam-does-not-teach-confrontation

Manuty, M. N. (1989). *Perceptions of social change in contemporary Malaysia: A critical analysis of ABIM's role and its impact among the Muslim youth* (Unpublished doctoral dissertation). Temple University, Philadelphia, PA.

Muhd Amin, R., Yusuf, S. A., & Haneef, M. A. (2011, December). *The effectiveness of an integrated curriculum: The case of the International Islamic University Malaysia*. Paper presented at 8th International Conference on Islamic Economics and Finance, Qatar. Retrieved from http://conference.qfis.edu.qa/app/media/326

Muslim American Society Greater LA. (2015).*What is the MAS* Usrah*?* Retrieved from http://www.masgreaterla.org/index.php/departments/tarbiya/mas-usrah

Mustari, M. I., & Mohd Salleh, S. (2010). *Persepsi pelajar terhadap program* Usrah *di SMKA (P) Al-Mashoor*. Retrieved from http://eprints.utm.my/10478/1/PERSEPSI_PELAJAR_TERHADAP_PROGRAM_USRAH.pdf

Nahon, D., & Lander, N. R. (2013). Working with men in groups from an integrity model perspective. *Journal of Men's Studies*, *21*, 162–177. doi:10.3149/jms.2102.162

Nassar-McMillan, S. C., & Hakim-Larson, J. (2003). Counseling considerations among Arab Americans. *Journal of Counseling & Development*, *81*, 150–159.

Nofal, N. (1993). Al-Ghazali. *International Bureau of Education, XXIII*, 1–19

Nordin, M., Ahamd, J., & Tamuri, H. (2011). Pelaksanaan program *Usrah* di Sekolah Menengah Kebangsaan Agama (SMKA) Sheikh Haji Ahmad Said. *Prosiding Nadwah Ulama Nusantara (NUN), IV*, 25–26. Retrieved from http://www.ukm.my/nun/Artikel%20EDITED%20OK%20(PDF)/68%20514-518%20Muhammad,%20Jamil%20%26%20Ab%20Halim.pdf

Pedersen, P. (2000). *A handbook for developing multicultural awareness*. Alexandria, VA: American Counseling Association.

Rosenthal, L. (1985). A modern analytic approach to group resistance. *Modern Psychoanalysis*, *10*, 165–182.

Shechtman, Z., & Tanus, H. (2006). Counseling groups for Arab adolescents in an intergroup conflict in Israel: Report of an outcome study. *Journal of Peace Psychology,12*, 119–137. doi 10.1207/s15327949pac1202_2

Shuriye, A. O. (2011). The role of credited co-curricular programmes on the internationalization and infusing values into student's personality: The IIUM Model. *Journal of Emerging Trends in Educational Research and Policy Studies, 2*, 100–107. Retrieved from http://jeteraps.scholarlinkresearch.org/articles

Smither, R., & Khorsandi, A. (2009). The implicit personality theory of Islam. *Psychology of Religion & Spirituality. 1*, 81–96.

Stuff. (2014). *Haya: Modesty, the innate character of Islam*. Retrieved from http://religion4humanity.blogspot.com

Sue, D. W., & Sue. D. (2012). *Counseling the culturally different: Theory and practice*. Hoboken, NJ: John Wiley and Sons.

Tamuri, A. H. (2007). Islamic education teachers' perceptions of the teaching of akhlaq in Malaysian secondary schools. *The Journal of Moral Education, 36*, 371–386. doi:10.1080/03057240701553347

Usrah. (2003). *Introduction to the* Usrah *system*. Kuala Lumpur, Malaysia: International Islamic University Malaysia.

Williamson, T. (2006). *Countries and their cultures—Malaysia*. Retrieved from: http://www.everyculture.com/Ja-Ma/Malaysia.html

Windwalker, T. (2013a). *The life of gay people in Malaysia, the female perspective*. Retrieved from http://1dad1kid.com/gay-people-in-malaysia-the-female-perspective/

Windwalker, T. (2013b). *The life of gay people in Muslim Malaysia*. Retrieved from http://1dad1kid.com/the-life-of-gay-people-in-muslim-malaysia/

Yalom, I. D., & Leszcz, M. (2005). *The theory and practice of group psychotherapy*. New York, NY: Basic Book.

Zinck, K., & Littrell, J. M. (2000). Action research shows group counseling effective with at-risk adolescent girls. *Professional School Counseling, 4*, 50.

Transcending Traditional Group Work: Using the Brazilian Martial Art of Capoeira as a Clinical Therapeutic Group for Culturally Diverse Adolescents

Isaac Burt
Florida International University

Many culturally diverse populations, such as angry youth, relapse into aggressive behaviors because of poor behavioral self-efficacy and socialization skills. To supplement traditional treatments, there is need for culturally sensitive and effective programs. Martial arts, when integrated with culturally sensitive clinical components, are a viable addendum to therapy. Martial arts represent a paradigm shift from talk therapies to more interactive, socially involving group methods. Combining the movement of martial arts with culturally sensitive therapeutic principles can make a significant difference with culturally diverse populations. Capoeira (a Brazilian martial art) is a potential multicultural group approach for behavioral change.

According to Gladding (2012), group work is an effective counseling approach to use with difficult client populations, such as angry adolescents. In particular, groups provide youth with structure and direction during difficult mental and physical growth (Burt & Butler, 2011). However, due to factors such as ethnicity, gender, and anger level, not all adolescents respond well to conventional group methods (Gladding, 2012). An example of orthodox group methods is traditional sit-down talk therapy. As stated by Graham and Harris (2013), canon counseling procedures and methods may not be appropriate for the current generation of culturally diverse youth. Furthermore, culturally diverse youth who also struggle with anger present difficulties that can frustrate group facilitators and counselors alike (Brandt, Sidway, Dvorsky, & Weist, 2013). For the purposes of this article, culturally diverse youth can be ethnic minorities, or individuals having ancestries from an international background.

When clients possess both cultural diversity and anger, research indicates conventional counseling methods may not be appropriate (Clauss-Ehlers, Serpell, & Weist, 2013). As such, counselors must use creative methods to serve this population better (M. E. Young, 2013). Practitioners and researchers have proposed various alternatives to assisting clients, ranging from rope courses to community involvement (Grothaus, 2013). However, one method in particular has received noteworthy recognition, which is intersecting clinical mental health counseling with martial arts in a group format (Burt, 2012; Burt & Butler, 2011; Hackney, 2013; Twemlow et al., 2008). Research in this innovative method suggests clinical group martial arts reduces anger and fosters positive youth development (Hackney, 2013). Additionally, clinical group martial arts can also assist in reducing self-injurious behaviors (Potik & Schreiber, 2013). While research indicates a group-centered clinical martial arts approach is useful, a variation of the method using the Brazilian martial art of Capoeira indicates promise (Burt & Butler, 2011). Specifically, Capoeira promotes relaxation, mindfulness, and personal reflection as well as providing a sense of physical wellbeing through exercise (Capoeira, 2006).

EXPLANATION OF CAPOEIRA

Capoeira participants label this martial art as a game and not a fight, and use the term play rather than competing. Additionally, there are no winners or losers in Capoeira (Capoeira, 2006). This is because each participant needs to work with the other in order for the martial art to look aesthetically appealing (da Conceição, n.d.). Of primary importance is the idea of non-contact, as practitioners avoid hitting one another through dodging (Downey, 2005). The principle of avoiding conflict is paramount, as practitioners transpose this belief in everyday life (Capoeira Brasil webpage, www.capoeirabrasil.com). In essence, practitioners seek to avoid conflict in Capoeira and their lives (Capoeira, 2006).

Working with others collaboratively, encouraging diversity, and understanding personal strengths and limitations are the foundations on which Capoeira stands (Capoeira, 2003). Capoeira practitioners (called Capoeiristas) develop a distinct philosophy of looking at life, and understanding reality (da Conceição, n.d.). A phenomenological view matures in those practitioners who devote themselves to Capoeira practice (Capoeira Brasil webpage, www.capoeirabrasil.com). Through this dedication, a distinctive worldview develops in Capoeiristas that mirror the philosophy of Capoeira (Capoeira, 2003). The fundamental belief on which Capoeira philosophy lays is to not allow anger to overcome oneself (Burt, 2012). Instead, the Capoeirista learns to channel negative behaviors positively. An example of positive channeling is the following brief example. In Capoeira, a practitioner may want to kick at the same time as another does, resulting in a clash. Clearly, both practitioners cannot do the same thing simultaneously, as the two are opposing. The Capoeirista learns from the experience, and instead of becoming angry, can try something new to avoid future clashes (Joseph, 2005). Similarly, in life clashes may occur when a Capoeirista wants to do something that conflicts with others (Downey, 2005). Thus, the Capoeirista begins to develop a less ego-centered perspective, and is more aware of other people (Almeida & Porter, 2007).

Capoeira also provides encouragement, as the group claps, shouts, and praises Capoeiristas who try or accomplish new movements (Joseph, 2012). According to Bandura (2008), this kind of social encouragement is crucial. For instance, some culturally diverse and angry adolescents have a negative self-image and live up to negative expectations (Seligman, 1991). When these adolescents act in a manner perceived as potentially disruptive, some adults quickly rush in to stop the behavior (Nadal, Escobar, Prado, David, & Haynes, 2012). Research indicates, however, allowing people to express themselves increases behavioral self-efficacy (Bandura, 2012). Allowing culturally diverse angry adolescents to express themselves assists in creating client buy-in and satisfaction (Burt, Patel, & Lewis, 2012). Additionally, group cohesion can increase, as culturally diverse members feel less anxious (Burt, Patel, Butler, & Gonzalez, 2013). Thus, social engagement and participation are critically important to the social milieu in Capoeira (Essien, 2008). According to the Capoeira Brasil webpage (www.capoeirabrasil.com), without these cooperative elements, Capoeira would not be the group art it is today.

THEORETICAL FOUNDATION FOR A CLINICAL GROUP MARTIAL ART

Although Capoeira has several underlying therapeutic components, a truly clinical group martial art must have a theoretical underpinning (Twemlow et al., 2008). Research indicates social cognitive theory (SCT) is a useful model for group martial arts (Burt & Butler, 2011). According to Bandura (1986), social cognitive theory (SCT) incorporates the concept of *reciprocal determinism*. Operationally defined, reciprocal determinism is the triadic relationship between personal factors (emotions/cognition), behaviors, and environment (Bandura, 2012). A bi-directional effect exists between the three concepts, as each one influences the other in fluctuating levels. Adding to this, Orpinas and Horne (2004) asserted reciprocal determinism is a fundamental component for successful and effective group counseling. Bandura (2008) supported Orpinas and Horne, and went further by stating reciprocal determinism assists in increasing adolescents' self-efficacy. Increases in self-efficacy help to create trust, group cohesion, and increase ability to deal with problems (Burt et al., 2013).

While unintentional, Capoeira also emphasizes this interaction among personal factors, environment, and behaviors (Lewis, 1992). Further, Bandura (2008) declared these three interactional factors are critical in creating a prosocial environment. Operationally defined, a prosocial environment is a milieu facilitating behavior that is positive, and encourages social acceptance and group cohesion (Kellner, Bry, & Salvador, 2008). SCT and reciprocal determinism are critical components in creating a prosocial environment, which is influential in having effective group counseling (Burt et al., 2012). Thus, any clinical group martial art would need these components in order to be successful (Twemlow et al., 2008). While Capoeiristas do not assign a label to reciprocal determinism per se, the idea does exist. Instead of attempting to categorize this phenomenon, a Capoeirista would simply state they have a better awareness and control of themselves and the environment (Capoeira, 2006).

The following brief depiction illustrates how a group facilitator could use SCT/reciprocal determinism to accentuate Capoeira's natural therapeutic elements. In groups, establishing trust can produce anxiety, especially during early stages (T. L. Young, 2013). Similarly, in Capoeira practicing martial arts with someone new can become intense or stressful, due to the physical and mental nature of the art (Essien, 2008). To reduce problems with initial group apprehension, facilitators normally have members go through activities that reduce anxiety and increase participation (Ware, Ohrt, & Swank, 2012). Canon methods such as icebreakers and overly structured activities, however, may not be appropriate with culturally diverse angry adolescents (Butler, Shillingford, & Snow-Alexander, 2011). Research indicates traditional methods such as structured activities may actually increase anxiety with culturally diverse populations (Vereen, Hill, & Butler, 2013).

The experiential nature of Capoeira, however, provides a novel, more experiential method of dealing with anxiety a group facilitator can use. Capoeira allows individuals to experiment with anxiety in a corporal manner (Almeida & Porter, 2007). For example, Capoeira philosophy states that one should not allow anxiety or anger to take over and let these emotions lead to negative mental thoughts or inaccurate self-doubt (da Conceição, n.d.). If one feels depressed or anxious after practicing Capoeira, because of being nervous, this is a natural occurrence expected in life (Capoeira, 2003). Sadness may occur because of being tense and scared in trying something new, and feeling vulnerable (Capoeira Brasil webpage, www.capoeirabrasil.com). This feeling, nonetheless, should not deter and take away hope. According to Capoeira, (2006):

> Capoeira is not about winning or losing; it creates thoughts about what went wrong, it develops pondering about what environmental opportunities there are to become better, how to use people around you to assist, and to train more appropriately next time. (p. 97)

In the preceding brief example, a facilitator can use reciprocal determinism in the following way. The facilitator might emphasize to a member(s) how: The environment (practicing Capoeira), has an effect on the personal factors of a person (depression/anxiety) and behaviors (performing poorly) that can come from these factors. The facilitator can have group members relate this experience to their life by connecting their present behavioral/emotional states to situations in the past. Research suggests when members connect experiential experiences in a group to real life, self-awareness develops (Burt & Butler, 2011). With culturally diverse individuals, the effect of self-awareness can be even greater, especially with angry adolescents (Butler et al., 2011).

To demonstrate the potential effectiveness of Capoeira, this article has a dual fold intention. The first purpose is to describe the viability of Capoeira as a clinical group martial art. The second goal is to illustrate how group facilitators can use Capoeira with culturally diverse populations. In order to accomplish these tasks, the remainder of this article includes three parts. The first part describes multicultural competencies and group framework. This section also includes group dynamics for a clinical group martial art. Contained within group dynamics are recommendations for the appropriate type of facilitator, participants, group size, and development. The second segment provides a description of the clinical group martial art. The third part involves limitations in using a clinical group martial art. The article concludes with implications and future directions suggested for facilitators working with culturally diverse, angry populations.

MULTICULTURAL COMPETENCIES AND GROUP FRAMEWORK

To be able to provide group services to culturally diverse populations, facilitators need to have a number of requisite knowledge and skills (Singh, Merchant, Skudrzyk, & Ingene, 2012). Lack of adequate knowledge and skills can result in miscommunication, misinterpretations, or stereotyping (Hays, Arredondo, Gladding, & Toporek, 2010). As such, facilitators need to have the following:

1. An ability to be a reflective practitioner, which includes an awareness of self and others (i.e., group members).
2. An understanding of strategies and skills essential to group counseling, such as effectively using modeling and conflict resolution (Gladding, 2012).
3. Appreciation for members' culturally diverse worldviews.
4. Welcome bilingualism and embrace language differences (Singh et al., 2012).
5. Have knowledge about the historical significance of members' ethnicity and culture, and be aware of any historic oppression.
6. Demonstrate an empathetic understanding of how members' identifiable characteristics (nationality, race, culture) can affect interpretations of events, and reactions to situations.
7. Establish if the group would be more effective as either a (a) *culture-specific* group (cluster of group members sharing mutual familiarities due to cultural background, (b) an *intercultural learning group* (group exploring differences that intersect between culturally different populations, or (c) *other-content focused group* (groups dedicated to other issues but still identify and address cultural diversity affecting group cohesion and functioning) (Merchant, as cited in Singh et al., 2012).

In regards to group framework, three factors are critically important. First, there must be a martial artist (Capoeirista), who provides the physical training (Twemlow et al. 2008). Second, a group facilitator will oversee the clinical aspects and functioning of the group. This facilitator will also supervise and provide training to the Capoeirista. Due to not having a background in counseling, the Capoeirista needs supervision (Burt, 2012). Third, the facilitator, while not teaching Capoeira, will be there throughout the group sessions to provide a presence, and participate. Participation can be through playing instruments, singing, or actually learning Capoeira. However, the bulk of what the facilitator will do is to provide *learning intervals* to the group members. This is a time where the training stops for a portion of the group, and the facilitator focuses on behavior, emotions, and connecting these experiences to everyday life. The facilitator actively monitors and engages members while they are involved in practice. An average duration for a clinical group martial art is 1 hr, once a week for 8 weeks (Twemlow et al., 2008).

Appropriate Type of Group Facilitator

A facilitator who has worked in a variety of therapeutic settings with youth, such as a behavioral center, private practice, or community clinic is an appropriate choice. Culturally diverse individuals are a distinct population, which have unique needs and concerns (Graham & Harris, 2013). Due to these distinct characteristics, a facilitator who uses an integrative approach may be more effective with culturally diverse groups (Burt et al., 2013). Adding to this, a group facilitator will need to have several of the following characteristics Gladding (2012) asserted are essential for culturally diverse facilitators: (a) humor, (b) flexibility, (c) creativity, (d) internal discipline, (e) strong sense of self, (f) energetic enthusiasm, and (g) empathy.

Humor is critical because many culturally diverse, angry youth may have experienced oppression. As such, being able to use and tap into appropriate humor is essential to ease this population's concerns (Vereen et al., 2013). Young persons also rarely follow a schedule and can be unpredictable and capricious. Thus, flexibility and creativity are imperative as well (Gladding, 2012). A clinical group martial art, additionally, requires much stamina. A clinical group martial art is a non-traditional, very active modality. Therefore, the facilitator rarely gets to sit down while the group is in session. Due to this fact, a high internal discipline, coupled with a strong sense of self is essential. Facilitating a group with youth requires a large amount of energy, as well as empathy to assist individuals as they struggle with anger, oppression, and racism (Twemlow et al., 2008).

Group Development

Recruitment, screening, selection, and size. This group will consist of culturally diverse, angry adolescents. Corresponding with the operational definition stated earlier in this article, this population could comprise different races, ethnicities, or nationalities. Participants can be males or females from a residential facility, community center, or school. Depending on group locale, the facilitator will have to adjust the group accordingly. A group at a residential facility will have different rules, parameters, and behavioral populations than a community center or school (Burt, 2012). Moreover, restrictions may emerge limiting the type of recruitment allowed due to the location as well. Some commonalities, however, do exist that are widely established, such as recruiting through word of mouth, flyers, or the Internet. Criteria for inclusion can include individuals experiencing problems with aggression, impulse control, and oppositional behavior in the school, home, and community (Hill & Meyer, 2003).

The focus of this clinical group martial art is to identify and address anger in culturally diverse youth. As such, it is critical to have potential members who meet the criteria. To correctly identify potential members, the facilitator needs to use the recommendations of adults (e.g., parents, teachers, administrative staff, counselors) (Kellner et al., 2008). The facilitator can conduct small, informal interviews with adults to attain important information. Due to biases, however, adult opinion can be troublesome at times (Brandt et al., 2013).

Succinctly stated, adult recommendations, in and by themselves, might not be enough.

To reduce biases and ensure appropriate members, facilitators can use informal or formal assessments (Gladding, 2012). An informal assessment can be as simple as a self-made questionnaire, inquiring about behavior and cultural diversity. A formal assessment can be as intricate as the State Trait Anger Expression Inventory 2 Child and Adolescent (STAXI–2 CA; del Barrio, Aluj, & Spielberger, 2004). Having both (interviews and assessment) can provide protection against incorrect or biased selection processes. Once a list of potential members develops, the facilitator should interview adults a second time. This second small interview with adults is a precautionary measure to ensure potential members actually need services. As stated by Butler et al. (2011), some assessments are not appropriate for all culturally diverse populations. Moreover, people's opinions and views are sometimes capricious (Bandura, 2008). As such, having a three-tier system consisting of an interview, assessment, and second interview helps in reducing biases (Burt, 2012). Through adult recommendations and informal/formal assessment, the facilitator will give these selected persons personalized printed and oral invitations. The facilitator can give interested persons a consent form for the parent/guardian to approve and sign. The consent forms need to have information regarding confidentiality, participants' rights, and ability to decline participation.

Due to the physical nature of the group, the facilitator may have to screen out individuals with significant physical limitations (e.g., pervasive developmental delays; see Hill & Meyer, 2003). Additionally, participant age can range from 8–17 years of age. Research suggests however, keeping ages as close as possible due to physical and cognitive developmental differences between children and adolescents (Twemlow et al., 2008). If separation is not possible, then the facilitator must monitor closely to avoid frustration from younger members and boredom with older ones. Once a member of the group, the facilitator needs to design a coding system to eliminate any information that might identify members. Lastly, corresponding with Gladding (2012), group size should range from six to ten members.

DESCRIPTION OF THE CLINICAL GROUP MARTIAL ART

Sessions 1 and 2

The objective of Session 1 is to begin to develop trust by formally introducing the group to the facilitator and Capoeirista. The group facilitator has much to do in this first session, as members may be unsure of how to behave (Gladding, 2012). To alleviate initial confusion and anxiety, the facilitator can begin discussing the parameters of the group. First, the facilitator must emphasize to the members the difference between this clinical group martial art and sport martial arts (Twemlow et al., 2008). For instance, the facilitator starts to discuss with the members the goal of the group is to improve behavior and self-awareness, as opposed to teaching them how to fight. Although the facilitator explains this beforehand, it may need restating. The facilitator further states the group will address psychosocial and interpersonal problems that are affecting them in the home, community, and school. Group members understand they are involved in therapy, and this group utilizes Capoeira as a therapeutic martial arts framework. As such, members know they are involved in a therapeutic modality that addresses individual and group goals (Baker, 1995).

Hackney (2013) suggests the facilitator should be firm in establishing a solid foundation for rules and protocols. Members need to know they have personal accountability, and are responsible for their involvement. Thus, the facilitator emphasizes that breaking protocols by hitting others is a fundamental rule not to breach (Potik & Schreiber, 2013). The facilitator reiterates to members that this group can present them with an opportunity to work on their personal goals while with others. After taking time to discuss parameters of the group, the facilitator allows the Capoeirista to take over and begin teaching Capoeira.

During this time, the facilitator can walk around observing the group, or participate. Regardless of what the facilitator decides to do, he/she must continually observe the group and provide assistance when necessary to the Capoeirista. The group ends with the facilitator having each member state a positive affirmation (Burt et al., 2012). The goal of the positive affirmation is for the members to state something positive they learned, or to thank someone in the group. After the first session, research declares the facilitator should meet with the Capoeirista afterwards and process the group, while planning for the next session (Twemlow et al., 2008).

The second session begins with the facilitator reiterating the rules and protocols from the previous session. Burt et al. (2013) and Kellner et al. (2008) emphasized the need for groups to have an opening experiential activity. An opening activity has several purposes. Facilitators can use it to decrease anxiety, increase participation, or as a method to plant seeds to draw upon later in the session. For the second session, the facilitator discusses the idea of *machismo* (being macho), and what that looks like for members in their individual cultures. Males, as well as females can partake in this activity, as machismo affects both genders (Butler et al., 2013). The purpose of this activity is to openly discuss distortions/stereotypes adolescents may have. Joseph (2012) asserted that cognitive distortions and culturally diverse people's interpretations of them is one of the major problems facing them in life. Since the members are taking a martial art, it is critical the group discusses and addresses attitudes on machismo. Members respond, and the facilitator leads the group in identifying their own inconsistencies and errors in cognitive processing (Hackney, 2013).

After the opening activity, the Capoeirista can begin to teach Capoeira. In this session, the facilitator wants to become further involved, and talk with members more as they are training. The facilitator wants to monitor the group and address proper member socialization. Remaining active and continually assessing members' ability to transfer skills learned to the outside is also critical in this session. Any information members stated about the experiential activity, the facilitator wants to discuss it again at the end of the session. The purpose is to see if, through training, members have any new insights. To end the session, the facilitator has the group do positive affirmations. After the group ends, the facilitator debriefs with the Capoeirista and plans for the next session.

Sessions 3 and 4

The third session focuses on what Bernard (1991) stated is crucial for adolescents, which is the need for affiliation with a group. The opening experiential question concentrates on groups the members identify with. What makes the groups important, and how they fit into their lives is a focal point. The facilitator engages members in a discussion asking where they perceive the martial arts group in their lives. Since a clinical group martial art should be proactive, the facilitator listens to attributes members deem important. After listening, the facilitator should ask members how they could contribute in order to make the group develop into something they consider significant. Having members take ownership helps to increase accountability, satisfaction, and client commitment (Gladding, 2012). Since the emphasis of the group is positive goal attainment and development, members should focus on solutions as opposed to problems (Potik & Schreiber, 2013). Thus, members can take on responsibility of the group. Members discuss what they want from the group, but the facilitator does not tell them how to go about doing it. Instead, the facilitator provides suggestions, while the members decide what they want to contribute for the group to develop into something special. The group ends with positive affirmations, while the facilitator and Capoeirista process and plan for the next session.

Another critical component Bernard (1991) identified as important for youth is the need for them to feel powerful. The fourth session focuses on this factor. The opening experiential question has members discuss what makes them feel in control. This is a delicate session, as some members may disclose personal weaknesses and vulnerabilities (Burt, 2012). Facilitators need to be ready for member disclosure, and have a non-judgmental stance and appropriate empathy (Thompson, 2011). This is the halfway point of the group, and as such, falls into the transition stage (Gladding, 2012). If the facilitator handles the situation improperly, then members may not feel comfortable. As a result, the group may not recover or progress.

As the group discusses what makes them feel strong, the facilitator can once again reiterate the fundamental difference between the clinical group and sport martial arts. Laypersons sometimes believe martial arts are violent and the power attained from training people use to intimidate others physically (Baker, 1995). Popular media and TV sometimes portray this image, which can distort members' perceptions (Burt & Butler, 2011). The anticipated product of the clinical group martial art is not to fight, but to develop an inner philosophy and control over their thoughts and emotions. The facilitator can discuss the history of Capoeira here and examine how early Capoeiristas used non-violent methods through a martial art to attain their goals. Success in sport martial arts centers on how hard a person can kick, or how they can control an opponent (Burt & Butler, 2011). A clinical group martial art focuses on interpersonal growth, while learning more about oneself through a physical outlet (Capoeira, 2006). Through this dialogue, the objective is for members to develop positive ways to feel powerful. Once the facilitator has completed this discussion, the Capoeirista can begin teaching. To end the session, the facilitator guides the group in positive affirmations. As with previous sessions, the facilitator debriefs with the Capoeirista and plans for the next week.

Sessions 5 and 6

Session 5 deals with what Bernard (1991) asserted drives youth to gravitate towards negative influences, which are feelings of inadequate security. Very similar to Session 4, facilitators have to be prepared for member disclosure. In these sessions, members are testing the waters and determining if those waters are safe (T. L. Young, 2013). Thus, facilitators must provide an environment conducive for safe member disclosure (Ware et al., 2012). Comparable to Session 4, the facilitator asks the group what makes them feel insecure, instead of powerful. The facilitator creates a dialogue with members, and leads a discussion on personal values and fears. Next, the facilitator explains one of the group's goals is to increase self-efficacy and decrease insecurity.

The facilitator informs the group that one of the purposes of the clinical group martial art is to cultivate socialization and improve cognitive skills. The facilitator restates the purpose of the group is not to simply learn Capoeira. Alternatively, the objective is to provide opportunities to engage positively with others and increase socialization and behavioral skills (Bernard, 1991). The facilitator leads a discussion about how members have learned to be accountable and responsible for their actions. Proceeding on, the facilitator emphasizes that interactions between each other are just as important as learning the movements in Capoeira. The facilitator encourages the members to continue to participate in improving their social and cognitive skills. One method to continue to participate is to ask questions about movements in Capoeira when confused. According to Capoeira (2003), asking questions and being honest when confused are skills that people can use in everyday life. For example, members could be confused with topics in school, but do not feel comfortable asking questions. They may prefer not to ask questions because they do not want to appear incompetent (Gladding, 2012). Members can practice these skills in a safe environment, and then transfer those abilities to the real world. Lastly, to close out the session, the facilitator discusses termination, and what members can do to transfer the new skills into their lives.

The sixth session addresses the need Bernard (1991) stated adolescents struggle with, which is lack of activities, or boredom. The facilitator spearheads a discussion on what bores members, and what they do to alleviate boredom. The members then discuss if the group has fulfilled their needs and limited boredom. According to the literature, a clinical group martial art builds members' sense of physical and emotional stability (Potik & Schreiber, 2013). According to Capoeira (2006), the philosophical aspect serves to alleviate boredom and encourage positive behaviors over a lifetime. The facilitator then addresses if the group has assisted members in other parts of their lives. As the group session concludes, the facilitator discusses termination again, in order to prepare members.

Sessions 7 and 8

The seventh session deals with the effect of role models and modeling has on youth. Twemlow et al. (2008) suggested in a clinical group martial art, the behaviors the instructor displays have a tremendous effect on members' conduct. In a clinical group martial art, members scrutinize, analyze, and dissect the behavior of the instructors (Hill & Meyer, 2003). The members examine instructor behavior in an attempt to ascertain the most appropriate manner of conduct (Capoeira, 2003). Watching positive role models can increase behavioral self-efficacy and self-esteem, and lower levels of performance anxiety (Bandura, 2008). As the group begins to go through the processes of termination, the facilitator asks members to describe behaviors by both the facilitator and Capoeirista. A discussion ensues detailing what they saw, how it affected them, and if they could model themselves after the instructors. Modeling is an important aspect of a clinical group martial art, as a healthy, prosocial environment teaches more than just kicks and movements (Capoeira, 2006). As the session concludes, the facilitator addresses this is the next to last session, and that the group is about to end.

The eighth, and final, session is one delegated for wrap-up and paperwork. Due to the group ending, facilitators should avoid bringing up new behavioral material (Gladding, 2012). Instead, this session can focus on what members learned, how they progressed, and what they can do in the future to keep their new skills (T. L. Young, 2013). Further, the facilitator can design methods for the group to say their goodbyes in a positive, therapeutic manner. Since this may be the first time these group members had a constructive activity, it may be difficult for them to acknowledge the group is ending (Burt et al., 2012). A group facilitator must understand that some members may not want the group to close (Gladding, 2012). Furthermore, Thompson (2011) recommended a facilitator be firm, but have an empathetic understanding in acknowledging the group is ending. If the facilitator used assessments, this session is necessary to determine if the group was successful.

LIMITATIONS

Physical ability is certainly a limitation of a clinical group martial art. For both the facilitator and members, having a good degree of fitness and stamina is beneficial. Although physical ability can be a limitation, it is not the most important component. As the group progresses, dexterity, speed, and control develop as well. One of the principles of Capoeira is that the only true competitor is the person him/herself (Essien, 2008). As such, mastering the philosophical component of Capoeira is of primary importance (Almeida & Porter, 2007). Without grasping the philosophical principles on which Capoeira lays, not even the quickest or strongest person is an effective Capoeirista (da Conceição, n.d.). Another limitation is that group members may not want to participate in a group considered international, or foreign. However, an effective way to avoid this issue is to not force the group on members. According to Burt and Butler (2011), helping members to understand the history and philosophy of Capoeira is critically important. Understanding the history, then connecting that to their lives aids vicarious modeling, which can lead to the dissolution of barriers and engagement in the group.

SUMMARY AND IMPLICATIONS

There is a need for culturally sensitive interventions for the new generation of clients (Butler et al., 2011; Vereen et al., 2013). Due to the "browning of America," clients are emerging that are vastly different from past populations (Sundstrom, 2008). For group facilitators, the challenge is to incorporate traditional training and methods with contemporary approaches in order to assist these clients (Villalba, Ivers, & Ohlms, 2010). Culturally diverse client populations are more commonplace, and no longer relegated to large, metropolitan cities (Sundstrom, 2008). As people move from different countries, they may encounter difficulties adjusting to the lifestyle (Joseph, 2012). Sometimes there are culture clashes as the dominant culture struggles to adapt to the minority culture, and vise versa (Brandt et al. 2013). Once clashes occur, some culturally diverse populations seek counseling to help in adjusting and dealing with issues (Graham & Harris, 2013). As M. E. Young (2013) suggests, contemporary group facilitators and counselors must use and adapt to modern methods and clients. Capoeira, a martial art from Brazil, has inherent therapeutic principles that make it attractive to use with culturally diverse populations (Burt & Butler, 2011).

Steen (2011) suggested group facilitators should continually monitor and assess their groups, in order to increase effectiveness and ensure appropriate facilitation. Gladding (2012) supports this idea, and adds that group facilitators may not know how effective their groups are without using appropriate measures. Measures can be report cards (indicating academic /behavioral progression and attendance), discipline referrals, evaluative reports from caregivers/school administrative staff, and self-evaluations. Additionally, informal evaluations by the facilitator are useful as well (Kellner et al., 2008). These informal evaluations can be behavioral tracking, observational data, baseline data, surveys, or questionnaires. Formal assessments such as the STAXI–2 CA, Behavioral Assessment Scale for Children 2 (Reynolds & Kamphaus, 2004) are also helpful in accessing behavior.

In conclusion, a clinical group martial art is not only innovative, but it can potentially assist culturally diverse youth in a number of ways. For example, a clinical group martial art can provide for improved social etiquette through increased discipline, direction, and guidance in a non-confrontational approach (Baker, 1995). Most youth seem intrigued by martial arts, and as a result, a clinical group martial art looks appealing (Twemlow, 2008). Innovative group approaches that reach out to populations are rapidly becoming popular, due to social justice advocates (Butler et al., 2011). Thus, holistic approaches meeting the client where they are at developmentally are becoming the norm (Goodrich & Luke, 2010). Additionally, future researchers may want to investigate more non-traditional group methods to determine what interventions are the most efficacious. Lastly, members learn more responsibility, as they are accountable for their group and actions. Members are responsible for equipment, washing mats after practice, properly working with partners, and participating fully (Baker, 1995). Through these components, the goal is for culturally diverse, angry youth to develop and grow.

REFERENCES

Almeida, P., & Porter, M. (2007). *Capoeira: The essential guide to mastering the art.* London, England: New Holland.

Baker, P. C. (1995, Summer/Fall). Going to the MAT for rehab: Martial arts therapy at St. Joseph Mercy hospital. *Rehab Review*. Retrieved from http://www.martialartstherapy.com/newsprintarticles/rehabreview.html

Bandura, A. (1986). *Social foundations of thought and action: A social cognitive theory.* Englewood Cliffs, NJ: Prentice Hall.

Bandura, A. (2008). The reconstrual of "free will" from the agentic perspective of social cognitive theory. In J. Baer, J. C. Kaufman & R. F. Baumeister (Eds.), *Are we free? Psychology and free will.* (pp. 86–127). Oxford, England: Oxford University Press.

Bandura, A. (2012). On the functional properties of perceived self-efficacy revisited. *Journal of Management, 38*, 9–44. doi:10.1177/0149206311410606

Benard, B. (1991). *Fostering resiliency in kids: Protective factors in the family, school, and community*. Portland, OR: Northwest Regional Educational Laboratory.

Brandt, N. E., Sidway, E., Dvorsky, M., & Weist, M. D. (2013). Culturally responsive strategies to address youth gangs in schools. In C. S. Clauss-Ehlers, Z. N. Serpell, & M. D. Weist (Eds.), *Handbook of culturally responsive school mental health: Advancing research, training, practice, and policy* (pp. 177–186). New York, NY: Springer.

Burt, I. (2012). An innovative approach to working with angry adolescents using therapeutic principles and martial arts. *VISTAS 2012*. Retrieved from http://counselingoutfitters.com/vistas/vistas12/Article_55.pdf

Burt, I., & Butler, S. K. (2011). Capoeira as a clinical intervention: Addressing adolescent aggression with Brazilian martial arts. *Journal of Multicultural Counseling and Development, 39*, 48–57.

Burt, I., Patel, S. H., Butler, S. K., & Gonzalez, T. (2013). Integrating leadership skills into anger management groups to reduce aggressive behaviors: The LIT model. *The Journal for Mental Health Counseling, 35*, 124–141.

Burt, I., Patel, S. H., & Lewis, S. V. (2012). Anger management leadership groups: A creative intervention for increasing social and relational competencies with aggressive youth. *The Journal of Creativity in Mental Health*, 7, 249–261. doi:10.1080/15401383.2012.710168

Butler, S. K., Shillingford, M. A., & Snow-Alexander, M. (2011). African American male students and the achievement gap: Building a successful student/client. *Interamerican Journal of Psychology, 45*, 177–184.

Capoeira, N. (2003). *The little Capoeira book*. Berkeley, CA: North Atlantic.

Capoeira, N. (2006). *A street-smart song: Capoeira philosophy and inner life*. Berkeley, CA: North Atlantic.

Clauss-Ehlers, C. S., Serpell, Z. N., & Weist, M. D. (2013). Introduction: Making the case for culturally responsive school mental health. In C. S. Clauss-Ehlers, Z. N. Serpell, & M. D. Weist (Eds.), *Handbook of culturally responsive school mental health: Advancing research, training, practice, and policy* (pp. 3–15). New York NY: Springer.

da Conceição, S. (n.d.). *Dancing through difficulties: Capoeira as a fight against oppression*. Retrieved from http://www.capoeirakarkara.com/Capoeira%20Paper.pdf

del Barrio, V., Aluja, A., & Spielberger, C. (2004). Anger assessment with the STAXI-CA: Psychometric properties of a new instrument for children and adolescents. *Personality and Individual Differences*, *37*, 227–244. doi:10.1016/j.paid.2003.08.014

Downey, G. (2005). *Learning Capoeira: Lessons in cunning from an Afro-Brazilian art*. New York, NY: Oxford University Press.

Essien, A. (2008). *Capoeira beyond Brazil: From a slave tradition to an international way of life*. Berkeley, CA: Blue Snake Books.

Gladding, S. (2012). *Groups: A counseling specialty* (6th ed.). Upper Saddle River, NJ: Pearson.

Goodrich, K. M., & Luke, M. (2010). The experiences of school counselors-in-training in group work with LGBTQ adolescents. *The Journal for Specialists in Group Work*, *35*, 143–159. doi:10.1080/01933921003705966

Graham, J. A., & Harris, Y. R. (2013). Children of color and parental incarceration: Implications for research, theory, and practice. *Journal of Multicultural Counseling and Development*, *41*, 66–81.

Grothaus, T. (2013). School counselors serving students with disruptive behavior disorders. *Professional School Counseling*, *16*, 245–255. doi:10.5330/PSC.n.2013-16.245

Hackney, C. H. (2013). Martial arts as a pathway to flourishing. In J. D. Sinnott (Ed.), *Positive psychology: Advances in understanding adult motivation* (pp. 145–158). New York, NY: Springer.

Hays, D. G., Arredondo, P., Gladding, S., & Toporek, R. L. (2010). Integrating social justice in group work: The next decade. *Journal for Specialists in Group Work*, *35*, 177–206.

Hill, B., & Meyer, B. L. (2003). *Therapeutic martial arts: The effects of a therapeutic martial arts program on youth in residential psychiatric treatment*. Retrieved from http://www.rivercityaikido.com/TherapeuticMartialArts.html

Joseph, J. (2005). Transgressing boundaries and crossing borders: As Capoeiristas Brasileiras (female Brazilian practitioners of an Afro-Brazilian martial art). *Women & Environments International*, *68*, 31–33.

Joseph, J. (2012). The practice of Capoeira: Diasporic Black culture in Canada. *Ethnic and Racial Studies*, *35*, 1078–1095. doi:10.1080/01419870.2012.661866

Kellner, M. H., Bry, B. H., & Salvador, D. S. (2008). Anger management effects on middle school students with emotional/behavioral disorders: Anger log use, aggressive and prosocial behavior. *Child & Family Behavior Therapy*, *30*, 215–230.

Lewis, J. L. (1992). *Liberation: Deceptive discourse in Brazilian Capoeira*. Chicago, IL: The University of Chicago Press.

Nadal, K. L., Escobar, K. M. V., Prado, G. T., David, E. J. R., & Haynes, K. (2012). Racial microaggressions and the Filipino American experience: Recommendations for counseling and development. *Journal of Multicultural Counseling and Development*, *40*, 156–173.

Orpinas P., & Horne A. M (2004). A teacher-focused approach to prevent and reduce students' aggressive behavior: The GREAT Teacher Program. *American Journal of Preventive Medicine*, *26*, 29–38.

Potik, D., & Schreiber, S. (2013). Carrying body and soul and embracing the one: Qigong group in a day-care psychiatric department. *Body, Movement and Dance in Psychotherapy*, *8*, 108–120. doi:10.1080/17432979.2013.772074

Reynolds, C. R., & Kamphaus, R. W. (2004). *Behavioral assessment scale for children*. Bloomington, MN: Pearson.

Seligman, M. E. P. (1991). *Learned optimism*. New York, NY: Knopf.

Singh, A. A., Merchant, N., Skudrzyk, B., & Ingene, D. (2012). *Association for Specialists in Group Work: Multicultural and social justice competence principles for group workers*. Retrieved from http://www.asgw.org/pdf/ASGW_MC_SJ_Priniciples_final_ASGW.pdf

Steen, S. (2011). Academic and personal development through group work: An exploratory study. *The Journal for Specialists in Group Work*, *36*, 129–143.

Sundstrom, R. R. (2008). *The browning of America and the evasion of social justice*. Albany: SUNY Press.

Thompson, E. H. (2011). The evolution of a children's domestic violence counseling group: Stages and processes. *The Journal for Specialists in Group Work*, *36*, 178–201.

Twemlow, S. W., Biggs, B. K., Nelson, T. D., Vernberg, E. M., Fonagy, P., & Twemlow, S. W. (2008). Effects of participation in a martial arts-based antibullying program in elementary schools. *Psychology in Schools*, *45*, 947–959.

Vereen, L. G., Hill, N. R., & Butler, S. K. (2013). The use of humor and storytelling with African American men: Innovative therapeutic strategies for success in counseling. *International Journal for the Advancement of Counselling*, *35*, 57–63. doi:10.1007/s10447-012-9165-5

Villalba, J. A., Ivers, N. N., & Ohlms, A. B. (2010). Cuento group work in emerging rural Latino communities: Promoting personal-social development of Latina/o middle school students of Mexican heritage. *The Journal for Specialists in Group Work*, *35*, 23–43.

Ware, J. N., Ohrt, J. H., & Swank, J. M. (2012). A phenomenological exploration of children's experiences in a social skills group. *The Journal for Specialists in Group Work*, *37*, 133–151.

Young, M. E. (2013). *Learning the art of helping* (5th ed.). Cranbury, NJ: Pearson.

Young, T. L. (2013). Using motivational interviewing within the early stages of group development. *The Journal for Specialists in Group Work*, *38*, 169–181.

Therapeutic Factors and Members' Perception of Co-Leaders' Attitudes in a Psychoeducational Group for Greek Children With Social Anxiety

Andreas Brouzos
University of Ioannina

Stephanos P. Vassilopoulos
University of Patras

Vasiliki C. Baourda
University of Ioannina

The purpose of this study was to investigate therapeutic factors and perception of co-leaders' attitudes in elementary children. The Critical Incident Questionnaire was collected from participants during 8 sessions of 3 psychoeducational groups for social anxiety, whereas the Barrett-Lennard Relationship Inventory was administered twice. It was found that affective and behavioral therapeutic factors decreased in the working and ending stages, while cognitive therapeutic factors increased significantly as the groups progressed. Moreover, children were able to form a positive perception of co-leaders' attitudes early on, and perceptions further ameliorated as the groups progressed.

During the past few years there has been a rise in group interventions used in schools, especially guidance and psychoeducational groups (Gerrity & DeLucia-Waack, 2006; Kulic, Horne, & Dagley, 2004). The group format is recognized as an effective mode of treatment or prevention for many cognitive, affective, academic, and social problems that children and adolescents might encounter (Hoag & Burlingame, 1997; Kulic et al., 2004). Group work in schools allows more children to be reached in a cost-effective manner (Akos, Goodnough, & Milsom, 2004; Bell, Raczynski, & Horne, 2010). Moreover, the group format is a logical choice for children and adolescents given the importance of socialization and peer relationships between the ages of 6 and 12 (Akos, Hamm, Mack, & Dunaway, 2006; Kulic et al., 2004). In that sense, groups provide children with an accepting and supportive environment, where they can try out new behaviors and skills and learn to interact in effective ways with others with whom they share the same concerns (Akos et al., 2004; Akos et al., 2006). Despite the empirical evidence that demonstrates the effectiveness of group interventions, research investigating the mechanisms responsible for these effects is scarce (Davies, Burlingame, Johnson, Gleave, & Barlow, 2008; Kazdin, 1995; Nickerson & Coleman, 2006). In this study we sought to investigate group processes in a psychoeducational group for socially anxious Greek students, which was found to be efficacious.

One of the most common psychological problems that children report is anxiety, which affects approximately 10–20% of school age children (Barrett, Dadds, & Rapee, 1996; Kendall et al., 1997). Social anxiety, which is defined as a persistent fear of one or more social or performance situations in which the person is exposed to unfamiliar people or to possible scrutiny by others (*DSM–5*; American Psychiatric Association, 2013), has a prevalence rate of 1–2% among school-aged children (Bernstein, Borchardt, & Perwien, 1996) and it has been diagnosed in children as young as 8 years old (Beidel, Turner, & Morris, 2000).

Research has shown that social anxiety impedes the emotional, social, and academic functioning of children and has long-term negative effects in adulthood (Beidel et al., 2000; Kendall et al., 1997). More specifically, young children with social phobia report feeling fear and anxiety when they are interacting with peers or adults (e.g., going to parties) and when they are performing tasks in public (e.g., writing on the classroom board; see Beidel, Turner, & Morris, 1999; Beidel et al., 2000). Children with social anxiety report higher trait anxiety, perceive their academic and cognitive competencies more poorly (Beidel, Turner, & Morris, 1995), engage in more negative self-talk (Kendall, 1994), and experience higher levels of depression (Beidel et al., 2000). Often these children report feelings of loneliness, have fewer friends, demonstrate social skills deficits (Beidel et al., 1999; Rapee & Spence, 2004), are teased more often, and are less liked by their peers (Rapee & Spence, 2004).

Given the pervasiveness of social anxiety symptoms in children as well as its long-lasting effects in adulthood, interventions specifically designed to address social anxiety in school age children are needed (Beidel et al., 2000; Kendall, 1994). Group treatment based on a cognitive-behavioral approach that includes psychoeducation and social skills training has proven to be efficacious in reducing social anxiety symptoms in school-aged children and adolescents (Barrett et al., 1996; Beidel et al., 2000; Kendall et al., 1997). More recently, our group conducted a psychoeducational intervention in Greece, which was delivered in a school setting and was efficacious in reducing social anxiety symptoms, negative interpretations for ambiguous events and in increasing benign interpretations and self-reported likeability in school children with social anxiety symptoms (Vassilopoulos, Brouzos, Damer, Mellou, & Mitropoulou, 2013).

Several researchers have emphasized the need for more group process research (Shechtman, 2007; Silverman et al., 1999). In addition, children and adolescents have unique characteristics that differentiate them from adults. Therefore, group processes in groups comprised of children and adolescents may differ from adult groups (DeLucia-Waack, 2000; Shechtman, 2007). Nonetheless, there are only a few studies of group process in groups of children and adolescents (Kazdin, 1995; Nickerson & Coleman, 2006; Shechtman, 2007) and even fewer regarding the processes in psychoeducational groups (Shechtman, Bar-el, & Hadar, 1997). Moreover, with almost 75% of group interventions for children and adolescents taking place in the school setting (Hoag & Burlingame, 1997) there is a growing need for process research in this context.

Research in group processes has traditionally examined mechanisms such as the therapeutic factors, group climate, and therapeutic alliance (Davies et al., 2008), as well as specific leader and member interactions and attitudes (Kazdin, 1995) like Rogers's core conditions of change (Garfield, 1990). The therapeutic factors are considered among the most important mechanisms of change that take place in the group setting (Yalom & Leszcz, 2005) and research shows there are linked to group outcomes (e.g., Shechtman, 2007). Considerable work in the area of group therapeutic factors has been performed by Yalom (Yalom & Leszcz, 2005), who developed a model of 11 therapeutic factors. Building on Yalom's work, other researchers have proposed that we can study the perceptions of group members regarding the therapeutic factors by classifying their descriptions of important session events into predetermined categories. Bloch, Reibstein, Crouch, Holroyd, and Themen (1979) proposed a model which includes 10 therapeutic factors belonging to three broader clusters. More specifically, acceptance, catharsis, and instillation of hope are classified as affective factors because they involve emotional expressions. Altruism, learning from interpersonal actions, and self-disclosure are behavioral because they involve learning by doing. Finally, guidance, self-understanding, universality, and vicarious learning are cognitive because they involve thought processes. Based on this model, Kivlighan, Multon, and Brossat (1996) developed a rating system which produced four therapeutic factor dimensions: Emotional Awareness–Insight which refers to affective experiences related to gaining insight, Relationship–Climate which refers to the relationship formed between members or members and therapist, Other versus Self-Focus which refers to a member's focus outside of himself or herself, and lastly Problem Definition–Change which refers to understanding a problem and changing behaviors.

Various studies now show that the therapeutic factors are affected by the type of group, the stage of group development, and the personal characteristics of group members (Kivlighan & Goldfine, 1991; Shechtman & Gluk, 2005; Yalom & Leszcz, 2005). Yalom and Leszcz (2005) hypothesized that group members would be more likely to value guidance, instillation of hope, and universality in the early stages of group development, and that altruism and cohesion would be valued consistently throughout the group's existence. Kivlighan and Goldfine (1991), studying interpersonal growth in group members, found that acceptance was equally important in the first and last stages of group development, and that universality and hope decreased over time while catharsis and guidance increased. Moreover, they found that affiliative group members valued cognitive therapeutic factors, while less affiliative members valued behavioral factors. Kivlighan and Mullison (1988) also reported that universality was more important in early stages of group development, whereas learning from interpersonal actions became more important in later stages. They additionally found that in the early developmental stages, members valued cognitive factors, while later on they tended to value the behavioral ones. Finally, MacKenzie (1987) found that in the early stages of group development, group members were more likely to endorse acceptance, instillation of hope, universality, and self-understanding, whereas in later stages they endorsed learning from interpersonal actions and vicarious learning.

Regarding the age of group members, some researchers have suggested that some therapeutic factors, like cohesion, develop in different patterns in children and adolescent groups (Bratton, Ceballos, & Ferebee, 2009). Nonetheless, there has been little research regarding the presence of therapeutic factors in groups of children (Shechtman, 2003). Shechtman and Gluk (2005) investigated the endorsement of therapeutic factors in psychotherapy groups of school-aged children presenting emotional, social, and behavioral problems and found that children endorsed the relationship-climate as the most important factor, which includes encouragement, support, acceptance, and liking the group. Altruism, universality, learning from feedback, self-disclosure, and catharsis were ranked next by the children. Finally, the component of problem identification-change received the lowest ratings. The authors concluded that the therapeutic factors refer to all children regardless of gender, even though there was a gender difference on emotional awareness-insight, in that girls scored higher than boys. A second study, which examined the therapeutic factors that adolescents value in counseling or psychoeducational groups, found that in both types of intervention, boys and girls equally valued interpersonal learning and catharsis as the most important therapeutic factors (Shechtman et al., 1997). Still, studies that have investigated group process in Greece are currently lacking. The further investigation of the endorsement of therapeutic factors in a psychoeducational group of Greek children was the first aim of the current study.

The therapeutic alliance between group members and leader has recently received much attention in light of studies that demonstrate it is a strong predictor of the therapeutic outcome in various types of groups (Crits-Christoph, Johnson, Connolly Gibbons, & Gallop, 2013; Duncan et al., 2003; Woody & Adessky, 2002). Building on Bordin's (1979) conceptualization of therapeutic alliance in individual therapy, group alliance concerns "the active collaboration on therapeutic issues that occurs between members, between members and therapist(s) and between members and the group as a whole" (Gillaspy, Wright, Campbell, Stokes, & Adinoff, 2002, p. 320). Many scholars have pointed out that the therapeutic alliance is closely linked to Rogers's core conditions of unconditional positive regard, empathic understanding, and congruence (Kirschenbaum & Jourdan, 2005). A large number of studies investigating those core conditions found they are related to therapeutic outcomes, providing further support for the hypothesis that the core conditions and the concept of therapeutic alliance are interdependent and overlapping and all play an important role in the therapeutic process and outcome (Kirschenbaum & Jourdan, 2005; Lambert & Barley, 2001). For example, there is evidence that therapist's empathic style is more effective than a confrontational style in the treatment of substance use disorders (Crits-Christoph et al., 2013), and group leaders' empathy level in general is thought to be predictive of group outcome (Johnson, Burlingame, Olsen, Davies, & Gleave, 2005). Moreover, Oetzel and Scherer (2003) have underlined the importance of therapist's empathy, unconditional regard and congruence in building a positive therapeutic relationship when working with adolescents. Nevertheless, research investigating the perception of group leaders' attitudes and behaviors in children's groups is scarce. This was the second aim of the current study.

To sum up, in this study we examined the endorsement of therapeutic factors in a non-clinical population of elementary school children with moderate to high social anxiety, who participated in a school-based psychoeducational intervention in Greece. Furthermore, we examined the development of children's perception of the group leader's empathy, positive regard, congruence, and unconditionality. To our knowledge this is the first study of group processes in Greece in general. We hypothesized that participants would endorse different therapeutic factors in different stages of group development, as suggested by the literature review reported above. Based on the suggestion put forward by Kivlighan and Lilly (1997) that group members who are relatively healthy (i.e., not severely disturbed) form a positive relationship to group leaders from the first group sessions, we also hypothesized that children would be able to form a positive perception of co-leaders' attitudes early on, which would further ameliorate as the group progressed.

METHOD

Participants

The participants were 13 boys and 27 girls 10–12 years old (M = 10.83) who attended an elementary school in the city of Ioannina, Greece. From these students, 18 were attending the fourth grade, 13 the fifth grade, and 9 the sixth grade. The students were chosen based on their scores on the Social Anxiety Scale for Children-Revised (SASC–R), a self-report measure of child social anxiety (La Greca & Stone, 1993) that was administered to students before the intervention. Only children who scored at or above the mean on the SASC–R participated in this study.

The participants were assigned to three groups of 9–16 members. Two of the groups consisted of students from both the fourth and the fifth grade, while the third group consisted of 9 students from the sixth grade. Written informed consent and verbal assent were obtained from parents and participating children, respectively.

Measures and Analyses

Critical Incident Questionnaire. The Critical Incident Questionnaire (CIQ; Kivlighan & Goldfine, 1991) is used to assess important therapeutic factors for group members during a group session. The questionnaire is open-ended and reads as follows: "Of the events that occurred in this group session today, which one do you feel was the most important to/for you personally? Describe the event—what took place, the group members involved, and their reactions. Why was this important to you?" With this method researchers can tap directly into each member's perspective of what makes the group effective

(DeLucia-Waack, 1997; Lese & MacNair-Semands, 2000; MacKenzie, 1987).

The CIQ was translated into Greek and administered to all group members at the end of each meeting. The answers of the members were analyzed using the rating system method described by Bloch et al. (1979). More specifically, two independent raters classified the members' responses into the ten therapeutic factors proposed: Acceptance, catharsis, instillation of hope, altruism, learning from interpersonal actions, self-disclosure, guidance, self-understanding, universality, and vicarious learning. This method has been used in a number of studies with satisfactory reliability (Kivlighan & Goldfine, 1991; Nitza, 2011).

Two postgraduate students were trained in this rating system. The training included discussion of the definitions of the therapeutic factors followed by the joint rating of the answers of the first meeting until they had reached 100% agreement. They then independently rated the answers for the rest of the meetings, reaching an initial 90% agreement in their ratings. In the cases of disagreement in the coding, the two raters coded the item in question following discussion, finally reaching total agreement in the classification of the members' answers.

There is a consensus among researchers that all groups progress through a number of developmental stages (MacKenzie, 1997) and the development of psychoeducational groups usually includes three stages: a beginning stage, a middle or working stage, and an ending stage (Jones & Robinson, 2000). Accordingly, the therapeutic factors were grouped according to the stage of the group development: beginning stage (the therapeutic factors of the first two meetings), working stage (the factors of the third, fourth, fifth, and sixth meetings), and ending stage (the factors of the last two meetings). The number of times each therapeutic factor was mentioned by the group members in each stage was divided by the total number of answers in that stage and multiplied by 100 to compute the percentage value of each factor in each developmental stage. This method was chosen because of unequal sample sizes for each developmental stage (Shechtman et al., 1997). In order to ascertain whether there was a relationship between the therapeutic factors and the developmental stage of the group, the Pearson's chi-square test was used. This is a statistic measure that examines whether there is an association between two categorical variables by comparing the frequencies observed in certain categories to the frequencies one would expect to get in those categories by chance (Field, 2013).

Barrett-Lennard Relationship Inventory. The Relationship Inventory was developed by Barrett-Lennard in 1962 to assess the perceived quality of therapeutic relationships based on Roger's core conditions of empathy, congruence, unconditionality, and positive regard (Kolb, Beutler, Davis, Crago, & Shanfield, 1985). Since its initial construction, the questionnaire has been revised and used extensively in clinical and field settings, where it was found to have good internal consistency and test-retest reliability (Kirschenbaum & Jourdan, 2005).

In the current study we used the short version of the questionnaire which consists of 40 items (Barrett-Lennard, 1995): 10 items for empathy that assess the degree to which the therapist manages to communicate personal comprehension of the client's experience; 10 items for regard that measure the degree to which the therapist communicates caring and respect for the client; 10 items for congruence that assess the degree to which the therapist is being himself and not pretending, and 10 items for unconditionality that measure the degree to which the therapist communicates caring and respect for the client constantly regardless of the circumstances (Lambert & Barley, 2001). The present measure has been translated into Greek and then back-translated by a bilingual translator and modified until cross-language equivalence was established under the supervision of the first author (Brouzos & Kouzouni, 2010). In addition, two experts in person-centered counseling confirmed the measure's face validity. For the purposes of the current study, instead of the original Likert scale, which ranged from –3 (*strongly disagree*) to +3 (*strongly agree*), a modified 6-point Likert scale ranging from 1 (*strongly disagree*) to 6 (*strongly agree*) was used to make it more simple and straightforward for children. Furthermore, the wording was adapted to the developmental level of the participants.

The Barrett-Lennard Relationship Inventory was administered twice. First, it was administered at the end of the third session, where children received thorough instructions to complete it at home and return it the next group meeting. This was due to time limitations that prevented children from completing the questionnaire on site. Only two children failed to return the questionnaire completed. Second, 1 week after the completion of the intervention, the questionnaire was re-administered to group members to complete it during the class hour.

The reliability of each factor for each group leader was measured using Cronbach's alpha (see Table 1). The unconditionality factor had unacceptable low reliability and was excluded from further analyses. Following previous studies (e.g., Kolb et al., 1985), a composite score was also calculated by summing the scores of all 40 items after reversing the scoring for the negatively worded items, in order to have a measure of the members' aggregate perception of the co-leaders' attitudes. This aggregated score has also the additional advantage that it included the items of the unconditionality factor that was excluded from the analyses.

Table 1 Reliability of the Factors of the Barrett-Lennard Relationship Inventory Measured by Cronbach's Alpha

	First Leader		*Second Leader*	
	Measurement 1	*Measurement 2*	*Measurement 1*	*Measurement 2*
Regard	0.818	0.798	0.862	0.774
Empathy	0.739	0.762	0.788	0.703
Unconditionality	0.400	0.667	0.110	0.634
Congruence	0.728	0.601	0.551	0.679
Aggregated Attitude	0.871	0.853	0.869	0.881

The data for Barrett-Lennard Relationship Inventory factors were analyzed using paired samples t-test for each group leader. To investigate possible differences in attitude perception between boys and girls, an independent samples t-test was conducted for each factor separately. Also, one-way ANOVAs were used to investigate any differences in attitude perception between the three individual psychoeducational groups participating in the study.

Procedure

Participation in the study was voluntary. First, participants for the groups were identified and verbal informed assents were obtained. Participating children were also asked to give a consent form to their parents. All children but one (who was excluded from the study) agreed to take part. The three groups were co-facilitated by two masters' students from the Counseling program in the Department of Primary Education at the University of Ioannina, Greece. Both facilitators were female and had attended a postgraduate group counseling course. One of the facilitators was a school teacher with previous experience in facilitating psychoeducational groups of elementary school children and the second facilitator was a psychologist. Both facilitators received supervision on a regular basis.

The group sessions took place in the school library once a week for 8 consecutive weeks. Each session lasted 45 min and consisted of four parts. The first part consisted of the introduction of the session's topic followed by a discussion among the members and the facilitators. In the second part, the facilitators introduced one or two structured activities that the children carried out individually or in small groups. In the third part the activity was processed. The final part included the processing and closing of the session. For an overview of the intervention see Vassilopoulos et al. (2013).

RESULTS

Therapeutic Factors

From a total of 292 answers, 148 were classified in the categories of the therapeutic factors described by Bloch et al. (1979). Statistical analyses with the χ^2 criterion revealed significant statistical differences in the presence of the therapeutic factors during the three stages of group development, as is shown in Table 2.

During the first stage of group development, learning from interpersonal action was the most frequently mentioned factor, followed by acceptance, instillation of hope, and catharsis. Self-disclosure, guidance, and altruism were reported in relatively small percentages, while self-understanding, universality, and vicarious learning were not reported at all by group members.

In the working stage, it was the factor of guidance that was most frequently reported. The factors of learning from interpersonal action, self-understanding, acceptance, vicarious learning, self-disclosure, catharsis, and instillation of hope were all reported in small percentages, and the factors of altruism and universality were not mentioned at all by group members.

During the ending stage, guidance continued to be the most frequently mentioned factor followed by vicarious learning. Self-understanding, catharsis, acceptance, learning from interpersonal action, and self-disclosure were reported in small percentages. The

Table 2 Percentages of Therapeutic Factors by Developmental Stage of the Group

Therapeutic factor	*Beginning Stage*	*Working Stage*	*Ending Stage*
Acceptance	13.89%	5.56%	4.55%
Altruism	5.56%	0.00%	0.00%
Catharsis	11.11%	1.11%*	9.09%
Guidance	5.56%	67.78%**	50.00%##
Instillation of hope	13.89%	1.11%**	0.00%
Learning from interpersonal action	41.67%	10.00%**	4.55%##
Self-disclosure	8.33%	2.22%	4.55%
Self-understanding	0.00%	6.67%	9.09%
Universality	0.00%	0.00%	0.00%
Vicarious learning	0.00%	5.56%	18.18%#

Note:
*$p<.05$ between the working and the beginning stage
** $p<.001$ between the working and the beginning stage
# $p<.05$ between the ending and the beginning stage
$p<.001$ between the ending and the beginning stage

Table 3 Percentages of Hierarchies of Therapeutic Factors by Developmental Stage of the Group

Hierarchies of Therapeutic factors	*Beginning Stage*	*Working Stage*	*Ending Stage*
Affective	38.89%†	7.78%*††	13.64%††
Behavioral	55.56%$^{\&}$	12.22%$^{*\&}$	9.09%$^{\#\,\&}$
Cognitive	5.56%	80.00%*	77.27%$^{\#}$

Note:
* $p<.001$ between the working and the beginning stage
$^{\#}$ $p<.001$ between the ending and the beginning stage
$^{\&}$ $p<.001$ between the behavioral and cognitive therapeutic factors
† $p<.01$ between the affective and cognitive therapeutic factors
†† $p<.001$ between the affective and cognitive therapeutic factors

factors of altruism, instillation of hope, and universality were not mentioned by group members during this stage.

Statistical analyses with the χ^2 criterion revealed an increased presence of affective and behavioral therapeutic factors in the beginning stage of group development as opposed to an increased presence of cognitive factors in later stages. During the beginning stage of group development, most of the therapeutic factors mentioned by group members were behavioral, followed by affective factors, while the cognitive factors were mentioned in significantly lower percentages ($p < .01$). However, during both the working and the ending stage the reference to cognitive factors increased significantly ($p < .001$) while the reference to affective and behavioral factors decreased ($p < .001$; see Table 3).

Perception of Group Co-Leaders' Attitudes

The change for regard did not reach significance from pretest to posttest, even though there was an increase in mean ratings for both group co-leaders. A significant increase was noted for empathy, but only for the first co-leader. Regarding the second co-leader, although there was an increase of the perceived empathy at posttest, this did not reach significance. For both group co-leaders a significant increase was found for congruence at posttest. Finally, regarding the aggregated attitude, which consisted of all 40 items of the Barrett-Lennard Relationship Inventory, a significant increase was found for both group co-leaders (see Table 4).

The analysis did not reveal any significant differences between the three psychoeducational groups participating in the study concerning

Table 4 Perceptions of Co-Leaders' Attitudes at Pretest (After the Third Group Meeting) and Posttest (One Week After the Termination of the Intervention)

		Pretest *M* (± *SD*)	*Posttest* *M* (± *SD*)	*t*	*df*	*p*
Regard	First Leader	5.32 (±0.64)	5.46 (±0.62)	−1.310	31	0.200
	Second Leader	5.15 (±0.79)	5.34 (±0.73)	−1.386	25	0.178
Empathy	First Leader	4.77 (±0.69)	5.3 (±0.66)	−2.470	31	**0.019**
	Second Leader	4.66 (±0.76)	4.84 (±0.64)	−1.422	22	0.169
Congruence	First Leader	4.82 (±0.78)	5.27 (±0.55)	−4.142	32	**0.000**
	Second Leader	4.60 (±0.66)	5.08 (±0.66)	−4.021	23	**0.001**
Aggregated Attitude	First Leader	4.82 (±0.49)	5.24 (±0.40)	−5.811	27	**0.000**
	Second Leader	4.65 (±0.52)	5.04 (±0.51)	−3.925	18	**0.001**

Note: Values in boldface are statistically significant.

their scores for the two group leaders at pre- and posttest ($p > .05$). Similarly, regarding gender differences, the independent samples *t*-tests that were performed on pre- and posttest scores did not reveal any significant differences ($p > .05$), with the exception of a significant difference on empathy scores for the first group leader at posttest between boys ($M = 50.75$, $SD = 8.09$) and girls ($M = 56.65$, $SD = 3.65$), $t(13.117) = -2.416$, $p = .031$.

DISCUSSION

The purpose of this study was to investigate the endorsement of therapeutic factors in each stage of group development, as well as the development of group members' perceptions of co-leaders' attitudes towards them. Our first hypothesis regarding the relative importance of different therapeutic factors in different group stages was supported by the results. Affective and behavioral therapeutic factors decreased in the working and ending stages, while the presence of cognitive therapeutic factors increased significantly as the groups progressed. More specifically, guidance and vicarious learning increased in the second and third group stage compared to their endorsement in the first stage, whereas installation of hope and learning from interpersonal action decreased as the groups progressed.

The high percentages of cognitive therapeutic factors combined with the relatively low presence of affective and behavioral factors can be interpreted by the fact that the intervention was psychoeducational in nature and based on the cognitive-behavioral theory. Previous research reveals that cognitive therapeutic factors predominate in cognitive-behavioral group therapies (Shechtman, 2003; Shechtman & Pastor, 2005) and especially in psychoeducational groups that place an emphasis on teaching group members specific skills and behaviors (Brown, 2011; Shechtman & Pastor, 2005).

A previous study of therapeutic factors in a psychoeducational group with children showed that guidance predominated during the working group stage (Shechtman & Pastor, 2005), which was accounted by the fact that the main goal of psychoeducational groups is to educate members and help them acquire specific skills. The present study provides further support for this notion through the finding that guidance was the most frequently mentioned therapeutic factor during the working and ending group stages. Thus, leaders of psychoeducational groups appear to rely on directive guidance to educate members and attain the group goals. Another possible interpretation for the high occurrence of guidance is that guidance was the most easily recognized factor by the children due to cultural characteristics. More specifically, the psychoeducational group was conducted within the school context which, in Greece, places a premium on information-packed lecturing and student's attentive listening (see relevant discussion below).

In the present study, instillation of hope was reported mainly during the beginning stage and references to it reduced in later stages of group development. This finding is consistent with the literature which suggests that instillation of hope is very important, especially during the first stage of group development, because it helps members believe that they can improve for the better (DeLucia-Waack, 2006; Kivlighan & Goldfine, 1991; Yalom & Leszcz, 2005).

Nevertheless, some of our findings were unexpected in the light of previous research. Many researchers have underlined the importance of acceptance for children participating in psychoeducational and counseling groups during the beginning and working stage of group development, as well as the significance of universality for the first stages of group development (Akos et al., 2006; Kivlighan & Goldfine, 1991; Shechtman, 2007). In the present study, universality was not reported at all by group members and acceptance was reported mainly in the beginning stage of group development and appeared to decrease over time. This may be due to the fact that the group facilitators emphasized the educational aspect of the groups rather than the similarities between group members or the development of social relations between them. (However the group leaders did try repeatedly to make connections between children, especially during the first two sessions). Another possibility may be that the members took for granted their similarities and the existence of an accepting climate between them, since they were peers coming from the same cohort, thus omitting references to universality and minimizing references to acceptance.

The therapeutic factor of catharsis does not usually appear in psychoeducational groups since it is not thought to be consistent with their goals (Corey, Corey, & Corey, 2010). In the present study, members experienced catharsis in direct reference to the group activities they performed during the second, third, and seventh group session, in which activities aimed at the experience and expression of feelings. These findings provide support to the notion that specific leader functions and interventions might help foster specific therapeutic factors (Morran, Stockton, Cline, & Teed, 1998). More specifically, they suggest that it is possible for leaders of psychoeducational groups to provoke intense cathartic feelings in members by including activities that aim at the expression of intense emotions. This is particularly important for cultures like the Greek culture where the expression of one's emotions and feelings is not only an acceptable way of interpersonal communication but also contributes to the development of strong ties between people. Thus, leaders must be prepared to process such emotions in order to facilitate affective, behavioral, cognitive or/and social changes in children (Corey et al., 2010).

Many researchers have stressed the significance of interpersonal and vicarious learning that take place within a group setting for the personal growth of group members (Akos et al., 2006). In the current study, learning from interpersonal action was pronounced during the first stage and decreased over time, while vicarious learning was pronounced at the ending stage. These results stand in contrast with past studies which evidenced an absence of a connection between these factors and specific stages of group development (Kivlighan & Goldfine, 1991).

The increase in vicarious learning indicates that as group cohesion builds up, members start to learn by observing each other. Interestingly, reports of this factor were made during the third, fourth, seventh, and eighth group session, as members participated in small group activities that gave them the opportunity to interact. However, the increase of vicarious learning was combined with a decrease of learning from interpersonal action. Other researchers have proposed that these two therapeutic factors should be considered as two facets of the same factor (MacKenzie, 1987). Nevertheless, our findings suggest that they probably represent the two ends of a continuum. Indeed, by definition, learning from interpersonal action takes place when group members try to connect with each other in a positive, constructive way, whereas vicarious learning occurs when group members learn something important for themselves by observing other group members (Bloch et al., 1979). Therefore, it makes sense to assume that learning from interpersonal action is more pronounced during the first group stage, when members try to establish a relationship between them, and once this relationship is in place the members can begin to safely observe each other's behaviors and learn from them.

Regarding the second hypothesis, findings on the aggregated attitude score show that group members formed a positive perception of both group leaders early on and that this perception further improved as the group progressed. The relatively high scores of aggregated attitude at pretest (third group session) provide further support for the notion that group members who are relatively healthy develop a positive relationship with group leaders, even from the first sessions (Kivlighan & Lilly, 1997). Moreover, analyses of the Barrett-Lennard Relationship inventory factors revealed an elevated score for the perception of positive regard at pretest, which was further increased at posttest, even though the change was only marginal and did not reach significant level.

The results also revealed that there was a significant rise in the perception of empathy, but only for the first leader. This finding can be explained in the light of different tasks performed by each co-leader in the groups. The first leader had the main responsibility of leading the teams (opening each session, introducing and processing the activities, and closing the session), whereas the second leader assisted as needed. Due to their different levels of involvement in leading the groups, it is possible that group members perceived the second co-leader as more detached and less empathic.

Finally, group members perceived the team leaders as being congruent in their attitudes throughout the intervention, and this perception increased significantly over time. Also, the analyses showed that there were no gender differences or differences between the three individual psychoeducational groups regarding their members' perceptions of leaders' attitudes towards them. This finding shows that group co-leaders functioned rather consistently and might have displayed the same attitude towards all three groups. Furthermore it suggests that group members, regardless of their gender, perceive group leaders' attitudes in pretty much the same way.

Limitations

This study is not without limitations. First, the sample was small and as a consequence we could not investigate the differential endorsement of therapeutic factors between boys and girls. More research is needed with larger samples not only to replicate the present study's findings, but also to examine possible gender differences in the endorsement of therapeutic factors.

Second, during the classification of the critical incidents, it was noticed that the classification of Bloch et al. (1979) was limited. More specifically, there were answers that could not be classified into any category despite the fact that they contained information that could prove useful for the evaluation of the specific group session or the intervention in general. MacKenzie (1987) suggested that the therapeutic factor categories proposed by Bloch and colleagues need to become more focused conceptually and that further categories are needed to depict negative issues that arise in groups. Moreover, MacKenzie (1987) argued that categories such as "guidance" are not suitable for cognitive-behavioral interventions which are more directive in nature. Other approaches to measuring therapeutic factors, such as the Group Counseling Helpful Impacts Scale (Kivlighan et al., 1996), might prove to be more suitable.

Third, the therapeutic factors were exclusively assessed from the perspective of group members. Future studies should try to assess therapeutic factors in psychoeducational groups for children using multiple perspectives, such as members, leaders, and trained observers. Finally, the use of the Barrett-Lennard Relationship Inventory constitutes both a limitation and a strength of the present study. It is a limitation because no other studies have used this questionnaire before to study group processes, which limits the comparability of the current results with past studies. But it is also a strength, because it is a well-established measure and there is currently no other measure that could tap into all core attitudes that have been shown to lead to therapeutic change.

Conclusions and Implications

Despite the aforementioned limitations, the current study is among the few studies that investigated group processes in a psychoeducational group that has been shown to reduce social anxiety in children (Vassilopoulos et al., 2013) and, to the best of our knowledge, it provides the first investigation of group processes overall in Greece. The results appear to suggest that group leaders can affect the emergence of specific therapeutic factors in psychoeducational groups by facilitating the activities of each session and their processing, thus supporting Shechtman's (2007) notion that leaders use different skills according to the goals of the group and their theoretical orientation. More specifically, the results of the the present study show that the therapeutic factor of catharsis might emerge when group members are engaged in activities that involve expression of emotions, whereas the therapeutic factors of vicarious learning and learning from interpersonal actions are likely to emerge when group members are engaged in group activities that involve interpersonal interaction. A clear implication of these findings is that when designing psychoeducational groups, counselors should be aware of the therapeutic factors that might prove beneficial for their group members—depending on the group developmental stage and the cultural context in the which the intervention is taking place—and select activities that are more likely to lead to the emergence of those factors.

A second implication relates to the fact that only children who presented moderate to high scores on a social anxiety measure participated in this study. Social anxiety has been conceptualized as an inability to relate to others, and individuals suffering from social anxiety have often difficulty in establishing and maintaining interpersonal relationships due to beliefs of personal inadequacy, skills deficits, and debilitating fears of negative evaluation by others (Alden & Taylor, 2004). In addition, participation in a counseling group is a particularly anxiety-provoking situation for these individuals, in the sense that it involves multiple and intense interpersonal contacts with unfamiliar persons (Vassilopoulos & Brouzos, 2012). The fact that children high in social anxiety were able to perceive co-leaders as showing positive regard and empathy towards them is very encouraging and suggests that these children might benefit from the leader-member therapeutic alliance developed within the structured format of a psychoeducational group.

A final implication has to do with the suitability of psychoeducational groups as a mode of school-based intervention in Greece. Greek culture is typically portrayed as a collectivistic, large power distance, and high-context culture (Jandt, 2010). The educational policy of Greece still follows the traditional banking model of education and continues to place a premium on information-packed lecturing and student's attentive listening. Short-term, directive, and goal-oriented counseling that provides concrete advice and guidance has been suggested as the intervention of choice for collectivistic societies (Dwairy, 2002). Thus, the fact that school age children in the current study valued the opportunity to receive directive guidance suggests that psychoeducational groups are not only compatible with their day-to-day experience in the classroom, but also constitute a culturally appropriate mode of intervention for Greek students. Finally, given the role that the therapeutic factor of catharsis might have played in the program, we argue that psychoeducational groups are a welcome type of intervention, especially where the Greek educational system is concerned, for which the social and emotional education has yet to find its way into the national curriculum.

REFERENCES

Akos, P., Goodnough, G. E., & Milsom, A. S. (2004). Preparing school counselors for group work. *The Journal for Specialists in Group Work, 29*, 127–136. doi:10.1080/01933920490275637

Akos, P., Hamm, J. V., Mack, S. G., & Dunaway, M. (2006). Utilizing the developmental influence of peers in middle school groups. *The Journal for Specialists in Group Work, 32*, 51–60. doi:10.1080/01933920600977648

Alden, L. E., & Taylor, C. T. (2004). Interpersonal process in social phobia. *Clinical Psychology Review, 24*, 857–882.

American Psychiatric Association. (2013). *Diagnostic and statistical manual of mental disorders* (5th ed.). Washington, DC: Author.

Barrett, P., Dadds, M., & Rapee, R. (1996). Family treatment of childhood anxiety: A controlled trial. *Journal of Consulting & Clinical Psychology, 64*, 333–342.

Barrett-Lennard, G. T. (1995). *The Relationship Inventory (Form MO-40, ver. 2)*. Unpublished manuscript, The Centre for Studies in Human Relation, Perth, Australia.

Beidel, D. C., Turner, S., & Morris, T. (1995). A new inventory to assess childhood social anxiety and phobia: The Social Phobia and Anxiety Inventory for Children. *Psychological Assessment, 7*, 73–79. doi:10.1037/1040-3590.7.1.73

Beidel, D. C., Turner, S., & Morris, T. (1999). Psychopathology of childhood social phobia. *Journal of the American Academy of Child & Adolescent Psychiatry, 38*, 643–650.

Beidel, D. C., Turner, S. M., & Morris, T. L. (2000). Behavioral treatment of childhood social phobia. *Journal of Consulting & Clinical Psychology, 68*, 1072–1080. doi:10.1037/0022-006x.68.6.1072

Bell, C. D., Raczynski, K. A., & Horne, A. M. (2010). Bully Busters abbreviated: Evaluation of a group-based bully intervention and prevention program. *Group Dynamics: Theory, Research, and Practice, 14*, 257–267. doi:10.1037/a0020596

Bernstein, G. A., Borchardt, C. M., & Perwien, A. R. (1996). Anxiety disorders in children and adolescents: A review of the past 10 years. *Journal of the American Academy of Child and Adolescent Psychiatry, 35*, 1110–1119.

Bloch, S., Reibstein, J., Crouch, E., Holroyd, P., & Themen, J. (1979). A method for the study of therapeutic factors in group psychotherapy. *The British Journal of Psychiatry, 134*, 257–263. doi:10.1192/bjp.134.3.257

Bordin, E. S. (1979). The generalizability of the psychoanalytic concept of the working alliance. *Psychotherapy: Theory, Research & Practice, 16*, 252–260.

Bratton, S. C., Ceballos, P. L., & Ferebee, K. W. (2009). Integration of structured expressive activities within a humanistic group play therapy format for preadolescents. *The Journal for Specialists in Group Work, 34*, 251–275. doi:10.1080/01933920903033487

Brouzos, A., & Kouzouni, K. (2010). Teacher-student relationship: A pilot application of the Barrett-Lennard Relationship Inventory to 5th and 6th graders. In A. V.

Kosmopoulos & S. P. Vassilopoulos (Eds.), *The pedagogical relationship* (pp. 245–258). Athens, Greece: Grigoris. (in Greek)

Brown, N. W. (2011). *Psychoeducational groups: Process and practice* (3rd ed.). London, England: Routledge.

Corey, M. S., Corey, G., & Corey, C. (2010). *Groups: Process and practice* (8th ed.). Belmont, CA: Brooks/Cole, Cengage Learning.

Crits-Christoph, P., Johnson, J. E., Connolly Gibbons, M. B., & Gallop, R. (2013). Process predictors of the outcome of group drug counseling. *Journal of Consulting and Clinical Psychology, 81*, 23–34. doi:10.1037/a0030101

Davies, D. R., Burlingame, G. M., Johnson, J. E., Gleave, R. L., & Barlow, S. H. (2008). The effects of a feedback intervention on group process and outcome. *Group Dynamics: Theory, Research, and Practice, 12*, 141–154. doi:10.1037/1089-2699.12.2.141

DeLucia-Waack, J. L. (1997). Measuring the effectiveness of group work: A review and analysis of process and outcome measures. *The Journal for Specialists in Group Work, 22*, 277–293. doi:10.1080/01933929708415531

DeLucia-Waack, J. L. (2000). Effective group work in the schools. *The Journal for Specialists in Group Work, 25*, 131–132. doi:10.1080/01933920008411456

DeLucia-Waack, J. L. (2006). *Leading psychoeducational groups for children and adolescents*. Thousand Oaks, CA: Sage.

Duncan, B. L., Miller, S. D., Sparks, J. A., Claud, D. A., Reynolds, L. R., Brown, J., & Johnson, L. D. (2003). The Session Rating Scale: Preliminary psychometric properties of a "working" alliance measure. *Journal of Brief Therapy, 3*, 3–12.

Dwairy, M. (2002). Foundations of psychosocial dynamic personality theory of collective people. *Clinical Psychology Review, 22*, 343–360.

Field, A. (2013). *Discovering statistics using IBM SPSS statistics* (4th ed.). London, England: Sage.

Garfield, S. (1990). Issues and methods in psychotherapy process research. *Journal of Consulting & Clinical Psychology, 58*, 273–280.

Gerrity, D. A., & DeLucia-Waack, J. L. (2006). Effectiveness of groups in the schools. *The Journal for Specialists in Group Work, 32*, 97–106. doi:10.1080/01933920600978604

Gillaspy, J. A., Wright, A. R., Campbell, C., Stokes, S., & Adinoff, B. (2002). Group alliance and cohesion as predictors of drug and alcohol abuse treatment outcomes. *Psychotherapy Research, 12*, 213–229. doi:10.1093/ptr/12.2.213

Hoag, M. J., & Burlingame, G. M. (1997). Evaluating the effectiveness of child and adolescent group treatment: A meta-analytic review. *Journal of Clinical Child Psychology, 26*, 234–246. doi:10.1207/s15374424jccp2603_2

Jandt, F. E. (2010). *An introduction to intercultural communication: Identities in a global community* (6th ed.). Thousand Oaks, CA: Sage.

Johnson, J. E., Burlingame, G. M., Olsen, J. A., Davies, D. R., & Gleave, R. L. (2005). Group climate, cohesion, alliance, and empathy in group psychotherapy: Multilevel structural equation models. *Journal of Counseling Psychology, 52*, 310–321.

Jones, K. D., & Robinson, E. H. M. (2000). Psychoeducational groups: A model for choosing topics and exercises appropriate to group stage. *The Journal for Specialists in Group Work, 25*, 356–365. doi:10.1080/01933920008411679

Kazdin, A. (1995). Bridging child, adolescent, and adult psychotherapy: Directions for research. *Psychotherapy Research, 5*, 258–277. doi:10.1080/10503309512331331376

Kendall, P. C. (1994). Treating anxiety disorders in children: Results of a randomized clinical trial. *Journal of Consulting & Clinical Psychology, 62*, 100–110.

Kendall, P. C., Flannery-Schroeder, E., Panichelli-Mindel, S., Southam-Gerow, M. A., Henin, A., & Warman, M. (1997). Therapy for youths with anxiety disorders: A second randomized clinical trial. *Journal of Consulting & Clinical Psychology, 65*, 366–380.

Kirschenbaum, H., & Jourdan, A. (2005). The current status of Carl Rogers and the person-centered approach. *Psychotherapy: Theory, Research, Practice, Training*, *42*, 37–51.

Kivlighan, D. M., & Goldfine, D. C. (1991). Endorsement of therapeutic factors as a function of stage of group development and participant interpersonal attitudes. *Journal of Counseling Psychology*, *38*, 150–158.

Kivlighan, D. M., & Lilly, R. L. (1997). Developmental changes in group climate as they relate to therapeutic gain. *Group Dynamics: Theory, Research, and Practice*, *1*, 208–221.

Kivlighan Jr., D. M., & Mullison, D. (1988). Participants' perception of therapeutic factors in group counseling: The role of interpersonal style and stage of group development. *Small Group Behavior*, *19*, 452–468.

Kivlighan, D. M., Multon, K. D., & Brossat, D. F. (1996). Helpful impacts in group counseling: Development of multidimensional rating system. *Journal of Counseling Psychology*, *43*, 347–355.

Kolb, D., Beutler, L., Davis, C., Crago, M., & Shanfield, S. (1985). Patient and therapy process variables relating to dropout and change in psychotherapy. *Psychotherapy: Theory, Research, Practice, Training*, *22*, 702–710.

Kulic, K. R., Horne, A. M., & Dagley, J. C. (2004). A comprehensive review of prevention groups for children and adolescents. *Group Dynamics: Theory, Research, and Practice*, *8*, 139–151. doi:10.1037/1089-2699.8.2.139

La Greca, A. M., & Stone, W. L. (1993). Social anxiety scale for children-revised: factor structure and concurrent validity. *Journal of Clinical and Child Psychology*, *22*, 17–27.

Lambert, M. J., & Barley, D. E. (2001). Research summary on the therapeutic relationship and psychotherapy outcome. *Psychotherapy: Theory, Research, Practice, Training*, *38*, 357–361.

Lese, K. P., & MacNair-Semands, R. R. (2000). The Therapeutic Factors Inventory: Development of a scale. *Group*, *24*, 303–317. doi:10.1023/a:1026616626780

MacKenzie, K. R. (1987). Therapeutic factors in group psychotherapy: A contemporary view. *Group*, *11*, 26–34. doi:10.1007/bf01456798

MacKenzie, K. R. (1997). Clinical application of group development ideas. *Group Dynamics: Theory, Research, and Practice*, *1*, 275–287.

Morran, D. K., Stockton, R., Cline, R. J., & Teed, C. (1998). Facilitating feedback exchange in groups: Leader interventions. *The Journal for Specialists in Group Work*, *23*, 257–268. doi:10.1080/01933929808411399

Nickerson, A. B., & Coleman, M. N. (2006). An exploratory study of member attraction, climate, and behavioral outcomes of anger-coping group therapy for children with emotional disturbance. *Small Group Research*, *37*, 115–139. doi:10.1177/1046496405284810

Nitza, A. (2011). Group processes in experiential training groups in Botswana. *The Journal for Specialist in Group Work*, *36*, 222–242.

Oetzel, K. B., & Scherer, D. G. (2003). Therapeutic engagement with adolescents in psychotherapy. *Psychotherapy: Theory, Research, Practice, Training*, *40*, 226–231.

Rapee, R. M., & Spence, S. H. (2004). The etiology of social phobia: Empirical evidence and an initial model. *Clinical Psychology Review*, *24*, 737–767. doi:10.1016/j.cpr.2004.06.004

Shechtman, Z. (2003). Therapeutic Factors and outcomes in group and individual therapy of aggressive boys. *Group Dynamics: Theory, Research and Practice*, *7*, 225–237.

Shechtman, Z. (2007). How does group process research inform leaders of counseling and psychotherapy groups? *Group Dynamics: Theory, Research and Practice*, *11*, 293–304.

Shechtman, Z., Bar-el, O., & Hadar, E. (1997). Therapeutic factors and psychoeducational groups for adolescents: A comparison. *The Journal for Specialists in Group Work, 22*, 203–213. doi:10.1080/01933929708414381

Shechtman, Z., & Gluk, O. (2005). An investigation of therapeutic factors in children's groups. *Group Dynamics: Theory, Research and Practice, 9*, 127–134.

Shechtman, Z., & Pastor, R. (2005). Cognitive-Behavioral and humanistic group treatment for children with learning disabilities: A comparison of outcomes and process. *Journal of Counseling Psychology, 52*, 322–336.

Silverman, W., Kurtines, W., Ginsburg, G., Weems, C., Lumpkin, P., & Carmichael, D. (1999). Treating anxiety disorders in children with group cognitive-behaviorial therapy: A randomized clinical trial. *Journal of Consulting & Clinical Psychology, 67*, 995–1003.

Vassilopoulos, S. P., & Brouzos, A. (2012). A pilot person-centred group counselling for university students: Effects on social anxiety and self-esteem. *The Hellenic Journal of Psychology, 9*, 222–239.

Vassilopoulos, S. P., Brouzos, A., Damer, D. E., Mellou, A., & Mitropoulou, A. (2013). A psychoeducational school-based group intervention for socially anxious children. *The Journal for Specialists in Group Work, 38*, 307–329. doi:10.1080/01933922.2013.819953.

Woody, S. R., & Adessky, R. S. (2002). Therapeutic alliance, group cohesion, and homework compliance during cognitive-behavioral group treatment of social phobia. *Behavior Therapy, 33*, 5–27. doi:10.1016/s0005-7894(02)80003-x

Yalom, I. D., & Leszcz, M. (2005). *The theory and practice of group psychotherapy* (5th ed.). New York, NY: Basic Books.

The Development of Relational Competences in High School Students by Means of Sociometric Methods

Regiane da Silva Macuch
Henrique Malheiro Vaz
University of Porto

This article reports results of an analysis of the relationship of young people in school, and their individual and group attitudes based on sociometric theory. This study adopted a mixed methodological approach with an intervention conducted with 60 youths over 3 years in Portugal and was based on the question "Is sociometry capable of giving support for the development of relational skills in young people within a school setting?" The results showed that sociometry can be a powerful tool to reduce conflicts and improve communication and a solid knowledge base for group counseling aimed at the development of identity of youth in a school setting.

Young people, as any other human group, tend to group themselves based on affinities, while trying to differentiate themselves and to express their individuality. Youth is a time in life rich in manifestations of sociability. Groups allow young people to identify themselves, as well as provide space for playing and sharing their secrets and experiences. For decades, numerous researchers underscored the importance of the development of relational skills. Young people in high schools yearn to connect and belong, yet opportunities to form meaningful relationships may be scarce (Dunphy, 1990; Loder & Hirsch, 2003; J. P. Newman & Kosson, 2006). Professionals who have used counseling and psychoeducational groups with young people in school settings have identified positive outcomes (Brigman & Campbell, 2003; Brigman, Webb, &

Campbell, 2007; DeLucia-Waack, 2006; Steen, 2011; Steen, Henfield, & Booker, 2014; Steen & Kaffenberger, 2007). However, little research has been conducted on the relationship between young people and their peers as well as on the development of the skills required to relate to each other.

In relationships between young people, the “others” have an important role to play in defining identity; youngsters see part of their identity reflected in the group and are very much concerned with peer assessment in the group (Brown, 2000; Coleman, 1980; Youniss & Smollar, 1985). Sometimes the youngster looks for people with different “ways of being” than those with which he or she was raised. By doing so, they bring into play their values and those of the parents and thus open the possibility of testing the construction of their own way of being in the world.

In order to understand how young people develop their relational abilities at school, this study was based on the premise that the identity and the competence to relate are not built on their own, but rather through relationships. In this regard Loder and Hirsch (2003), said, “Peer relationships and involvement in peer group activities are critical to healthy adolescent development” (p. 2). The construction of identity involves continuity and change, since human life is in fact the product of many relational plots over time. Thus, the concept of identity also changes with time. The relational competence, as an important element in the construction of the human being and its identity, is inserted in the “in-between” of social relations, since it does not belong exclusively to the individual, but to the collective as well (Buber, 1974; P. R. Newman & Newman, 1976). For Buber (1974), the meaning of inter-human relationship cannot be found in any of the partners in a relationship, nor in both together, but rather in the dialogue between the two.

In order to understand the concept of competence, we should consider the three characteristics presented by Perrenoud and Thurler (2002): personhood, context, and mobilization. The first feature indicates those who may or may not be competent. The second affirms that there is no competence without context. The third refers to the ability of making use of what is known, in order to accomplish what is intended.

Relating to people implies choosing. Choices represent important events in all relationships. The fact that people make choices in their interpersonal relationships, and the fact that they allow themselves to have these choices, enabled the physician Jacob Moreno, in the mid-1930s, to find a way to better understand social relationships and their underlying psychological mechanisms, which he called Sociometry. For Moreno, choices are mostly of an existential order and require no special justification, if they are spontaneous and true. Moreno considers that all human relationships are expressed by signs of choice, rejection, or neutrality. These signs, emotional and qualitative, can reveal a series of events that ensure the understanding of the psychological structure of a group and the established setups among its members (Moreno, 1934/1953/1978/1992).

Sociometry is interested in understanding the existing social relations in groups (networks). Relationship networks are not easily envisioned; they are established in two dimensions, one is visible and obvious, and the other is invisible, underlying, or psychological. Sociometry concerns itself with the second level, in other words, the emotional content of relationship (Silva Jr., 1997).

In this regard, this article will describe results of a mixed methodological approach study which focused on learning more about the development of relational dynamics of young people attending school in Portugal. Following the line of sociometric study, the author will describe how sociometric theory can be used as a framework for understanding relational dynamics that emerge when educational leaders facilitate counseling groups in school settings. The research was implemented in a high school for three years with over 60 students.

First, we will highlight tenets associated with sociometry and we will provide examples of how sociometry seems to influence dynamics and relational skills. While addressing sociometry, we will highlight its application to the research design as well as describe how interventions were selected in order to provide youth with opportunities to support the development of relational dynamics.

Sociometry as a Method of Research and Intervention

Parlebas (1992) recognized three trends in sociometry as a methodology of experimental research, namely a disciplined and rigorous approach that seeks to explore the socio-emotional structure of groups, interpersonal and relational dynamics, as a psycho-sociological and pedagogical instrument and as a therapeutic intervention that allows individuals to participate in the decision-making process that directly affects their life within the group. Sociometry confirms the existence of characteristic patterns of organization within a group, their expressions and settings or configurations. The results can be examined on three levels, the individual, the level of interpersonal relations, and, finally, the level of structures of personal groups. Sociometric analysis allows detection of the relational networks in groups, converting the qualitative resource into a quantitative trait, using graphic features that allow individuals to see the personal situation of each group member.

The basic proposal of sociometry is composed of two approaches for the analysis of interpersonal relation, an objective analysis and a perceptual analysis. The Objective Analysis consists of asking each individual in the group to answer the question "who do you choose to perform a particular task?" With this, a set of structures of group relations is revealed, showing both the way each individual is seen through the eyes of other group members, and how each person in the group chooses and is chosen. The Perceptual Analysis corresponds to the perception each individual has about his own position within the group. This analysis consists of asking each individual to answer the question "who do you think/feel/perceive would be chosen to carry out a particular task?", and then to explain the reasons why he/she believes to have been chosen and how he/she is perceived by the other group members. Perceptual analysis allows for understanding the person's ability to perceive and objectively show what the individual sees in the situations regarding the choices of others towards him- or herself. As important as choosing and being chosen, it is also fundamental to be able to perceive correctly.

Theory of Tele

Perceptual analysis is based on the theory of Tele (Moreno, 1934/1953/1972). Tele is the human ability to communicate emotions at a certain distance. The concept of Tele can be understood as an indicator of the dynamic flow of a group and necessarily implies having communication; in other words, being in a relationship is in fact to communicate. The basic process of Tele is reciprocity. As a *phenomenon of interaction*, Tele can be considered an intrapsychic factor, providing a "Telic potential" for the individual to maintain contact and Telic bonds and, as a *relational factor*, which has to do with the quality of connections between two people. Tele decides the clarity of a connection, and everything that interferes in this clarity is regarded by Moreno (1934/1953/1972), as a "transfer" or "pathology of the Tele" or the inability, on the part of an individual, to perceive clearly and objectively what happens in his/her relationships. Also Tele offers empathic insights when group members may not have the words to voice their needs, concerns, and desires.

Moreno (1934/1953/1972) advised on the need to take precautions during sociometric analysis. He described three concerns. The first concern has to do with the involvement of participants in the decision making process. The second concern is with the criteria used in its application, which must be allocated to real action projects, which are concrete and important to the group. The third point relates to the fact that the instructions given by the group leader must be sufficient and clear in order to release the spontaneity of the participants so they can respond. We will provide an example of how we applied the notion of Tele in analyzing the data. The researcher examined how adolescents engaged in Tele; we focused on understanding when the flow of Tele seemed to occur spontaneously as much as when Tele seemed blocked and offered support to each other to voice what was silenced. As Moreno (1934/1953/1972) described, we attempted to be mindful of these concerns by focusing on the description of relational procedures of the youngsters and on the analysis of in-depth data collected through multiple sources of information.

Another important indicator used by Moreno in his studies has to do with the sociometric status; that is, the strength of each element within the group. Coie, Dodge, and Coppotelli (1982) demonstrated the basic relationship among the characteristics that exist between positive and negative social skills and the nominations/appointments. The authors found five categories for the analysis of the Individual Sociometric Status: (1) popular (P), receives more nominations than most participants; (2) rejected (R), receives more nominations of rejection than of choice; (3) isolated (I), does not choose and is not chosen by anyone, and is not recognized by others as belonging to the group; (4) controversial (C), has medium indications for being chosen and rejected and (5) medium/mean (M), does not fit in the above categories.

METHOD

Context of Study

In Portugal, the secondary education structure, as defined by the Fundaments of the Educational System Law no. 46/1986, Law no. 115/1997, and the amendments of Law no. 49/2005 consists of mandatory schooling and encompasses a single 3-year study cycle (10th, 11th, and 12th grade), following the end of primary education. Until 2009, secondary education in Portugal was optional. With the passing of Law no. 85/2009 it became universal, free of charge, and mandatory.

What is nowadays known in Portugal as secondary education had its origins in the 16th century "crafts" teaching. At the end of the 18th century schooling became standardized and a responsibility of the state. In 1895 there was a major reform in schooling and the high school organization, and henceforth became the basis for today's secondary education. In 1948 there was another teaching reform, the new statuses for high school and technical education had been published, which would then collectively be known as secondary education. In 1973, the first Fundament of the Educational System Law was passed, marking the merger of regular high school with technical education. In 1986, the current Fundament of the Educational

System Law was passed, resulting in a reorganization of the schooling system. In the 1990s, secondary education was made accessible to the masses, consisting of over 70% of the youth population between 15 and 18 years old by the end of the decade. Today, Secondary Education in Portugal contains four types of courses: scientific- humanistic, technological, specialized artistic education, and professionals. It is currently arranged for furthering education and permit that youth enter the workforce.

The general objectives of secondary education in Portugal according to Law 46/1986 of Diário da República, 1a série - No 237 of 14/10/1986 are: (1) ensuring the development of reasoning, scientific reflection and curiosity, and the deepening of the fundamental elements of a humanistic, artistic, scientific, and technical culture; (2) providing the necessary knowledge for the understanding of aesthetical and cultural manifestations, and making the enhancement of artistic expression possible; (3) inciting the gain and the application of ever more in-depth skills; (4) training young people interested in solving the country's problems and promoting awareness of the problems of the international community; (5) providing contacts and experiences with the labor market; (6) favoring professional training and orientation; (7) and creating individual and group work habits.

The study plan of secondary school in Portugal consists of a technical, scientific and socio-cultural training, as defined by the Portuguese Ministry of Education, according to the National Agency for Qualification Plan of Study (2010) as being, (a) a noncompartmentalized global workload over the 3 years of training, to manage the school, in terms of pedagogic autonomy, with regard to the balance of the annual workload to optimize the overall modular management and training in the workplace; (b) the student chooses a foreign language. If the students are only studying one foreign language in primary education, a second language in secondary education is required; (c) basic scientific disciplines to lay down rules, according to the professionals skills to be acquired; (d) technological subjects, technical and professional qualifications of the offeree and structuring practice, and (e) training in the workplace seeks to acquire and develop relevant technical, relational and organizational skills for qualification. The Portuguese study plan is presented in Table 1.

The high school where this empirical research took place provides three professional courses in scenic, artistic, and theatrical arts: Performance and Interpretation, Set and Props Design, Lighting Design, and Sound. The choice for the school where the research took place originated in the reading of a thesis entitled "Zero Project: School at the theater," which dealt with the meaning of work in an artistic professional school (Vaz, 2007).

Table 1 Study Plan

Training Component	*Subjects*	*Total Training Hr/Cycles (a)*
Sociocultural	Portuguese language	320
	Foreign language I, II, or II (b)	220
	Integration area	220
	Information technology	100
	Physical education	140
Scientific	2 to 3 subjects (c)	500
Technical	3 to 4 subjects (d)	1,180
	Work-related training (e)	420
Total workload hr		3,100

The courses in the chosen school were organized by modules of training and work in a nuclear context, which corresponds to the practical exercises that replicate the professional context of staging a play (design, execution and presentation). Training is completed in the third and final year with the Professional Aptitude Test (Vaz, 2007), where students will demonstrate the knowledge and skills developed during the course.

A peculiar feature of this school has to do with the age profile of students. In its early years of operation, the school received older students (above 21 years) coming from the labor market and seeking a formalization/certification for their practical knowledge. With schooling being mandatory up to the 12th year, the age of the enrolled students was decreasing, to the point where today it coincides with the age group of 14 and 15 years, which equates to those fresh out of the 9th grade of education. This age shift generated a need for academic change, in order to meet the demands. For the school to continue to account for its professionalization profile which already existed, it needed to adapt its language to the level of understanding and maturity of these younger students (14 and 15 years old), which was not always forthcoming and was reflected in the number of students quitting school before the conclusion of training.

Participants

The young school students in the study started in school in 2007 and graduated in 2010. They all came from different regions of Portugal, especially from the North. Students were admitted to school via a two-stage entrance examination, specific to the course intended that took place between May and July 2007. The students were divided into three courses (see Table 2).

Table 2 Student's Distribution by Age and Gender (at the Beginning and at the End of the Course)

	The Beginning of Course/2007			*The End of the Course/2010*		
Course—Gender	*Masculine*	*Female*	*Total*	*Masculine*	*Female*	*Total*
Stage and crafts Design	5	13	18	1	7	8
Light and sound design	13	7	20	6	4	10
Acting	11	11	22	6	10	16
Total	29	31	60	13	21	34

Based on Table 2, one can see that the number of students who concluded the training in 2010 was 34 out of 60, in other words, almost half of the youngsters did not finish the training within the expected time for various reasons. However, those students who left the groups were not followed in this study, mainly due to the dropout itself. Though we consider the dropout index in need of further analysis, it will not be done in this article.

Methodological Procedures

This descriptive research used a mixed methodological approach (Tashakkori & Teddlie, 2003) associated with an experimental method of intervention (Creswell, 2009/2010) over the course of a 3-year study period, based on sociometric theory. Its premise was to find solutions for practical issues through observation, analysis, and objective description. We would add the qualitative study done by Monteiro (1995), as this is an amazing study with children and youths who live on the streets of Brazil, as support to design this study.

The methodological procedures used were participant observation of day-to-day school activities and work projects undertaken; formalized and nonformalized interventions done by the researcher; implementation of questionnaires for self-assessments and of others about the work done during work projects; application of objective and perceptual Sociometric tests throughout the three years; procedures for self-assessment and that of others among participants; and, feedback meetings between the researcher and students throughout the process.

This case study was considered as a complex whole that required specific considerations for each moment or phase, and that due to the complexity and size, will be listed in this article only in an abridged form. The phases of warm-up, action, and sharing of the socio-psychodramatic sessions (Moreno, 1946/1975) were used as metaphors for the organization and analysis of the research–intervention (see Table 3).

Table 3 Empirical Research Phases

	Warm-Up			
Phases	*Nonspecific*	*Specific*	*Dramatization*	*Sharing*
Date	May–September/2007	October/2007–July/2008	September/2008–July/2009	September/2009–July/2010
Period School	Pre-Registration	10th year	11th year	12th year

The warm-up phase refers to the four phases from the period of pre-entry to the end of the 1st year of school. The Nonspecific warm-up created a predisposition, or in other words, served to help understand the territory. It consisted of initial conversations with the pedagogical director of the school for submission and approval of the research, informal conversations with the school community, monitoring of entrance exams, and observations during the integration week for new students within the school environment. The Specific warm-up phase prepared for action. In other words, it focused on a clearer identification of context, through the monitoring of some theoretical and practical classes of the others teachers. It also prepared for the very first sociometric exercises, for the initial analysis of interpersonal relationships that were established between youths in school, in other words, how they met and were accepted.

The Dramatization phase, where the action itself took place, is where the objective and perceptual sociometric applications were performed using the following criterion "Who do I choose to form a theater company with?" Observation was conducted in classroom and projects took place in work settings. The assessments were made after the project's execution.

In the Sharing phase, the closing process of the research in the school took place. The third and final sociometric application was held, including the monitoring of the last project in the workplace, and the final considerations about sociometric results, and, finally, the monitoring of trials for the students' Professional Aptitude Test was held in the school.

The obtained Sociometric Data was processed with Excel Spreadsheets by Microsoft.

Results and Discussion

For presenting the results, the data about sociometric tests conducted between October 2008, June 2009, and March 2010 with the

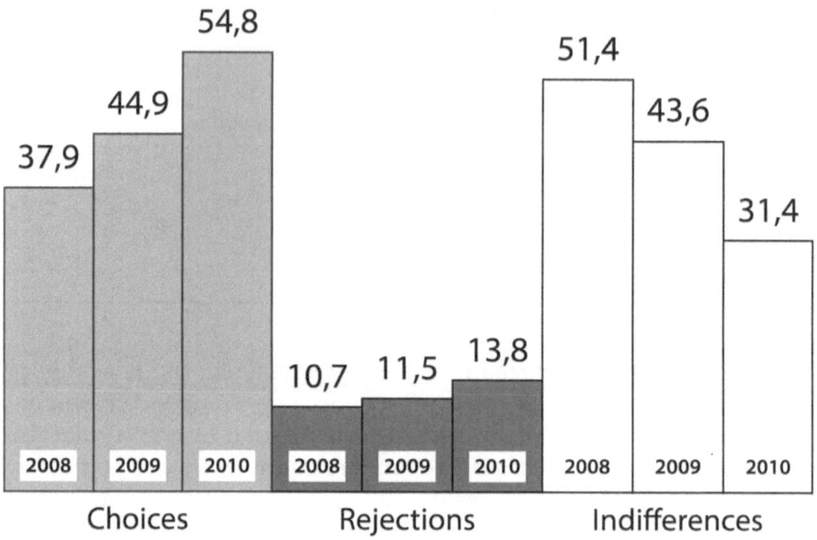

Figure 1 **Comparison among three objective sociometric applications (percentage values).**

criteria "The Creation of a Theater Company" were used. In this analysis, we observed a number of regularities, convergences, and divergences about the youngsters and their groups, which will be presented in the discussion. The real names of the youngsters were changed to pseudonyms to protect their identity. The evolution of choices, rejections, and indifferences among students can be seen in Figure 1.

Based on Figure 1, we can notice how the youngsters were interacting with work projects. The choices grew from 37.9% to 54.8%, the indifferences decreased by 20%, and rejections were concentrated between 10.7% and 13.8% during the project period. In Figure 1, one can see the gradual increase of choices, the reduction of indifferences, and a clearer definition of rejection. The group went from a simple organizational structure, with a predominance of indifferences, to a positive complex organizational structure with the predominance of choices. The evolution of the choices increased over an 18-month period. The reduction in "indifference reactions" shows that the relationships between the youngsters became more apparent from the increased time spent together working on projects, which can be confirmed from the evolution of reciprocal choices. This reveals the improvement in the capacity of emission as well as perception by the youngsters (see Figure 2).

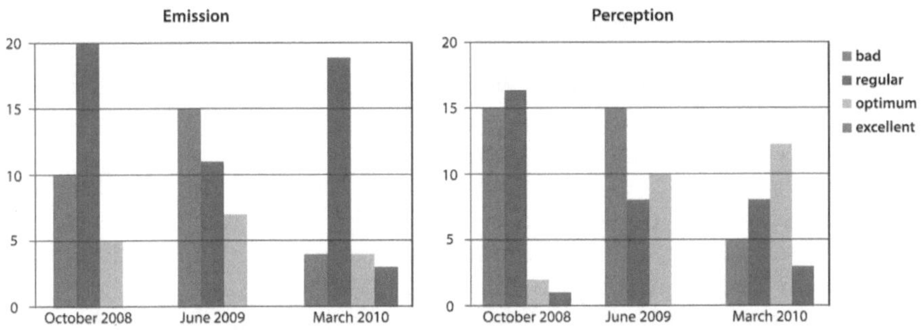

Figure 2 Comparison between perception and emission.

According to Moreno (1937) the Group Structure can be understood in accordance with the indications issued in sociometric testing: predominance of neutrality indicates a simple structure; predominance of choices indicates a complex positive structure and prevalence of rejections indicates a complex negative structure.

In this study, the identification of these configurations allows for a greater understanding of the dynamics that interfered between youth. As an objectively observable phenomenon, such settings allow for the intervention of professionals working with young people in schools in a more coherent and adjusted way according to the level of development of the group.

Moreno (1934/1953/1978/1992) concluded that reciprocity relationship increases the higher the Group Telic Index (GTI), which also increases cohesion within the group. In order to bring about an increase in the Telic index of youngsters, one has to invest in the development of self and outer-observation attitudes, to make it possible to identify feelings sprouting from the situations experienced in interpersonal relationships. In March 2010, the correct perceptions increased significantly. For most of the youths, the perception index was above the rate of correct emission. This reveals that they were able to perceive better than communicate, as shown in Figure 2.

Those youths who had a low perception index were also the most rejected by the group. This fact deserves consideration: Can the development of activities that stimulate the ability of perception change the rejected status of youths in school? Moreno found that sociometric status tends to be maintained even if the person leaves the group. Thus, rejected individuals, even if they change groups, tend to maintain their rejected status in other groups. Therefore, for rejected persons, one must carefully analyze whether group change does not represent another rejection for the individual, while keeping someone in a group might mean a greater chance of improvement and inclusion (Eisenhart & Holland, 1983).

In this sense, care and attention are necessary when trying to change a rejected person in the group, because often a simple change will continue to represent rejection. In this case, it is preferable to keep the person in the same group and pursue other minimally healthy partnerships so the person can establish the idea that he or she can increase the capacity of communication within the group, rather than simply swap groups and cause an even greater rejection.

Regarding the sociometric status that each person has within the group, it can be obtained from nominations/appointments by their peers. In Table 4, one can see the sociometric status of young people.

Table 4 Sociometric Status

Stable Statute				*Buoyant Statute*			
Name/ Application	*October 2008*	*June 2009*	*March 2010*	*Name/ Application*	*October 2008*	*June 2009*	*March 2010*
Bernarda	P	P	P	Alice	P	R	R
Carina	P	P	P	Amália	P	M	M
Eduardo	P	P	P	Anita	P	M	M
Julia	P	P	P	Ana	P	P	M
Monteiro	P	P	P	Isaura	M	R	R
Paschoal	P	P	P	Ramires	M	R	R
Sonia	P	P	P	Rosa	M	R	R
Claudete	M	M	M	Vanessa	M	M	R
Camila	M	M	M	Morgana	M	P	P
Cristal	M	M	M	Gualter	M	P	P
Mariana	M	M	M	José	M	R	M
Pero	M	M	M	Márcia	R	P	M
Homero	R	R	R	Maria	R	R	M
Inês	R	R	R	Regina	R	C	R
Susana	R	R	R	Humberto	C	C	P
Nilton	R	R	—	Breno	C	C	M
Serguei	R	R	—	Josué	C	C	R
Carmelo	P	P	—	Timor	C	C	R
Elcio	P	P	—	Lisa	C	P	P
Francisco	P	P	—	Timóteo	C	M	P
				Marialva	M	R	—
				Riana	M	—	—
				Filomena	M	—	—
				Braga	R	—	—
				Moriana	R	—	-

Note: This table presents the evolution of each youngster's sociometric status throughout the three years of training.

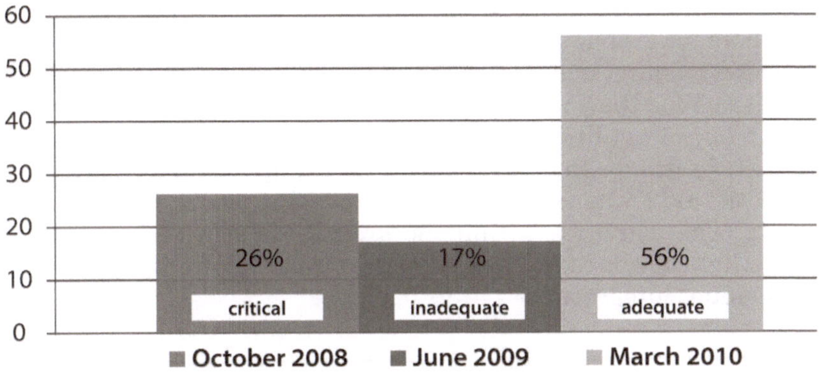

Figure 3 Group Telic Indexes.

Based on Table 4 it is possible to show that 15 youngsters had a stable sociometric status and other youngsters had oscillating sociometric status. Oliveira (1999) found that individuals with an isolated status show a lack of social involvement and greater loneliness than those who are rejected. The author cited that these rejected individuals are less gifted in the interpretation of social signals, which can enable them to make biased interpretations of others, because they interpret the positive responses received in a less favorable manner and negative responses less negatively. Even though they do have their social networks, these individuals generally choose peers with sociometric statuses similar to theirs, which tends to increase their problems. However, those who are controversial, although presenting leadership capabilities are also disruptive, have low self-esteem, a negative perception of the self, and are usually described by others as fun (Oliveira, 1999).

Already, the GTI allows us to understand the amount of Tele that the group maintains. This index was obtained by summing the individual indexes, and then dividing that by the number of possible choices. Throughout the process, this index ranged from Critical to Inadequate, and after to Adequate according to the classification adopted by Bustos (1979). Figure 3 shows the GTI at three different points in the research process.

Based on Figure 3, the sociometric application was first used in October 2008 and revealed the presence of a higher concentration of transfer or conflict in relationships among the youths. In June 2009, the predominance of troubled and unresolved relationships indicated an inadequate GTI. Although most young people had worked together in other theater projects, the observations showed that they suffered from complicated and tense group dynamics, which prevented further growth, both for individuals and for the group. This period, which refers to the second year of training at the school, represented a time of difficult decisions for the youths about coping with maturity and with the responsibility of not dropping out of the course, both individually and for the whole group. In March 2010, the groups showed more maturity and the GTI was more adequate, revealing more positive group dynamics. The activities within the groups were more beneficial for everyone. Tele flowed more easily and the groups showed more cohesion and individual integration.

Conclusions

The research presented in this article consisted of understanding the identity development and the relational dynamics of young people during their schooling in high school, based on Moreno's Sociometry as a qualitative method research and intervention (Creswell, 2009/2010; Tashakkori & Teddlie, 2002). The sociometric methodology (Moreno, 1934/1953/1972, 1934/1953/1978/1992, 1937; Treadwell, Kumar, Stein, & Prosnick, 1997) appeared to reveal the structure and underlying dynamics between individuals and the group, confirming its effectiveness today, despite having been created in the mid-20th century. For Moreno (1934/1953/1978/1992) "the old dichotomy, qualitative versus quantitative, is solved within the sociometric approach. The qualitative aspect of social structure is neither destroyed nor forgotten. It is integrated in quantitative reasoning, and works from the inside out, as a unit" (p. 157).

The group experience presented the youth with a series of learning experiences and knowledge, in an intense game between the individual and the collective (Buber, 1974; Parlebas, 1992). Much more than the professional preparation, the moments and spaces experienced by the youngsters in school were moments and spaces of life. The concepts of autonomy and involvement were important in the constant, interconnected, and simultaneous pursuit of learning how to relate. The engagement in interpersonal relationships occurred in the intersubjectivity and complexity of the process. The feedback among them as well as between the youth and the researcher acted as assistance in the process of identity construction and development of relational skills.

During the development of these youngsters in school, the self-assessment exercises and the goal-oriented analysis from the sociometric tests promoted the development of relational skills. The youngsters' evolution in the ability to have a voice and perception has become essential for monitoring the evolution of the group (Bustos, 1979; Coie et al., 1982; Orr & Hulse-Killacky, 2006). To see oneself and others in the relational game established between youth pairs

(Oliveira, 1999), enabled the expansion of the capacity of each one to communicate (Brigman & Campbell, 2003; Loder & Hirsch, 2003) and learn from both sides of a same process: autonomy-differentiation and integration-cooperation.

In that sense, Brigman and Campbell (2003) highlight the importance of receiving and giving feedback through encouragement in order to help discouraged students. Orr and Hulse-Killacky (2006), on the other hand, talk about voice, knowledge, mutual construction of meaning, and transfer of learning, all of which occurred in our study when youths chose among their peers whom to collaborate with in projects; which helped them give voice to their experiences and construct meaning through Tele. Sociometry promotes feedback giving with a focus on encouraging each other and on being a voice for one another, doing so by facilitating the learning and understanding of the skills of communicating and perceiving relational signs correctly.

The sociometric applications performed made it possible to understand the relational dynamics as a solid basis for the development of preventive pedagogical intervention strategies of group counseling in school, as previous literature has demonstrated (Bauman, Steen, & Smith, 2008; DeLucia-Waack, 2006; Steen, 2011; Steen et al., 2014; Steen & Kaffenberger, 2007). Because this study sought to understand the dynamics of relationships and communication and relational learning of youngsters in school, all the reflections produced can be important indicators for the construction of a Relational Competency Development Program in schools based on Sociometry.

The development of relational skills is a process requiring adaptive expertise to deal with the experiences of being chosen and rejected by youth peers (Macuch, 2010), as well as being faced with the events of life. Being confronted with oneself and others, mediated by time and space, whether in or outside of school, is a big challenge for youth.

Implications for Group Leaders

Envisioning a society that can recognize the concerns of the young implies not only a transformation of the structure of societies, but also a transformation in small groups as well as the individual. It is the school's task to promote that youth understand that the path of life is a path of learning, of overcoming barriers and discovering new horizons, both inwardly and outwardly.

Understanding the sociometric proposal is a great challenge in education. It is known that often educators have scarce opportunities during their academic education to address questions concerning relational competences at school from a practical perspective. Much is being said, but little is being done. Caution is required not to address these issues as secondary or palliative, since the school is still, by excellence, a relational space (Relvas, 1999).

The adult facilitator, be it the figure of the teacher, the counselor, the tutor, the principal, or any other school employee, plays a fundamental role in the educational process of youngsters as far as their relational competences are concerned. The adult facilitator can aid youngsters in recognizing and communicating emotions, helping them to become responsible for and conscious of their own emotional displays. But, for that to happen, one needs to know the youngsters. This is a process that begins in the early days of school. The more knowledge the facilitator has about the youngsters and their relations, the more efficient her or his pedagogical acting will be. To know about the young people implies having an attitude of permanent inquiry and attention to the interests and needs they express.

As a general conclusion, Sociometry, as is true with other approaches, is not confined to the first ideas of its creator Jacob Levy Moreno. He was a man ahead of his time, and today his sociometric proposals can be reviewed and reconsidered in light of new possibilities, since they remain current with regards to modern contexts. Studies in the field of social networks, for example, have surpassed the first sociometric interventions described by Moreno, but the essential aspects of sociometry for understanding these communications networks remain unquestionable.

REFERENCES

Bauman, S., Steen, S., & Smith, J. (2008). The training of professional school counselors for group work. *The Journal for Specialists in Group Work, 33*, 253–269.

Brigman, G., & Campbell, C. (2003). Helping students improve academic achievement and school success behavior. *Professional School Counseling, 7*, 91–98.

Brigman, G., Webb, L., & Campbell, C. (2007). Building skills for school success: Improving academic and social competence. *Professional School Counseling, 10*, 279–288.

Brown, R. (2000). Social identity theory: Past achievements, current problems and future challenges. *European Journal of Social Psychology, 30*, 745–778.

Buber, M. (1974). *Eu e tu*. São Paulo, Brazil: Centauro.

Bustos, D. (1979). *O teste sociométrico: fundamentos, técnica e aplicações* [The sociometric test: foundations, techniques, and applications]. São Paulo, Brazil: Brasiliense.

Coie, J. D., Dodge, K. A., & Coppotelli, H. (1982). Dimensions and types of status: A cross-age perspective. *Developmental Psychology, 18*, 557–570.

Coleman, J. C. (1980). Friendship and the peer group in adolescence. In Adelson, J. (Ed.), *The handbook of adolescent psychology* (pp. 408–431). New York, NY: Wiley.

Creswell, J. (2010). *Projeto de pesquisa: Método qualitativo, quantitativo e misto* [Research design: Qualitative, quantitative, and mixed methods approaches]. Porto Alegre, Brazil: Artmed. (Original work published 2009, in English).

DeLucia-Waack, J. L. (2006). *Leading psycho educational groups for children and adolescents*. Thousand Oaks, CA: Sage.

Dunphy, D. C. (1990). Peer group socialization. In R. E. Muuss (Ed.), *Adolescent behavior and society: A book of readings* (pp. 230–246). New York, NY: Random House.

Eisenhart, M. A., & Holland, D. C. (1983). Learning gender from peers: The role of peer groups in the cultural transmission of gender. *Human Organization, 42*, 321–332.

Loder, T. L., & Hirsch, B. J. (2003). Inner-city youth development organizations: The salience of peer ties among early adolescent girls. *Applied Developmental Science, 7*, 2–12.

Macuch, R. (2010). *As dinâmicas relacionais na escola secundária e o desenvolvimento de competências relacionais em jovens.* [Relational dynamics at high school and the development of relational competences in youngsters] (Unpublished doctoral dissertation). Faculty of Psychology and Education Sciences, University of Porto, Portugal.

Monteiro, J. M., Cody, J. J., Leitner, D. W., & Dollinger, S.J. (1995, April). *An ethnographic study of the kids on the streets of Fortaleza, Brazil: Family, school, peer group and community, self-concept.* Paper presented at the Annual Conference of AERA (American Educational Research Association), San Francisco, CA.

Moreno, J. L. (1937). Sociometry in relation to other social sciences. *Sociometry, 1*, 206–219.

Moreno, J. L. (1972). *Fundamentos de la sociometría* [Foundations of sociometry] (2nd ed.). Buenos Aires, Argentina: Paidós. (Original work published 1934, in English; revised 1953, in English)

Moreno, J. L. (1975). *Psicoterapia de grupo y psicodrama* [Psychodrama and group psychotherapy]. Mexico: Fondo de Cultura Económica. (Original work published 1946, in English)

Moreno, J. L. (1992). *Quem sobreviverá? Fundamentos da sociometria, psicoterapia de grupo e sociodrama* [Who shall survive? Foundations of sociometry, group psychotherapy and sociodrama]. Goiânia, Brazil: Dimensão. (Original work published 1934, in English; revised 1953 and 1978, in English)

National Agency for Qualification. (2010). *Young people/Vocational courses.* Retrieved from http://www.en.anqep.gov.pt

Newman J. P., & Kosson, D. (2006). Passive avoidance learning in psychopathic and nonpsychopathic offenders. *Journal of Abnormal Psychology, 95*, 252–256.

Newman, P. R., & Newman, B. M. (1976). Early adolescence and its conflict: Group identity vs. alienation. *Adolescence, 10*, 127–136.

Oliveira, C. (1999). *Os jovens e os seus pares: Estudo sociométrico e psicopatológico de uma população escolar* [Youths and their peers: Sociometric and psychopathological study of a school population] (Unpublished doctoral dissertation). University of Coimbra, Coimbra, Portugal.

Orr, J., & Hulse-Killacky, D. (2006). Using voice, meaning, mutual construction of knowledge, and transfer of learning to apply an ecological perspective to group work training. *The Journal for Specialists in Group Work, 31*, 189–200.

Parlebas, P. (1992). *Sociométrie, réseaux et communication* [Sociometry, networks, and communication]. Paris, France: Presses Universitaires de France.

Perrenoud, P., & Thurler, M. G. (2002). *As competências para ensinar no século XXI* [Competences for teaching in the 21st century]. Porto Alegre, Brazil: Artmed. Lei no 46/1986 de 14 de Outubro de 1986. Retrieved from http://dre.pt/pdf1sdip/1986/10/23700/30673081.pdf

Relvas, A. (1999). A escola de ontem face aos adolescentes de hoje: Como poderá ser amanhã? [Yesterday's school in light of today's adolescents: how will it be tomorrow?]. In M. Pinto, J. C. Tedesco, J. M. Pais, & A. P. Relvas, *As pessoas que moram nos alunos: Ser jovem hoje na escola portuguesa* [The people living in pupils: Being young at school in Portugal] (pp. 75–95). Porto, Portugal: Edições ASA.

Silva Jr, A. (1997). *Encontro X Confronto na busca de solução para conflitos detectados no sistema "ASJ" do teste sociométrico* [Meeting x confrontation in search of solutions for conflicts found in the ASJ system of the sociometric test] (Work of accreditation as Didata). Curitiba, Brazil: Federação Brasileira de Psicodrama, FEBRAP.

Steen, S. (2011). Academic and personal development through group work: An exploratory study. *The Journal for Specialists in Group Work, 36*, 129–143.

Steen, S., Henfield, M., & Booker, B. (2014). The achieving success everyday group counseling model: Implications for professional school counselors. *The Journal for Specialists in Group Work*, March, *39*, 29–46.

Steen, S., & Kaffenberger, C. J. (2007). Integrating academic interventions into small group counseling in elementary school. *Professional School Counseling, 10*, 516–519.

Tashakkori, A., & Teddlie, C. (2002). *Handbook of mixed methods*. London, England: Sage.

Treadwell, T. W., Kumar, V. K., Stein, S. A., & Prosnick, K. (1997). Sociometry: Tools for research and practice. *The Journal for Specialists in Group Work, 22*, 52–65.

Vaz, H. (2007). *Projecto Zero: A escola no teatro. Significado da instância trabalho numa escola profissional artística. Estudo de Caso* [Zero Project: School at the theater. Meaning of the work instance at a professional art school. Case study]. (Unpublished doctoral dissertation). Faculty of Psychology and Education Sciences, University of Porto, Portugal.

Youniss, J., & Smollar, J. (1985). *Adolescent relations with mothers, fathers and friends*. Chicago, IL: University of Chicago Press.

Development and Implementation of a Psychoeducational Group for Ghanaian Adolescents Experiencing Parental Divorce

Anthony K. Nkyi
University of Cape Coast

This article presents development and informal assessment of a 10-week psychoeducational program designed for 8 adolescent group members experiencing parental divorce in a rural community in Ghana. Group design, cultural considerations, program implementation, and impacts are described. The literature review pertaining to group work as an instrument for addressing parental divorce of adolescents is presented; group format and content within group sessions are discussed. The outcomes of this experience, as evidenced by a brief assessment questionnaire given before and after the group experience, indicate that completion of the group led to an increase in participants' knowledge of self-esteem, time management, anger management, peer relationships, educational goals, and psychological healing through spirituality. Implications for culturally informed group facilitation are discussed.

Studies indicate that the stress of parental divorce can have negative effects on the academic, social, and emotional development of children and that these children are at risk for a variety of negative developmental outcomes (Cecen-Erogul & Dingiltepe, 2012; Glenn & Kramer, 1985; Johnson & Wiechers, 2002). Children whose families have experienced divorce report higher rates of stress and risk factors than children of intact families (Cecen-Erogul & Dingiltepe, 2012; Winslow, Wolchik & Sandler, 2004). Studies report an increasing number of children and youth in Ghana being left to fend for themselves; leaving them increasingly at risk of being subjected to child labor, sexual exploitation, and teenage pregnancies (L. O. Gyekye, Arthur & Dankwa, 1996). Some of the short-term effects of divorce on children include guilt, anger, depression, anxiety, withdrawal, less social and school competence, and health problems such as eating disorders (Long & Forehand, 2002). As a result, a number of these children are likely to be more stressed, because they have no control over what is happening. In fact, some might even begin to exhibit a drop in self-esteem and self-confidence. This emotional turbulence interferes with other aspects of their lives.

Although most children adapt well to this transition, approximately 20% to 25% develop mental health or adjustment problems, a figure that is twice the rate experienced by children from continuously married families (Winslow et al., 2004). Female and male adolescents from single parent families have lower life satisfaction and psychological health than adolescents from intact families (Cecen-Erogul & Dingiltepe, 2012). Hetherington and Kelly (2002) indicated that about 75–80% of children from divorced families and stepfamilies do not have serious problems. Besides, it may be troubled marriages and not divorce that actually create problems. Kelly and Emery (2003) found that children display similar problems if their parents have a troubled marriage and remain together. This suggests that the problems of the children of divorce often begin years before the actual divorce. Regardless, divorce is stressful. Although most children possess the resilience to adjust, some children are more vulnerable than others (Guttmann & Rosenberg, 2003). Divorce causes changes in the family system and the quality of parent-children relationships, and increases the risk of straining emotional ties between parents and children. Given the high prevalence of divorce in a rural community in Ghana, the low levels of support received, and the risks to their adjustment, a psychoeducational group was developed that could offer them the ability to communicate effectively with others, express their feelings, and connect with peers facing similar challenges. The group could also serve to teach members coping strategies, and build on their life skills and self-esteem.

Divorce Across the Globe

Divorce is defined as the disruption of the intimate relationship between a man and a woman, a splitting apart of two interdependent people into two independent agents (Schaie & Willis, 2002). Over 1 million children in the United States experience divorce annually, with one out of every two first marriages ending in divorce (Clarke, 1995). One of the results of divorce is the rise in the number of single parent families. In 2006, 12.9 million families in the United States of America were headed by a single parent, 80% of which were headed by a female (Navarro, 2008; United States Census, 2006). In 2005, a general household survey report indicates that about 1 out of 4 families with dependent children in the United Kingdom are single-parent families, 8 to 11% of which have a male single-parent (United Kingdom Statistics, 2006).

Researchers report a rise in the rates of divorce in sub-Saharan Africa (Takyi, 2001; Takyi & Gyimah, 2007) leading to single parent households. The status of single parenthood in Ghana has resulted from desertion, separation, divorce, or death of the other spouse (L. O. Gyekye et al., 1996). By desertion, a partner abandons the spouse and children without consent in violation of their legal or moral obligation. In a study conducted by Boateng (1996) 50 percent of single female parents in Ghana were divorced, 30% were deserted, 14% were victims of transfer (where a partner leaves the spouse and children to secure job position elsewhere), and 2% were widowed, all leading to single parenthood. According to the Ghana Statistical Service (2012), of the population aged 12 years and older, 42.9% were married while 42.0% had never been married. In addition, 10.2% had been married before but at the time of the census were separated, widowed, or divorced. The study further indicates that a higher proportion of males (48.9%) than females (35.6%) had never been married. On the other hand, females were more likely to be married (43.9%) than males (41.7%). Again, the proportion of females divorced or widowed was higher than that of males (Ghana Statistical Service, 2012). Furthermore, divorce in Ghana has led to the disruption of the family and is characterized by a large number of broken homes, early child bearing and single parenthood, child delinquency, child labor, school drop-outs, and an increasing number of street children, posing serious problems to the society as a whole (L. O. Gyekye et al., 1996).

During group work with 10 single parents in a rural community in Ghana, Nkyi (2013) indicated that single parents appear to experience low income and economic disadvantages. He concluded that due to economic hardships and psychological distress, coupled with lack of resources, income generation and other economic programs that reduce poverty are of much importance to single parents. Studies indicate that experiencing parental divorce has been shown to increase the risk for alcohol use and likely tobacco use for adolescents (Griesbeck, Amos, & Currie, 2003; Menning, 2006). Indeed, Amato (1993, 2000) has reported that the family emotional stressors that often accompany marital discord may explain the increase in risk for substance use frequently observed among adolescents of divorced parents. Nkyi (2014), however, reported no significant differences in drug or alcohol use between children whose parents were divorced and those with intact families in Ghana.

Lauer and Lauer (1997) observed that children are likely to be more stressed, because they have no control over what is happening to them and see no long-term benefit to the disruption. As a result, they may also exhibit a decrease in self-esteem and self-confidence. The stress of divorce may lead young children to regress to more immature kinds of behavior (Clarke-Steward & Brentano, 2006). Divorce may also precipitate a major crisis that requires professional help (Gillis, 1992). It is important to note that not all children experience these effects and may experience them at varying degrees, with some children actually exhibiting fewer problems following their parents' divorce.

Studies indicate that children experiencing parental divorce talk with friends and peers long before they talk with adults about emotional issues (Campbell, 2008). In a study by McIntosh (2000), parents indicated that they had little understanding about how the children in their families addressed separation issues. Arguably, stress experienced by children at separation would be reduced if parents were more open to hearing from children and listening to their opinions.

Benefits of Group Work for Adolescents Experiencing Divorce

Studies on effective groups designed for treating the psychological, social, and academic problems associated with children of divorce have been well documented (Cercone & DeLucia-Waack, 2012; DeLucia-Waack, 2011; Rose, 2009). Adolescents experiencing parental divorce gain many benefits from the psychoeducational group model. Psychoeducational groups offer members the opportunity to share their confusion, anger, guilt, resentment, anxiety, depression, and helplessness with others who are facing similar issues and thus serve as a powerful healing force (M. S. Corey & Corey, 2006). Members have the opportunity to learn from the feedback of other group members. The psychoeducational group format provides a means for learning and practicing social skills as well as managing psychological problems that may result from parental divorce.

Religion plays a significant role in the cultural practices of the Ghanaian community because of the belief that all human actions and thoughts have religious meaning and are influenced by a religious point of view (K. Gyekye, 1996). The religious is not distinguished from the non-religious or the secular from the non-secular. For example, when someone is mentally ill, it is unusual for his or her people to seek orthodox medical care. They would rather consult the native medicine person since the cause of the problem, in their estimation, is certainly from the spirit world. Regarding the norms of conversation, every Ghanaian is expected to conform to these norms because one loses face and affronts the face of his/her listeners when one fails to use the right euphemistic expressions in communication (Agyekum, 2010). For example, the Akan, a large ethnic group of Ghanaians, would say "wayi wokete agu abontene" meaning "you have been divorced." This indirect manner of referring to the divorce helps both the speaker and the listener save face. Communal values (e.g., caring for others, sharing, and solidarity) find their expressions in the family and guide the Ghanaian people's social relations, attitudes, and behaviors between the individual and the community. Some adolescents may not yet know these values. Thus, incorporating some of these cultural practices into the group work will enhance adolescents' spirituality and communication skills to understand some of the unique cultural practices in the Ghanaian culture. Shectman, Vuerebrand, and Hertz-Lazarowitz (1994) suggested that small therapy groups have the potential to provide a social climate of cohesiveness and belonging as well as feelings of acceptance. They also promote development norms of self-expressiveness and self-disclosure, and opportunities for constructive feedback that often to lead to positive interactions. Thus, a small psychoeducation and therapy group was the selected format to deliver the intervention. This article summarizes outcomes of a group psychoeducation program for Ghanaian adolescents facing parental separation or divorce. The intervention incorporates the cultural adaptations integrated into the sessions in order to make the CBT and other traditional, Western practices suitable for this group of children. It was believed that integration of the Ghanaian cultural values with Western-based, psychoeducational cognitive-behavioral interventions could help the participants deal with life stressors resulting from parental divorce.

GROUP DEVELOPMENT PROCESS

The Setting

The setting for the program was a small town in the central region of Ghana with a population of approximately 5,000 people. It is about 35 kilometers north of Cape Coast, the capital of the Central Region of Ghana, situated 165 kilometers west of Accra on the Gulf of Guinea. The location was chosen due to convenience, because it is a rural community and participants were available and willing to engage in the psychoeducational group therapy experience. The author coordinated the group and was the primary leader of the group sessions. The group took place at the local school classroom of the small community.

Participants

A total of 37 potential participants were interviewed during the screening process to enter the 10-week group program. Two prerequisites for joining the group were to be an adolescent whose parents were divorced or were in the process of divorce and to have parents agreed to the child's participation. The other criteria were attendance at an individual screening and orientation meeting and the child's ability to read, speak, and write in the English language. Of these 37 potential members, 27 individuals were excluded from the group because they did not meet the conditions and the criteria and were not aligned with the purpose and goals of the group work. Out of the 10 participants selected, 2 members were also disqualified because they were absent for the first two sessions of the group.

The group was comprised of 6 female and 2 male adolescents between the ages of 13 and 16 from the junior and high schools, some of whom live with their biological mothers, grandmothers, and other maternal family members. The interview and screening were based on a questionnaire that included demographic information (e.g., age, education level, availability of social support, sexual abuse history, and effects of separation/divorce on the present situation). The leader selected candidates who understood the benefits and goals of the group; were ready and willing to abide by the group rules, were ready to maintain the confidential nature of others' disclosures, and could read and write English. Parents/guardians were fully informed of the extent and nature of the study and gave their permission to allow their children to participate in the group work. No fee was required for participating in the group. Once all the members had been selected, there were two preliminary sessions designed to be acquainted with one another and to prepare the members for the group work.

OUTCOMES ASSESSMENT

Data were gathered before and after the group experience via questionnaire that measured the participant's personal reactions, ideas, and attitudes about their well-being and growth as a result of their experience of parental divorce or separation, and knowledge about certain topics to be discussed during the group process. The questionnaire was comprised of 10 statements (see Appendix A) developed by the author and group leader and included suggestions solicited from scholar practitioners involved in adolescent research. Next, the questionnaire was pilot tested with a small group of adolescents experiencing divorce (n = 15). Final revisions were made to the questionnaire after the pilot testing. Students rated each statement using a four point, Likert-type scale with values given to each answer, thus: 1 = *Strongly Disagree*; 2 = *Disagree*; 3 = *Agree*; 4 = *Strongly Agree*. Their answers were compared at pre- and posttest to evaluate improvements as a result of the group experience.

Group Goals

Goals for the group were adapted from goals described by Cercone and DeLucia-Waack (2012) and O'Gorman (2011) and aimed to: (a) normalize common experiences of children of divorce; (b) clarify divorce-related issues and help children improve their understanding of what a divorced family is; (c) provide a safe and supportive environment to express feelings of anger, sadness, and grief; (d) develop problem-solving, communication, anger management skills, and promote positive perceptions of themselves; and (e) help children achieve healthy relationships with their parents.

Procedures

As previously discussed, the criteria for joining the group were to be adolescents experiencing family separation or divorce and attendance at an individual screening and orientation meeting. Those who qualified after the screening and the interview were accepted into the group study. The author advertised for the group through contacts with religious groups in the rural community 6 weeks prior to the group's projected starting date of June 2013. After completion of the interview, screening and selection of the participants, and parents/guardians informed consent and child assent were given, children joined in the group work.

The leadership team was comprised of the main leader (author) and three other co-facilitators trained by the leader and who were certified trained teachers with Bachelor's Degrees in education. The leader's qualification was 6 years of professional counseling experience with adolescents.

The leader served as an educator and facilitator. As an educator, he encouraged the members to think for themselves. He educated by providing information and facilitating interaction by bringing up topics, clarifying comments, and encouraging members to share. He helped the members to create a trusting climate that enabled them to be more involved in the sessions. He taught participants general group guidelines and ways to participate actively, showed empathy, understanding, and shared insights with the group. He employed the skills of blocking and redirecting to avoid rambling during the sessions. The leader summarized the themes of the group discussions at the opening and closing of each session. The leader combined cognitive-behavior therapy (integration of cognitive, behavioral, affective, social, and contextual strategies for change); person-centered counseling (e.g., active listening, reflection, empathy, inspiring; enthusing; praising success) and active teaching techniques (e.g., psychoeducation, feedback, modeling, role play, and problem solving; see G. Corey, 2005; Gladding, 2005).

Group Format

The group was comprised of 8 members and was closed. The group met on Sundays, once a week, for 90 min for a total of 12 weeks (3 months including the screening and interview process). The leader used the first 40 min to educate the members about a scheduled topic, while members discussed the topic and asked questions during the next 30 minutes, and gave feedback to each other for the final 20 min. This was a structured group led by the leader and three co-facilitators. In order to provide culturally appropriate experiences and integrate Ghanaian spiritual and religious practices, each session started with prayers (see Appendix B for an example).

Each week the members participated in a check in to indicate how the week went. They were asked to tell the group one "UP" and one "DOWN" event for the week. An "UP" was something that happened during the week that was particularly positive and good. A "DOWN" was something that happened during the week that was particularly negative and bad. The members participated in feedback. Feedback was very structured and each member followed a script with the statement: "can I please give you feedback?" All feedback had to be positive. Members and group facilitators were allowed to give feedback to a peer member or to the group as a whole. The psychoeducational format included the use of cognitive restructuring techniques, interpersonal communication skills training, and strategies for enhancing coping skills (Choate & Henson, 2003).

After parental divorce, children's view of the world and appraisal of themselves as persons changes drastically (Amato, 1994). Some of the common assumptions held by some of the members are that they will not be able to go to school due to financial problems and some feel they are unloved. A member provided objective evidence that some people in their extended family did not love him. Other members shared assumptions such as "I am not lucky," "Where is God?," "Why do I experience such problems?"

One of the major focuses of the structured groups was on changing cognitions. Cognitive restructuring exercises concentrated on changing self-talk and disputing irrational beliefs. Self-talk is defined as sub-vocal speech that usually serves to direct one's actions and evaluate one's behavior (Meichenbaum, 1977). The leader encouraged the members to converse with one's self. The leader introduced cognitive restructuring in the session. The goal of the cognitive restructuring was to reduce distress by having the members identify, evaluate, and modify these negative thoughts. The leader helped the members to (a) identify the sequence of change (b) recognize their inappropriate self-talk, (c) restructure the content of their self-talk, and (d) to repeat their readjusted self-statements.

The leader distributed a handout on self-talk that contained examples of negative self-talk in the left column. In the right column, an example is provided on how to change the negative self-talk to positive or coping self-talk. The leader asked members to read the first example and describe the differences between the types of self-talk. The leader also asked for personal examples of negative self-talk (e.g., I am not loved, I am a failure, I am hopeless) and demonstrated ways to change these to positive or coping self-talk (e.g., I am loved, I am a conqueror, I am hopeful). He further asked the members how negative self-talk affected their feelings about themselves. Next, members worked as a group to discuss the available evidence in favor or against each possible interpretation and end up with the most rational or helpful one(s). The group leader and the other facilitators pointed out how the way we interpret an event can negatively affect our thoughts and behaviors. Next, participants were asked to select a positive or coping thought to help increase their self-esteem: *"I am strong," "I am not hopeless," "I can make it, even though my parents are divorced," "I can complete my education because I am loved."* The courage that some members had to disclose their thoughts and feelings seemed to help other group members take risks in disclosure which helped them reflect on their thoughts and then decide, with the group leader's support, how to cognitively and constructively restructure these thoughts.

Group activities were also designed to provide the members with opportunities to practice the learned skills in a variety of ways. The leader closed every weekly session by summarizing what occurred in the session and told the members to tell the group about what they heard and learned in the session. Participants were encouraged to share their experiences and insights gained that would be useful to them for the week. The leader also met the members individually three times before the termination of the group to help the individuals who needed some personal support that was not addressed in the group work.

OVERVIEW OF THE GROUP SESSIONS

Session 1: Introduction and Goal Setting

The first session of the group was structured and characterized by the establishment of group and individual goals. The leader then welcomed the group members warmly by addressing the need for inclusion.

The leader invited the members to introduce themselves by announcing his or her name. Participants were encouraged to define their present problems and their expectation of the group work. Confidentiality, attendance and punctuality, respect for each member, more intimate interaction with the group members, and member's rights and responsibilities were addressed. Each member was asked to list personal goals and topics he or she wanted to be discussed in the sessions. Poverty, self-esteem, anger, parents' divorce, making good friends, prayers, communicating well with others, and learning effectively were the major and common themes and topics that emerged. The topics for the sessions were built around these emerging themes.

Session 2: Impact of Divorce on Members

In the second session, each member was asked to provide three examples of challenges associated with divorce that entered their lives. The leader invited the members to write three negative things of divorce and effects on children. Each member read what she/he identified. Some of the experiences about divorce on children identified by the members included poverty, anger, inability to talk to father or mother, no good role models, inability to pursue further education, poor adjustment issues, and lack of support from either the father or mother. At the end of the session the group members were helped to understand how their positive thinking can affect their actions positively, and how their negative thinking about parents' divorce can affect their actions negatively.

Session 3: Time Management and Study Skills

The leader facilitated group discussion of general time management strategies, including the need for clarifying priorities. The leader and the co-facilitators distributed sheets of papers to group members to write their weekly study time table. Each member was called to read out his/her time table aloud to group members for feedback. Members were asked to write a new weekly time table during the week for the next session.

Session 4: Building of Self-Esteem

The fourth session focused mainly on helping the participants to identify the causes and barriers to good self-esteem, to understand themselves, and to discuss their strengths and weakness. Cognitive restructuring was employed to help the members change their thinking about who they think they are as a result of their parental divorce. Each participant used a worksheet to describe their qualities and strengths, read them aloud, and received compliments from the other group members.

Session 5: Communication Skill

According to Agyepong (2010), the acquisition of communicative competence is the overall knowledge and is one of the skills needed in speaking and listening or appropriate communication. The leader taught group members effective communication in our Ghanaian cultural community. For example, teaching them to mention the names of elders in the family and other people with the proper titles. We taught the members how to communicate well with the elderly and to identify their own style of communication (e.g., passive, aggressive passive-aggressive, and assertive). Culturally appropriate communication styles were emphasized and encouraged.

Session 6: Anger Management Skills

The leader employed anger management techniques to teach members how to control anger. Techniques include recognizing anger, taking a time out, deep breathing, and exercise, expressing anger appropriately, and thinking of the consequences of anger. Two members were asked to role play how to manage anger in an aversive situation. The first party was to recognize an aversive situation and make a time out. He was asked to say "Time out." First the first party insulted the other party and that resulted in an aversive situation. The first party then called a time out. The other person also returned the gesture and said "Okay, time out." The person who called time out left the aversive situation and returned 10 min later to work on the problem with the other party.

Session 7: Coping With Peer Pressure

The leader educated the group members about peer pressure and how to cope with it. The members generated some examples of situations in which they feel pressured by their peers (e.g., drinking of alcohol and the engagement in premarital sex). The leader and co-facilitators discussed ways to say "No" to peers. First look directly at the person and say, "No, thanks." Or say "I'm sorry, I won't do that." If the person persists, they were instructed to leave the person politely.

Sessions 8 and 9: Spirituality, Healing of Past Hurts, and Forgiveness

These sessions were focused on three main issues: (a) moral virtues (b) relationship with God through prayer and Bible studies; and (c) healing of past hurts. The leader indicated that the members should exhibit qualities of patience, kindness, fairness, humility, generosity, honesty, and respect for other people, especially the elderly. Prayer was emphasized as essential for God's help and protection in their life. The leader incorporated 1 week of Bible studies for the adolescents that included other children in the rural community. Regarding forgiveness, the leader assisted members to let go of the past hurts, rejections, hostilities, hates, and fears in their lives.

Session 10: Termination/Closure

The members completed the posttest survey before other agenda items were carried out. After the posttest survey, the leader, co-facilitators, and members reviewed the progress they had made in meeting their personal goals through review of the posttest survey. A candle (signifying light that overcomes darkness) was lit and put in the center of the group. Members prayed, thanking God and praying for each other. Members gave positive feedback to each other and ended with saying "Goodbye."

OUTCOMES

This group experience aimed to provide Ghanaian adolescents experiencing parental divorce with psychoeducational and therapeutic support. Basic demographic information was collected along with pre-and posttest questionnaire data based on the main topics of the group sessions. Each participant completed the pretest and posttest surveys to evaluate outcomes of the group intervention. The questions focused on the individual group members' feelings, attitudes, beliefs, knowledge, and behavior changes after the group intervention as compared to responses before group began. The participants' answers indicate the degree of group members' improvement and gains made in the group. While no inference of significance can be made given the small size of the group and the brief questionnaire given, we can confidently report the outcomes of this group experience were positive for the youths (see Tables 1 and 2).We will discuss the implications of these improvements next.

Table 1 Pretest Scores

Participants	*Q1*	*Q2*	*Q3*	*Q4*	*Q5*	*Q6*	*Q7*	*Q8*	*Q9*	*Q10*	*Total*
A	1	1	1	1	1	1	1	1	1	1	14
B	3	3	1	1	1	1	3	1	1	1	16
C	1	1	1	1	1	1	1	1	1	1	10
D	1	1	1	1	1	3	1	1	1	1	12
E	1	1	1	1	1	3	1	1	1	1	12
F	1	1	1	1	1	1	1	1	3	1	12
G	1	1	1	1	1	1	1	1	1	3	12
H	1	1	1	1	1	1	1	3	2	1	12
Total	10	10	8	8	10	12	12	10	10	10	100

Note: For purposes of convenience of interpretation the following scores categories are given:

Score categories	Total Scores
Strongly Disagree	1–10
Disagree	11–20
Agree	21–30
Strongly Agree	31–40

Table 2 Posttest Scores

Participants	*Q1*	*Q2*	*Q3*	*Q4*	*Q5*	*Q6*	*Q7*	*Q8*	*Q9*	*Q10*	*Total*
A	3	3	3	2	3	2	3	3	2	3	27
B	3	3	2	2	3	2	3	2	2	3	25
C	3	2	3	3	3	2	2	2	2	3	25
D	2	2	3	3	2	3	2	2	3	2	24
E	3	3	2	3	3	3	3	2	3	3	28
F	3	3	3	3	2	3	3	2	3	3	28
G	3	3	3	3	2	2	3	2	3	3	27
H	2	3	3	3	2	2	3	3	2	3	26
Total	22	22	22	22	20	19	22	18	20	23	210

DISCUSSION

Parental divorce is a difficult experience and can have many consequences for children's psychological development. Outcomes of the group work demonstrated the value of a structured, collaborative approach for enhancing the skills of adolescents experiencing parental divorce. A psycho-educational group intervention characterized by the integration of cognitive, behavioral, affective, social, and contextual strategies for change was employed (Jaycox, Zoellner, & Foa, 2002). This technique aimed to address the adolescents' erroneous cognitions and to engender emotional processing of the divorce.

The results of the study indicate that after the 10-week program, participants demonstrated improvements in many areas, including increased general satisfaction with self-esteem, time management, anger management, and religiosity/spirituality. On the statement "I know my good and bad qualities" (Self-esteem), all eight participants showed an improvement on posttest regarding personal good and bad qualities (self-esteem). Research on adolescents experiencing parental divorce and high maternal distress reported lower self-esteem (Amato, 2005; Amato & Afifi, 2006; Esmaeili & Yaacob, 2012). Adolescents may blame themselves for their parental conflict, which causes feelings of guilt and lower self-esteem. A possible explanation is that the adolescents' involvement of peer group work involved building strengths and sharing painful experiences. Activities such as role-playing gave group members the opportunity to discuss how to work through fears and consider all possible outcomes of any given situation. Another possible explanation for this is that self-esteem like self-concept is a relatively stable dimension that tends to resist change over a short period of time. Self-esteem has, however, consistently been shown to be a reliable measure of mental health, of the ability to cope with problems, to function under stress, to act efficiently, and to form relationships with others (Smilansky, 1992). It is therefore quite possible that even a slight positive change in self-esteem could have a positive ripple effect on the psychological functioning of the individual.

The posttest indicates gains for group members on the statements "I know how to manage and plan my time table well" (time management) and "I know what my goals for school are" (education goals). One possible explanation for the improvement in their time management and education goals may be that group counseling with adolescents has been shown to be effective for a variety of issues, including classroom behavior and self-control (Larkin & Thyer, 1999), and academic underachievement (Hong, Lin, Wang, Chen, & Yu, 2012). The psychoeducational activities could have influenced their behavior to learn to manage their time and have a positive outlook about their education. Furthermore, social activities coupled with problem-solving skills could have played a role in helping these adolescents understand the importance of education and enhanced their perception about taking their time seriously. The posttest improvement of members on time management and educational goals may indicate that these members previously lacked the motivation to study and had few or no goals in pursing their education before the program started. The lack of good role models coupled with their parental divorce may have affected their academic studies. Studies indicate that educational difficulties and academic achievement have been found to be a problem among children of parental divorce compared to children of intact two-parent families (Amato, 1994; Amato & Keith, 1991)

The group as a whole indicated a reasonable increase in their level of managing anger, moving from the "strongly disagree" category, to the "agree" category on the statement "I know what makes me angry and how to cope with anger" (anger management). This is of considerable importance because as members develop positive self-esteem, they are able to learn to manage their anger (Long & Forehand, 2002). Indeed, the negative concept they have about themselves vis-à-vis their parental divorce could contribute to the pain they go through. Sometimes students lack accurate perceptions of the skills or support they have, such adolescents will use defense mechanisms to cover up their pain. The use of problem solving skills, self-disclosure, and feedback could protect the members from the pain associated with the lowered self-image. When the individual members' overall evaluation of themselves, including feelings of general happiness and satisfaction are enhanced, they are more likely to feel connected and value themselves in spite of the loss they are going through.

One key area worthy of note that improved in the group is spirituality/religiosity among members. Spirituality is considered one of the primary constructs of health in Ghanaian culture. The limited evidence that exists suggests that spirituality may play an influential role in health-related behavioral choices and beliefs in these members' worldview. In Ghana, religion plays some role in moral practice and one's relationship with the Supreme Being (K. Gyekye, 1996). Our psychoeducational program offered teaching strategies that provided members with opportunities to develop a personal definition of Ghanaian cultural values, namely spirituality, and explored factors that contribute to discovering one's meaning and purpose in life. One possible explanation is the members' belief in God, their spiritual beliefs and practices and prayer could have enhanced their positive social behaviors and values. It appears that members were more open to the discussion of the core elements of spiritual and religious issues. This finding is also consistent with previous work in Lebanon and the United States of America (Edlund et al., 2010; Ghandour, Karam, & Maalouf, 2009) showing the protective nature of religiosity. This outcome indicates that for the Ghanaian adolescents in our group, their religious or spiritual life might have a significant impact on their mental health.

The session on divorce appears to have had little effect on the group. These adolescents may assume that they were unlucky to have experienced parental divorce. It appears that the extended family of Ghanaian children could play a role in the child's life that helps reduce social isolation and loneliness. Consequently, talking about their parents' divorce might have been of little concern to the group members. Adolescents' experience of parental divorce may not necessarily lead them to a long period of grief because of the extended families' involvement in the child's relationship. This is consistent with the findings by Nkyi (2014) that emotional deprivation is not a serious problem in Ghana because the traditional practice of extended family ties creates strong commitment for all family members. Nevertheless, it also appears behavior problems are fewer when the adolescent stays with extended family members even when there is divorce. Other possible explanation is that the members were afraid to give voice to their feelings as they did not want to bring "shame" to their families and might have felt pressure to "save face" of their families. It could be concluded that the group session on divorce may not have been enough to address all aspects of the members' needs.

An adolescent whose peer group engages in pro-social activities is also more likely to engage in socially sanctioned activities. Although research indicates that mastering the interpersonal skills is necessary to sustain meaningful peer relationships (Parker & Asher, 1987; Selman, Watts, & Schultz, 1997). Lerner (1982) suggests that one way in which youth become producers of their own development is by helping each other learn how to take feedback from others and respond to them. The response scores for this item appear to be low compared to other topics. It may suggest that more time is needed to build their skills with peers. Three months was too short to offer such adequate skills.

There are several characteristics of this program that need to be highlighted. The group was carried out with a population at risk because of experiencing parental divorce; characterized by grief, anger, low self-esteem, and low socioeconomic status. Studies conducted by Cercone and DeLucia-Waack (2012), DeLucia-Waack (2011), and Rose (2009) reported the effectiveness of group work for treating the psychological, social, and academic problems associated with children of divorce. Cognitive-behavioral interventions used to teach coping skills and strategies to deal with life stressors appear to be an effective technique that fit well into the psycho-educational approach that we used (Chen & Rybak, 2004). Research supports the effectiveness of cognitive-behavioral techniques for modifying children's self-perceptions when used by properly trained individuals (Hattie, 1992). The other strength of this psycho-educational program that is worthy of note is the structured format of the sessions (Chen & Rybak, 2004) that were built by the leader to achieve predetermined goals in a short time. Through structured activities, the psycho-educational model addressed the members' identified needs and built on their skills. The use of role plays, skill techniques, education, and group activities to teach coping skills and strategies to deal with life stressors among these members was appropriate. Furthermore, the psycho-educational group was supportive in nature and that may be why these members tended to respond better to this program (Remocker & Storch, 1992).

Conclusions and Implications for Group Counselors and Mental Health Professionals

This article has focused on psycho-educational group work with adolescents affected by parental divorce in a rural community in Ghana. Based on the outcomes of the group intervention, several implications for counselors and other health professionals could be drawn. First, interpersonal skills, socializing techniques, and strategies to practice new skills and behaviors are important. Such techniques might enable participants to challenge and modify maladaptive beliefs and behaviors related to safety, trust, self-esteem, and relationships. The negative impact of divorce on children could also be minimized. The ongoing formation of groups in communities might empower these adolescents to face crises and difficult situations. Such programs might equip them with much needed support. There appears to be a tendency for collectivistic communities with extended families (such as in Ghana) to overlook the importance of counseling and psycho-educational interventions. However, the outcomes of this experience appear to indicate that group members benefited from being able to learn to how to experience love, caring, and acceptance and perhaps even open a door to real relationship with others. In such programs we can instill hope through learning to attend to the needs and concerns of others, and giving them the opportunity to learn, gain self-esteem, and increase their sense of meaning in life.

Second, all culturally competent and effective counselor should be especially sensitive to the cultural dynamics that may impact their work with such groups. Integration of spirituality and religiosity in group work with Ghanaian clients could be of great value in the counseling process. The counselors' ability to communicate, to listen, and to be patient, creative, and sensitive to the needs of the clients has great impact on the group members. Counselors should recognize the culturally-appropriate ways of speaking to, and expressing themselves to these adolescents. Counselors should be aware of the social and age distance between themselves (the elder) and the adolescents across the entire social fabric. Thus, counselors working with Ghanaian adolescents must have the ability to listen and motivate the clients to speak. Building effective therapeutic relationships with clients to gain trust and confidence is essential.

The other implication for counselors and health professionals is the recognition of the financial and economic burdens in working with this group. The counselors' ability to offer clients financial help will have great impact on the counseling relationship (e.g., giving them money to buy food). Contrary to ethical guidelines in the United States of America, it is customary sometimes for counselors in Ghana to provide money to low income or poor clients. Some of the clients see a counselor as provider and a helper who should offer financial help to the client. Indeed, clients come to counseling with different needs that include material and financial needs that they expect the counselor to provide, sometimes. This was important as most of these adolescents live with their grandparents or their mothers in poor environments. It appears that a combination of culturally adapted cognitive-behavioral, person centered and psycho-educational set of techniques can be effective to assist Ghanaian adolescent children of divorce.

REFERENCES

Agyepong, K. (2010). *Akan verbal taboos in the context of the ethnography of communication*. Accra, Ghana: Ghana Universities Press.

Amato, P. R. (1993). Children's adjustment to divorce: theories, hypotheses and empirical support. *Journal of Marriage and the Family*, *55*, 23–28.

Amato, P. R. (1994). Life-span adjustment of children to their parents' divorce. *The Future of Children*, *4*, 143–164.

Amato P. R. (2000). The consequences of divorce for adults and children. *Journal of Marriage Family*, *62*, 1269–87.

Amato, P. R. (2005). The impact of family formation change on the cognitive, social and emotional well-being of the next generation. *Future of Children*, *15*, 75–96.

Amato, P. R., & Afifi, T. D. (2006). Feeling caught between parents: Adult children's relations with parents and subjective well-being. *Journal of Marriage and Family*, *68*, 222–235.

Amato, P. R., & Keith, B. (1991). Parental divorce and the well-being of children: A meta-analysis, *Psychological Bulletin*, *110*, 26–46.

Boateng, D. S. (1996). The changing family and national development in Ghana. In E. Ardyfio-Schandorf (Ed.), *The changing family in Ghana. Family and development programme* 1996. (pp.1–4). Legon, Ghana: Ghana University Press.

Campbell, A. (2008). The right to be heard: Australian children's views about their involvement in decision-making following parental separation. *Child Care in Practice*, *14*, 237–255.

Cecen-Erogul, A. R, & Dingiltepe, T. (2012). The comparison of adolescents from single parent families and intact families in terms of life satisfaction and quality of life. *Elementary Education online*, *11*, 1077–1086.

Cercone, K., & DeLucia-Waack, J. (2012). The effects of music and group stage on group leader and member behavior in psycho educational groups for children of divorce. *The Journal for Specialists in Group Work*, 37, 29–55. doi:10.1080/01933922.2011.606790

Chen, M., & Rybak, C. J. (2004). *Group leadership skills: interpersonal process in group counseling and therapy*. Belmont, CA: Thompson Brooks /Cole.

Choate, H. L., & Henson. A. (2003). Group work with adult survivors of childhood abuse and neglect: A psycho educational approach. *The Journal for Specialists in Group* Work, *28*, 106–121.

Clarke, S. C. (1995). Advance report of final divorce statistics, 1989 and 1990. *Monthly Vital Statistics Report*, *43*, 95.

Clarke-Stewart, K. A., & Brentano, B. (2006). *Divorce: Causes & consequences*. Nashville, TN: Abingdon.

Corey, G. (2005) *Theory and practice of counseling & psychotherapy* (7th ed.). Belmont, CA: Thomson Brooks/Cole.

Corey, M. S., & Corey, G. (2006). *Groups: Process and practice* (7th ed.). Pacific Grove, CA: Brooks/Cole.

DeLucia-Waack, J. L. (2011). Children of divorce groups. In G. Greif & P. Ephross (Eds.), *Group work with at-risk populations* (3rd ed., pp. 93–114). New York, NY: Oxford University Press.

Edlund M. J., Harris, K. M., Koenig, H. G., Han, X., Sullivan, G., Mattox, R., & Tang, L. (2010). Religiosity and decreased risk of substance use disorders: Is the effect mediated by social support or mental health status? *Social Psychiatry Epidemiology. 45*, 827–836.

Esmaeili, N. S. & Yaacob, S. N. (2012) Correlates of self-esteem among adolescents of divorced families. *Archives Des Sciences*, *65*, 52–59.

Ghana statistical service (2012). 2010 Housing and population census.Retrieved from http://www.statsghana.gov.gh/. . ./Census2010_Summary_report_of_final_resu

Ghandour, L. A., Karam, E. G., & Maalouf, W. E. (2009). Lifetime alcohol use, abuse and dependence among university students in Lebanon: Exploring the role of religiosity in different religious faiths. *Addiction*, *104*, 940–948.

Gillis, H. (1992). *Counseling young people: A practical guide for parents, teachers and those in healing professions*. Johannesburg, South Africa: Lynn Foundation

Gladding, S. T. (2005). *Counseling. A comprehensive profession* (5th ed.). Upper Saddle River, N.J.: Pearson Prentice Hall.

Glenn, N. D, & Kramer, K. K. (1985). The psychological well-being of adult children of divorce. *Journal of Marriage and the Family*, *47*, 905–912.

Griesbach D., Amos A., & Currie C. (2003). Adolescent smoking and family structure in Europe. *Social Science Medicine*, *56*, 41–52.

Guttmann, J., & Rosenberg, M. (2003). Emotional intimacy and children's adjustment: A comparison between single-parent divorced and intact families. *Educational Psychology*, *23*, 457–472.

Gyekye, K. (1996). *African cultural values. An introduction*. Accra, Ghana: Sankofa.

Gyekye, L. O., Arthur, A., & Dankwa, E. Y. O. (1996). Family law and customary practices for child maintenance and inheritance in Ghana. In E. Ardyfio-Schandorf (Ed.), *The changing family in Ghana. Family and development programme* (pp. 86–112) Legon, Ghana: Ghana University Press.

Hattie, J. (1992). *Self-concept*. Hillsdale, NJ: Erlbaum.

Hetherington, E. M., & Kelly, J. (2002). *For better or for worse: Divorce reconsidered*. New York, NY: W.W. Norton.

Hong, Z., Lin, H., Wang, H., Chen, H., & Yu, T. (2012). The effects of functional group counseling on inspiring low-achieving students' self-worth and self-efficacy in Taiwan. *International Journal of Psychology*, *47*, 179–191.

Jaycox, L. H., Zoellner, L., & Foa, E. B. (2002). Cognitive-Behavior therapy for PTSD in rape survivors. *Psychotherapy in Practice*, *58*, 891–906.

Johnson, C., & Wiechers, E. (2002). Intra-psychic of a group intervention programme on adolescents of divorce. *South African Journal of education*, 22,177–183.

Kelly, J. B., & Emery, R. E. (2003). Children's adjustment following divorce: Risk and resilience perspectives. *Family Relations, 52*, 352–362.

Larkin, R., & Thyer, B. A. (1999). Evaluating cognitive-behavioral group counseling to improve elementary school students' self-esteem, self-control, and classroom behavior. *Behavioral Interventions, 14*, 147–161.

Lauer, R. H. & Lauer, J. C. (1997). *Marriage and family: Making choices in a diverse society*. Stanford, CT: Thomson Wadsworth.

Lerner, R. M. (1982). Children and adolescents as producers of their own development. *Developmental Review, 2*, 342–370.

Long, N. J., & Forehand, R. (2002). *Making divorce easier on your child: 50 effective ways to help your children adjust*. New York, NY: McGraw-Hill.

McIntosh, J. (2000). Child-inclusive divorce mediation: Report on a qualitative research study. *Mediation Quarterly, 18*(1), 55–69.

Meichenbaum, D. (1977). *Cognitive-behavior modification*. New York, NY: Plenum.

Menning, C. L. (2006). Nonresident father's involvement in adolescents' smoking. *Journal Health Social Behavior, 47*, 32–46.

Navarro, M. (2008). The bachelor life includes family. *The New York Times*. Retrieved from http://www.nytimes.com/2008/09/07/fashion/07single.html?pagewanted=all&_r=0

Nkyi, A. (2014). Substance abuse among senior high school students in Ghana. *International J. Soc. Sci. & Education, 4*, 346–353.

Nkyi, A. K. (2013). Growth group for single parents in a community in Ghana. *Developing Country Studies, 3*, 100–108.

O'Gorman, S. (2011). Family-focused child therapy in marital separation. *The Australian and New Zealand Journal of Family Therapy, 22*, 237–248.

Parker, J. G., & Asher, S. R. (1987). Peer relations and later personal adjustment: Are low-accepted children at risk? *Psychological Bulletin, 102*, 357–389.

Remocker, A. J., & Storch, E. T. (1992). *Action speaks louder: A handbook of structured group techniques*. New York, NY: Churchill Livingstone.

Rose, S. R. (2009). A review of the effectiveness of group work with children of divorce. *Social Work with Groups, 32*, 222–229. doi:10.1080./01609510902774315

Schaie, K. W., & Willis, S. L. (2002). *Adult development and aging* (5th ed.). Upper Saddle River, NJ: R. R. Donnelley & Sons.

Selman, R. L., Watts, C. L., & Schultz, L. H. (Eds.). (1997). *Fostering friendship: Pair therapy for treatment and prevention*. Hawthorne, NY: Aldine de Gruyter.

Shechtman, Z., Vurembrand, N., & Hertz-Lazarowitz, R. (1994). A dyadic and gender-specific analysis of close friendships of preadolescents receiving group psychotherapy. *Journal of Social and Personal Relationships, 11*, 443–448.

Similansky, S. (1992). *Children of divorce: The roles of family and school*. Rockville, MD: BJE.

Takyi, B. K. (2001). Marital instability in an African society: Exploring the factors that influence divorce processes in Ghana. *Sociological Focus 34*, 77–96.

Takyi, B. K., & Gyimah, S. O. (2007) Matrilineal family ties and marital dissolution in Ghana. *Journal of Family Issues, 28*, 682–705. doi:10.1177/0192513X070280050401

United Kingdom Office for National Statistics. (2006). *Labour Market Statistics, Labour Market Review*. London, England: Office for National Statistics.

U.S. Bureau of the Census. (2006). *2006 Annual Social and Economic (ASEC) supplement current population survey*. Washington, DC: Author.

Winslow, E. B., Wolchik, S. A. & Sander, I. (2004). Preventive interventions for children of divorce. *Psychiatric Times, 21*, 45–48.

APPENDIX A
PRETEST AND POSTTEST QUESTIONNAIRE

This is a questionnaire designed to measure what you are thinking at this moment. There is of course, no right answer for any statement. The best answer is what you feel is true of yourself at the moment. Be sure to answer all of the items, even if you are not certain of the best answer. Again, answer these questions as they are true for you RIGHT NOW.

Scale: 1= *Strongly Disagree* 2= *Disagree* 3= *Agree* 4= *Strongly Agree*

1. SELF ESTEEM: I know my good and bad qualities
2. TIME MANAGEMENT: I know how to manage and plan my time table well.
3. EDUCATION GOALS: I know what my goals for school are.
4. ANGER MANAGEMENT: I know what makes me angry and how to cope with anger
5. COMMUNICATION SKILLS: I know how to express my feelings and needs in a way that respects the rights of others
6. PEER PRESSURE: I know how to make good friends.
7. SPIRITUALITY: I have no hurts against my parents.
8. DIVORCE EFFECTS: I feel comfortable to talk about my parents' divorce.
9. LIFE SATISFACTION: I have a bright future.
10. EVALUATION: I feel it is important to attend the program

APPENDIX B
PRAYER

O loving and creating God, bless families hurting with the pain of separation and divorce. We know that when two people are married, they mean it for life. Yet, at times, with some people, and in some very complex situations, it just doesn't happen that way.
Give peace and courage to all who have experienced the disruption caused by divorce or separation. Help us to accept our feelings of pain, rejection, and grief.

Help us, above all, to believe in your presence, and to believe in God as a source of strength and compassion.

Help all of us to be sensitive to emotional, spiritual, and physical needs of children who have divorced or separated parents. Enable us to reach out in love. May people be aware of the pain of separated and divorced families and always welcome them in spiritual and social activities.

Especially we pray, O God, that as we continue to recognize Jesus in the group work, we will grow in confidence and build our self-esteem.

God of power, you watched as Your Son Jesus died on the cross. Be with us and as we journey on together. Help our parents to get money to take care of us in our education. Comfort us and help us to remember that we are not alone, in each other and in you. Grant us the light of your love in the darkness of our situation today. Amen.

Conclusion

Reflections for the Future of International Group Work

Ana Puig, Bogusia Skudrzyk, Julieta Monteiro-Leitner, and A. Michael Hutchins

When our group of co-editors took on the challenge of creating this volume, we formed a task group that was to face many challenges. Some of these challenges came from the topics being explored; others came from within our forming community. We became fellow travelers, learning from and with each other. We discovered anew that group dynamics can be enhanced when we focus on how groups can be facilitated with room for a diverse range of perspectives. We discovered anew that traditional and non-traditional perspectives can complement and enhance each other. Perhaps most of all, we trusted the process as we knew that compassion for each other would carry us through.

Long before the dreams of editing a volume about international group work became a reality, we shared ideas and created plans. In honoring the inherent creativity of group work processes, we imagine … if were elements in nature, perhaps Michael would have been the wind. He listened and wisely shared his perspectives relevant to group work and social justice. He focused on the flow and shifts in dynamic that were new and needed to be understood. Perhaps Julieta would have been the sun; with warmth, she elaborated and shared her expertise in qualitative and quantitative approaches. Most of all she carefully illuminated the process of group work, be it here in the USA or in Brazil, with specific examples of stories shared by group members. With tenacity, Ana, in her calm ways, like water, knew how to smooth out the process of writing and rewriting—leaving the ideas intact yet presenting them in a clear way so others could find the perspectives refreshing. Bogusia, like fire, kept the passion for sharing alive. "*Why not?*" was her common question when we grappled with inclusion of so many perspectives.

Foremost, perhaps, these pages highlight that the power of love is the strongest force indeed; the flames may dim due to stormy events, yet the flames rekindle. Four of us come from four different parts of the universe and live and work in diverse parts of the United States. We each represent unique identities; we are different and we value this richness. We value the unifying yearning to help each other continue walking on the path of being fellow travelers, group workers who strive to create bridges among group members, bridges that support others on a journey that includes exciting, complicated, painful, and, at times, scary processes.

As we progressed through our editorial collaboration, each of us encountered personal challenges. We share but one poignant incident to illustrate the power of group work in action: In July 2014, Michael had a medical crisis that almost ended his life. The outcome of this crisis remains unclear, though he seems to be healing. As editorial colleagues, we became a source of love and support for him. Not only did we share in his part of the editorial process, but we also shared our ongoing love and support. When we step back, we recognize that it is love and the commitment to group work that drives this small community.

What the group did for Michael is similar to the task of choosing and reflecting on the articles in this volume. Groups have healing power. In different cultural communities, that power may take on different forms. Our challenge as co-editors was to find the healing power and common themes in the group manuscripts we reviewed. Indigenous peoples the world over have histories of healing. As we look at the way groups function in different cultures from our worldview, we are challenged to honor and respect that which currently exists while integrating and sharing that knowledge in new and loving ways. We are deeply grateful for the opportunity to have worked on this project among committed, passionate, and caring colleagues.

We would like to thank our contributors for their important and informative work. They have helped us to enhance our understanding of international group work, teaching, practice, consultation, and research, exploring the diverse practices and points of convergence among many cultures and countries represented here. The products of their efforts will help us move forward in our understanding and invite continued dialogue about international group work. It is our sincere hope to carry on this important conversation well into the future.

These writings illustrate international group work, outreach, and teaching efforts representing an exciting, fertile, and promising landscape. We hope the readers will find them informative and helpful, perhaps inviting ideas about adaptation of potentially beneficial group interventions and culturally sensitive pedagogical practices. We also aimed to present a sampling of research efforts that inform our understanding of global group practices and hope readers will walk away with new ideas about rigorous research yet to be conducted that might help us identify common underlying factors representing best group practices around the world. We also acknowledge aspects of these articles may give pause, raise concerns or yield dissenting opinions. Rich and deep discourse can result from these divergent perspectives. We hope good conversations will ensue. Let us all move forward with our love of group work!

Index

INDEX